MW00788246

THE
NATURALLY
HEALTHY
PREGNANCY™

Shonda Parker

Loyal Publishing
www.loyalpublishing.com

The Naturally Healthy Pregnancy™

Loyal Publishing, Inc.
P.O. Box 1892, Sisters, OR 97759

Third Edition

Copyright © 1998 by Shonda Parker

All rights reserved. No part of this book may be reproduced or transmitted in any form or by any means, electronic or mechanical, including photocopying, recording, or by any information storage or retrieval system, without written permission from Loyal Publishing, Inc., except for the inclusion of quotations in a review.

WARNING-DISCLAIMER

Loyal Publishing, Inc. and the author have designed this book to provide information in regard to the subject matter covered. It is sold with the understanding that the publisher and the author are not liable for the misconception or misuse of information provided. The purpose of this book is to educate. The author and Loyal Publishing, Inc. shall have neither liability nor responsibility to any person or entity with respect to any loss, damage, or injury caused or alleged to be caused directly or indirectly by the information contained in this book. The information presented herein is in no way intended as a substitute for medical care and counseling.

Cover Art by Robert Duncan, Robert Duncan Studios
Cover Design by Bill Chiaravalle
Clip-art courtesy of ArtToday.com

ISBN: 1-929125-12-7

00   01   02   03   04   05   06   07   08   /   12   11   10   9   8   7   6   5   4   3

TABLE OF CONTENTS

ACKNOWLEDGMENTS

The birth of this book...

Many years ago, a kind and committed English teacher, Robert Smith, put my first essay on the overhead projector in class to point out all the faults (and there were many), then he directed me to write it again. I did. He approved. Thank you, Mr. Smith, for opening for me an avenue of expressing what I thought, believed and experienced.

Another writing instructor, Karen Douglass, encouraged this expression by sharing her wisdom and teaching me that difficulties in life are instrumental to our growth and ability to share what we've learned with others. Thank you, Ms. Douglass, for your support in that difficult time.

Lou Anne King-Jensen, you are a treasure. The support, the encouragement, the reading and editing; I thank you for it all.

Vivian Mock, for all the many times you have read and edited this manuscript, I thank you. I thank you also for your valuable insight into the childbirth process.

Tana Basinger, your artistic ability amazes me. You have been able to bring my scattered ideas into a beautiful form. You have a wonderful gift. Thank you for sharing it with us in this book.

To all of the professional herbalists, naturopaths, midwives and nutritionists who have gone before me and shared their expertise with me through written works or interviews, thank you. Your experiences have been woven into the recommendations in this book in an attempt to provide moms with safe and healthy options for pregnancy.

My granny, Arlie, who inspired me with her seven birth stories; my mother, who by her strength, taught me perseverance; and Peggy Benoit, who sparked in me fascination and love with the birth process and sweet little babies, by allowing me to witness a woman in labor at her first birth.

And finally, my husband, Keith, who has withstood the test of living with a woman on a mission, I know that without your encouragement and love (that could only have been given by God), the woman who wrote this book would never have been, and

my babies, Zachary, Emily, Eryn, Eliana and Zebediah, your births shook my foundations, changed my structure and built my life...all my love...

PREFACE

Who among us does not wish to have a Naturally Healthy pregnancy? I have yet to find a pregnant woman who desired anything less. This book, a compilation of all I have learned during my own childbearing years, is meant to be used as a tool for achieving a Naturally Healthy pregnancy.

Since you are reading this book, you have received the happy news that a child is on the way, know someone who has, or perhaps are praying for this special blessing. You will see that we definitely advocate natural, drug-free childbirth as the safest and best way for mom and baby. You will also see that we lean toward giving birth at home. This is because we have come to believe that home is the place where a safe, natural, drug-free birth is most likely to occur. We do not believe giving birth in the hospital is wrong or that seeking medical doctors as professional care providers is wrong. A small percentage of women will find that birth at home would not be the best choice, due to physical difficulties.

Our hope for you as you read this book is that you will feel encouraged and motivated to become informed about the birth process and the body's natural physiological processes. Whatever decision you make regarding caregiver, place of birth and nutritional health should be an educated one. After all, we, as parents, are responsible before God for our choices regarding our children.

Our prayer for you is that you would be blessed by the sharing of our own pregnancy and birth experiences as well as those of the other women who have agreed to share of themselves with you and learn the importance of preparation for childbirth through education, whole foods nutrition and the wise use of herbs and other nutritional supplements to increase the body's ability to function as God designed.

Each pregnancy and birth has been a teaching bonanza for me. God has chosen this most teachable time for me as a tool for sanctification. May we, as women of God, submit ourselves to the Divine molding of our character with wholehearted joy, bearing the fruit of righteousness: Godly seed.

Blessings of health,

INTRODUCTION

Amy runs to the bathroom to throw up. She can hardly keep anything down, yet pharmaceutical medications carry a toxicity risk with their possible benefit of curbing her nausea. Sarah has developed varicose veins, yet the only suggestion by her physician is the use of support stockings and leg rest. Elizabeth's gums are puffy, swollen and bleeding. She regularly visits her dental hygienist, brushes and flosses twice daily, yet she wishes there were something more she could do. Amy, Sarah and Elizabeth are pregnant. They are moms concerned about providing their developing baby with a healthy, non-toxic womb in which to grow. These moms are experiencing some of the discomforts that may accompany pregnancy. Amy, Sarah and Elizabeth will be delighted to know our Creator has provided nutritional guidance as the foundation upon which healthy babies and moms grow. We may also thank Him for the provision of botanical medicines that have not only been used safely by women throughout history but have scientific "back-up" of their efficacy and safe use directives.

Nutritional medicine has been around since the beginning of time. All of us utilize nutritional medicine whether we realize it or not. When we have the flu, we naturally decline food and favor clear fluids. This natural fast allows our immune system to concentrate on overcoming our infection and healing rather than digesting heavy foods, and the increased liquids keep us hydrated as our fever burns off (and we sweat) the offending virus. Most of us can remember some nutritional direction given to us by our parents or grandparents during specific illnesses. My grandmother always went to her canning shed to get blackberry juice for our family member's bouts with diarrhea or to the chicken coop for eggs for her special shake to be given after an illness to "build you back up."

Food has long been employed as a healing aid. Food, or what is called food, can also be a disease-causing agent. We easily can picture salmonella-infected chicken as an illness-inducer. We have more difficulty seeing our white-bread ham sandwich loaded with salad dressing, iceberg lettuce and a cardboard-tasting tomato as a problem. A problem it is, nonetheless, as we will see in Part Two of this book. Since nutrition is a "hot" topic these days, "fat free," "lite," "natural," "vegetarian," and "organic" are terms we can read on products on supermarket shelves. As we begin to become interested in healthful eating habits and read some of the books available, it is easy to become confused by all the different dietary plans being promoted.

The "Naturally Healthy" approach is fairly simple. We believe that God's dietary plan is best since He is the one who created our bodies. We trust in His plan and hold all other diets up to the scrutiny of His written Word, the Holy Bible. In researching and trying one eating method after another, we found that they all seemed to have one thing in common: their promoters came from a disease state/poor nutrition to whatever foods or supplements seemed to work best for them and then began to promote that dietary method and/or supplement to everyone. I believe that, other than God's whole foods plan, we will not find one plan to fit all. Certain methods of eating (such as food combining) can be beneficial to those with certain health conditions such as digestive system difficulties; however, I believe it to be unnecessary for all people to follow the rules of food combining to be healthy. Nutrition as a tool of preventive health does not have to be strict adherence to eating methods devised by man. Nutritional medicine is quite simply eating those plants, fruits of the plant and animals that God called food.

Herbs certainly are given to man as food in the first chapter of Genesis, the beginning. Does it then follow that all herbs are to be our food? Are they to be thought of as medicine or food? The history of herb use certainly began in the Garden. Since everything was edible for food in the Garden except for the Tree of Knowledge of Good and Evil, it seems clear that there were no toxic plants just as the animals in the Garden were not carnivorous (meat eaters). Then the Fall of Man came. As man disobeyed his Creator, all of creation fell. Death and disease became a natural part of all living things. Plants that were once freely meant for food now may grow thorns that can inflict pain, and some have toxic constituents that can cause illness and/or death.

Simply because some plants have a chemical part or constituent that can cause us to be ill does not mean we are to eschew all plants. Potatoes which have greenish skins or eyes contain the toxin solanine which can cause diarrhea, dizziness, and stupor. Do we avoid potatoes because of this? Certainly not! We wisely avoid the potatoes with greenish skin or cut out the eyes. Peanuts contain an aflatoxin that is carcinogenic (cancer-causing), yet those of us who are not allergic to peanuts enjoy eating them. Herbal medicine, or botanical medicine, can be practiced in much the same way as we judge what foods we are to eat. We must responsibly educate ourselves on the history of the herb, how it has functioned for others, as well as keep abreast of current scientific research regarding the action of the chemical constituents and toxicity/safety information. I do not eat the newest food product on the market without first ascertaining other people's reaction to it and reading about any benefits or risks associated with that particular food.

Responsible herbalism is not an alternative to conventional, allopathic medicine; rather part of a "ladder-approach" system of medicine. The "ladder-approach" system of medicine functions by having patients-consumers begin with the least invasive/least risk healing method and progress as needed up the ladder. Of course, as we climb the ladder, our risk increases; however, the first or second step will not always allow us to reach the fruit of eradicated disease.

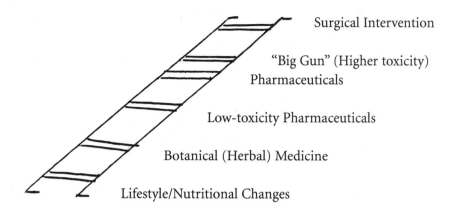

Surgical Intervention

"Big Gun" (Higher toxicity)
Pharmaceuticals

Low-toxicity Pharmaceuticals

Botanical (Herbal) Medicine

Lifestyle/Nutritional Changes

The "ladder-approach" also takes into account the fact that we will have to descend the ladder after reaching our fruit. When we have had to climb high into very invasive, therefore, more risky medical techniques, we will need to utilize the lower rungs on the ladder as we climb back down to restored health. Restoration to health requires a combination of methods and principles, and as always, we gratefully acknowledge that all healing comes from our Father God. He may allow our healing to come through the method we are utilizing, yet it is only He with the power to heal. We will explore this further in Part Three "A Biblical Prescription for Health." I feel compelled to add that the ladder-approach to health care is different for pregnant women. Any pharmaceutical drug carries with its benefit definite risks to mom and baby; therefore, mom and dad must become informed about nutritional and botanical medicine since these healing methods carry the least risk and, when used wisely, are the least invasive.

Herbal Consumerism

Botanical or herbal medicine provides us with a form of medicine we can practice at home. We have the choice of seeking the expertise of professional herbalists, naturopathic physicians, "herb-friendly" osteopathic or allopathic physicians, or simply doing self-study through reading professional herbals (books about medicinal herbalism) and attending conferences and symposiums led by those knowledgeable in the area of botanical medicine. Herbal medicine is the second rung on our "ladder-approach," and as such, this method of healing provides substantial results in health conditions that are generally self-limiting. Using medicinal herbs is also the preferred choice of many with chronic conditions due to the lack of effective, non-toxic pharmaceutical counterparts. A majority of those who use herbal medicine do so because of a frustration with standard allopathic treatment.

This frustration, I believe, is caused primarily by a misconception that elevates physicians to idol-status in the sky then plummets them to earth when they fail to live up to our imposed expectations. This misconception is our society's belief that doctors hold all the answers, can heal all illnesses and should become our best friend in the process: physician as M.Deity. The truth is that doctors know some of the answers (when we supply them with key information, our history and habits), can assist and direct healing of some illnesses (when we are responsible to educate ourselves, discuss options, weigh those opinions and evidence and follow through with the chosen treatment plan) and should become a partner with us in this healing process (the doctor/patient relationship need not be servant/master; ideally, two people come together with equally important information to share with one another to reach their goal together).

We may place our trust in God because He is faithful. Our thankfulness is directed to Him that He has endowed certain people with the desire to learn information and skills we do not possess. Our thankfulness is directed to Him also that He created this marvelous creation, our body, in such a way as to alert us when something is not right within us through pain or discomfort. The blending of body symptoms or dis-ease signals and specialized information and skills make for a positive health care relationship when both parties are open to learning from the other.

Whatever our reason for choosing herbal medicine, as we climb onto the second ladder rung, we do acknowledge that there is some risk in using herbs. With proper usage and education, this risk is minimal in comparison with the majority of pharmaceuticals. The risks involved in herbal medicine can be successfully minimized or eliminated through proper education and consumer responsibility. Education is imperative if we are to use herbal medicine as part of our family's health care. There are many fine books available on this subject, and most are as accessible as the local library (see Part 8, Resources). The Herb Research Foundation is a non-profit education organization for all of those interested in herbal medicine. The Herb Research Foundation provides research information about specific herbs and the health conditions they affect. HRF also publishes, with the American Botanical Council, the excellent quarterly magazine, *Herbalgram*, which updates consumers and professionals alike on the latest herb research, product industry news and current legal climate regarding botanicals. *See Part 8 for more information on HRF.*

Consumer responsibility is most likely to be active when the consumer is knowledgeable in the area of concern. We must move away from our passive "Do whatever you think is best" approach to health care and replace it with the proactive "I've found a number of sources documenting the positive effect of _____, let's try this for a couple of weeks and see what happens." I feel it important to add that there are times when upper-rung (on the ladder) intervention must occur quickly to save the life of mother and baby (for example, uterine hemorrhage). Once again, if we have done our homework, we will know which conditions require rapid intervention and those that permit time to work on the problem nutritionally and botanically.

When we look for guidance in the appropriate places, our self-education transforms our fear of the unknown into the power to choose. For instance, if I have read that the herb lobelia has toxicity risks when taken internally, yet I am also aware that taking too much lobelia will cause an emetic response (vomiting), it is highly unlikely that I will overdose myself. We can read responsible herb books and research articles to learn the standard dosages of herbs that have proven effective. We must unlearn gluttony which is the attitude of "If I like it and it works, more is better," instead, we must practice self-control and moderation.

Keys to responsible herbal care:

1. Know the herb(s) being taken: historical uses *and* scientific findings;

2. Follow dosages recommended by professional herbalists;

3. Know when to proceed to the next rung on the health ladder.

PART ONE

The Blessing of Birth

"Before I formed you in the womb I knew you;
Before you were born I sanctified you..." Jeremiah 1:5

GOD'S DESIGN FOR WOMEN

"And the Lord God caused a deep sleep to fall upon Adam, and he slept: and he took one of his ribs, and closed up the flesh instead thereof; And the rib, which the Lord God had taken from man, made he a woman, and brought her unto the man. And Adam said, This is now bone of my bones, and flesh of my flesh: she shall be called Woman, because she was taken out of Man, Therefore shall a man leave his father and his mother, and shall cleave unto his wife: and they shall be one flesh."
Genesis 2:21 - 24.

The Father of all Creation created us from man, yet He made us different from man in many ways, most noticeably in the area of reproductive abilities. Man, our husbands, provides the seed containing a blueprint for life and gender, and we provide a complementary blueprint and fertile ground, our wombs, for this new life to grow. God blessed pregnancy in *Genesis 1:27-28a*, "So God created man in His own image; in His image He created him; male and female He created them. Then God blessed them, and God said to them, 'Be fruitful and multiply; fill the earth and subdue it....' The ability to bear children is something that God called good, "Then God saw everything that He had made, and indeed it was very good" *Genesis 1:31*. Due to the sin of Adam, God's curse placed consequences on childbearing so that women would bring forth children in pain, sorrow and toil. There is debate upon the issue of whether the original meaning of the Hebrew words regarding the curse literally translates to physical pain for womankind. This book will not address this debated issue; rather, we will delve into God's design for women in childbearing.

Paul's letter to Timothy relates to us the important message, "But the woman being deceived, fell into transgression. Nevertheless she will be saved in childbearing if they continue in faith, love, and holiness, with self-control" *1 Timothy 2:14b-15*. This phrase "saved in childbearing" refers to Paul's admonition to women to learn from their husbands, to not be in authority over or teach men, because of a weakness toward being deceived and influencing men. God, in His infinite wisdom, knew our weakness and provided childbearing as a means of protection for us as women against being deceived by the world and then transferring that deceit to others. Childbearing is a gift of protection, not a curse. Pregnancy and childbirth, while sometimes uncomfortable or downright painful, is a gift from God.

As women, we are particularly prone to gathering together to share pregnancy and birth stories more aptly called "war stories." The woman with the worst experience wins the showdown, or does she? We all lose when we perpetuate the horror of pregnancy and childbirth. In essence, we take a gift of God, His means of protecting us, as well as providing dominion stewards, and call it a curse. Yes, pregnancy, childbirth and breast-feeding is physically and emotionally hard to bear, yet we must guard against taking a dim view of childbearing. Just as man has to work hard and pull weeds to bring forth the fruit of the ground instead of simply planting and watching the garden grow, so our female bodies must work hard, pulling weeds of health challenges to bring forth the fruit of the womb, instead of simply conceiving, birthing and watching our children grow.

The physical exertion of labor can be painful for some women. The issue of pain during labor depends largely on one's perception of pain. If I call a mild headache painful, then certainly, labor would be perceived by me to be painful. If garden-variety menstrual cramps (not those associated with a health condition) are thought of as part of the process of menstruation, they are not likely to be perceived as being painful. Most of us do experience more than just slight discomfort during labor. We would call the sensation felt during a contraction as pain. In looking back at the births of my children, I find that I perceive the good, strong contractions as being good, not painful, although technically they hurt. I perceive those parts of different labors where there were physiologic difficulties to overcome as being very painful and hard to bear. As soon as these variations in "normal" labor were corrected, contractions, while stronger in intensity and effectiveness, became bearable and good again. Certainly, when there is an area of tension or a variation in the normal process of labor and birth, pain is useful to us as a signal to attend to the area of need.

The unfortunate fact of today is that we, as women of God, have accepted the world's view of childbirth as a horrendous time of agony that we either must endure, or escape from through the use of drugs in order to have our babies. When we succumb to belief in the agony of labor rather than the truth of God's design, we steal the joy from God's blessing. Yes, pregnancy and birth is hard work, but it's still a blessing and gift from God. How much more enjoyable our childbearing years might be if we can view not just the fruit of the womb as a blessing but the gift of a womb as a blessing. We will look at two different mothers to illustrate this point.

Mother A desires a large family because she rests in the truth of children being a blessing and a heritage from the Lord. This mother discovers she is pregnant and responds to the news with these thoughts, "I do so love having my babies when they get here, but now I have months of fear and dread to go through before I can have my baby in my arms." Since she is trying to avoid thinking about her pregnancy and the impending birth, she does not change many, if any, of her lifestyle and nutritional habits to accommodate her growing baby. Other than hoping and praying that baby will be "okay," she does not spend time mothering this baby, her child, in her womb.

If she encounters health problems during the pregnancy, she avoids thinking about that, too, confident that they will resolve without her participation in the healing process. She chooses not to attend natural childbirth classes because she has given birth before and "knows how to do it," rather "get through it." Or she may go if forced by her caregiver, but she sits in her chair enduring the instruction, because the educator is just one of "those" types who must like pain and wants everyone else to like it too.

As the end of the pregnancy draws near and labor becomes imminent, Mother A fears for her very life. At this point, she may decide to "grit her teeth and endure the birth," or she may decide "Drugs are really not so bad, after all." Whatever her decision, Mother A has chosen to "opt out" of the joy of pregnancy and childbirth and "buy in" to a cheerless, fear-filled drudgery of mothering in the womb.

Mother B longs to be pregnant like Mother A; however, Mother B looks forward to her time of mothering while her child is still in her womb. She begins to change her lifestyle and dietary habits prior to her time of fertility so she will be in optimum health for pregnancy. Mother B's husband prays over her that areas they need to work on or change might be revealed so their pregnancy would be one of vibrant health. They yield to God's timing of conception, and He rewards them with the fruit of the womb; Mother B is pregnant.

Mother B rejoices in her pregnant condition. She prays for and talks to her baby often, even singing to her baby. She looks in the mirror at her growing body enjoying the presence of baby. Mother B and husband attend childbirth classes that give them, not only anatomy and physiology lessons and relaxation techniques, but instruct them in their spiritual responsibility during pregnancy, the birth and as parents. They are thankful for the classes because of an opportunity to address issues and make choices regarding their baby's birth experience. More importantly, their childbirth classes encourage Mother B in learning to "listen to" or recognize the physiological signals her body sends to enable her to work with the birth process.

As the pregnancy comes to an end and labor progresses, Mother B yields to the Creator's design, yields her body to the process of birthing her baby, meeting each contraction with the knowledge that the work she is accomplishing will bring her baby into her arms. Mother B's emotion comes from the prospect of possessing what she desires, her baby; Mother B is joyful. She may not be laughing and she may (most likely) be experiencing some pain with contractions, but her focus is not on "just getting through this," but on "going through this with her baby."

Mother B is not "better than" Mother A. Mother B has realized and put into practice the truth of God's design for women in childbearing. Mother B refutes the lie that says childbirth is a punishment. Mother A, while sincerely loving her children, has not yet learned to yield to birth. A yielding heart says, "This process is good. I will endeavor to learn how it works and follow its progress."

Much of our attitude toward childbirth today stems from belief that our babies are somehow separate from us, though joined with and dependent upon us, during labor. In order to experience joy in childbirth, we must recognize the joined-togetherness of mother and baby from conception. Our babies are not somehow "in there" and then mysteriously "out." Education about the birth process is important. Childbirth education classes are an important part of a mother's pregnancy; however, I am not saying that mothers must attend classes with each and every pregnancy. Moms who have learned the process of birth and learned to yield to that process may very well have earned an "exemption" from repeat classes.

A woman becomes a mother at the moment of conception with all attendant responsibilities that the role requires. As a parent, each and every one of our actions affects our children. Our responsibility becomes especially apparent during pregnancy. Mother and baby function as one yet at the same time are two separate creations of the Lord. During the process of labor and birth, mother must yield to God's design which directs the working together of mother and baby to get baby out of the womb into mother's arms. If mother is just enduring rather than working with the process, she is fighting the natural progression of labor which increases her pain and can lead to potential labor problems.

Another cultural attitude that may need changing, if we are to fully experience pregnancy and childbirth as God intended, is the belief that pregnancy is not a special time. In fact, many today view pregnancy as a downright nuisance and inconvenience. I am certainly not advocating we return to a time of not allowing women out of their homes during pregnancy and treating pregnancy as an illness. I do firmly believe that we should look upon pregnancy as a unique opportunity to mother in a quiet, gentle way.

Even the natural childbirth movement, which has been positive in that it has been responsible for educating and advocating a return to non-invasive birth, has promoted the idea of "Pregnancy does not have to change our life. We can live as usual; stop for a moment to give birth; and get right back to business." We, as mothers, will never again have such an opportunity to get to know and protect and nurture our children as during the time of pregnancy and the immediate postpartum period. Life must not go on as usual. We must submit to the changes of our bodies and live quieter lives. This is how we parent our pre-born and newborn children; by parenting in this manner, we serve God.

Preparing for the Blessing of a Child

"Lo, children are a heritage of the Lord: and the fruit of the womb is his reward. As arrows are in the hand of a mighty warrior; so are children of the youth. Happy is the man that hath his quiver full of them: they shall not be ashamed, but they shall speak with the enemies in the gate." Psalm 127:3 - 5

The Word of God is clear that children are a blessing. It is also clear that God's perfect desire for man/woman is to "be in health, even as his soul prospereth." *(III John 2)*. We are responsible to follow the natural principles set forth in the Word to be conducive to our health. These principles are outlined in Part 3, in the chapter "A Biblical Prescription to Health." It is clear that we are responsible for the maintenance of God's temple, our bodies.

While it is God who opens and closes wombs, we need to give our wombs and whole bodies all the nutrients needed to be a place of health and nourishment for these little blessings. Many women do not begin to prepare for pregnancy until after conception. This practice is not the ideal. It is far better to begin to prepare for the blessing of a child prior to conception.

Getting started early in preparing for pregnancy allows moms to eliminate poor habits slowly, change dietary habits slowly, so the family and mom is not in "whole food-shock" which commonly leads to a "junk food-relapse," and preparing before conception gives mom time to do any necessary lab tests to ascertain health status.

My own beginning in herbal medicine came as a result of being told by physicians that I would probably not be able to conceive and carry a child to term due to scar tissue formation from post-Cesarean infection that resulted in repeated miscarriages. The herbalist I visited and first learned from told me that I had to clean up my lifestyle and dietary habits before stimulating my body with herbs helpful for conception. She was right. After months of lifestyle and dietary changes as well as crying out to the Lord, our Emily was conceived and carried 10 days past due date. This taught me an important lesson in herbal medicine. Cleanse and build the whole body before attempting to work with herbs specific for fertility enhancement.

Eliminate habits detrimental to mom's or baby-to-be's health:

Smoking: Smoking depletes the body's supply of vitamins and minerals. It also is a constant irritant to the respiratory passages. Smoking has been implicated in numerous diseases. Smoking during pregnancy may lead to miscarriage, prematurity, intrauterine growth retardation leading to low-birth weight babies.[1] Although some women subscribe to the "I smoked during all my pregnancies, and none of that happened before" philosophy, these women and babies are the exception, not the rule. I realize those who smoke are addicted to those cigarettes and that it is difficult to overcome the addiction. I also believe that any addiction, nicotine, caffeine, drug or food, can be overcome with prayer, determination and the conviction to do what is best for baby. If dad is smoking, he should quit also. Second-hand smoke is still detrimental to mom and baby.

Alcohol: Alcohol consumption, even moderate amounts during pregnancy, has been identified as the causative factor in *fetal alcohol syndrome*. This syndrome is characterized by growth retardation, mid-facial hypoplasia - general flattening, short nose and upturned, small eyes. There may also be microcephaly, mental disorder, and/or abnormal palmar creases. The toxicity is believed to be caused by the alcohol itself or the breakdown products such as acetaldehyde.[2]

The damage done to babies due to FAS (fetal alcohol syndrome) should discourage fertile women from consuming alcohol. If a mom has become pregnant and has had a couple of alcoholic beverages, it is best not to spend the next nine months in despair. There are many factors that may damage baby's health beyond our control in our world today. The key is to avoid those that are possible to avoid; in other words, "don't drink if you are planning to be pregnant or if you are pregnant." Once again, dad should also take steps to avoid alcohol during the pre-conceptional time period. Alcohol may affect sperm health.

Caffeine: The studies that have been done on caffeine and its effect on fertility and pregnancy seem inconclusive in terms of lowering fertility and miscarriage. The effect of caffeine on the body is undisputed: caffeine is a stimulant affecting metabolism, adrenal function, circulatory ability and nervous system.[3][4] Caffeine stimulates the adrenal glands to produce more adrenaline, constricts blood vessels, causes the "shakes" from nervous system stimulation and speeds up the metabolism. Caffeine is a main ingredient in many diet plans because of these effects. This alone should cause one concern over ingesting caffeine during pregnancy because pregnancy is definitely not the time to be speeding metabolism to lose weight. Caffeine is "naturally" (found in nature) found in black tea, green tea (Camellia sinensis), coffee beans, cocoa (chocolate), cola or kola nut (Cola nitida), soft drinks, guarana (Paullinia cupana - caffeine content 2 1/2 times that of coffee), and mate (Ilex paraguensis).[5]

The pharmacological effect of caffeine can be experienced from 50mg upward, and doses exceeding 250mg are likely to be significant.[6] One study published in the *American Journal of Obstetrics and Gynecology* in January 1985 said that women who consumed more than 150mg of caffeine per day experienced an increase in spontaneous abortions (miscarriages).[7] One five-ounce cup of coffee can provide 150mg of caffeine depending upon how it is brewed. It also makes sense to eliminate caffeine because of its antagonistic effect on important vitamins and minerals. Caffeine lowers or prevents the absorption of nutrients from our food such as iron and zinc, both of which are extremely important for fertility and childbearing.[8] It is best to slowly wean oneself from caffeine to decrease the withdrawal symptoms of headache, fatigue and nausea.

Contraception: This one seems pretty obvious, but it is very important in the case of oral contraceptives to eliminate them at least three to six months before conceiving. Actually, for any health-oriented individual, they would not be a choice at all because of the legion of side effects. Oral contraceptives, also known as birth-control pills, can act as abortifacients as well.

Drugs: All drugs and medications that are not essential should be eliminated with the assistance of a health care provider. Those that are essential should be evaluated as to risk/benefit for mom and baby.

> **Make the change now to whole foods nutrition.**

Lab Work to be Performed:

Prenatal Lab Work-Up: It is my opinion that it is more beneficial to do this lab work prior to pregnancy with a follow-up during pregnancy than after the pregnancy has begun. This allows mom time to make necessary changes in diet to ensure a healthy conception and organ-development time for baby as well as alert caregivers to any health problems that need to be treated. A toxoplasmosis screen, in addition to regular labs, may also be beneficial to those who own cats.

Toxic Metal Screen: Environmental toxins known to be associated with the development of birth defects are toxic metals, methyl mercury, lead, cadmium, organochemicals, DDT, dioxin, agent orange and polychlorinated biphenyls (PCBs). Anyone living in a city or industrial environment or working in an industrial environment should be screened for toxic metals. This screening may be done through blood tests or a hair mineral analysis.[9] Blood tests are more reliable for what is currently circulating in the blood while hair analysis gives a better picture of low-levels or of toxic metal build-up in the system. A nutritionally-oriented care provider is the best choice for performing these tests because they have been trained to evaluate them and make recommendations based on these tests.

Food Allergy Tests: If a mom has been having digestive distress prior to pregnancy, food allergy tests may be of benefit to identify any allergens that should be avoided to increase nutrient absorption of other foods. Food allergies may be tested by skin tests (many doctors don't find this to be the best means), blood tests (some allergies won't show up by this method) and the elimination diet (most everyone agrees this is the best way though the hardest to do because favorite foods are being eliminated for a certain time period). I should mention that many adult food allergies show themselves as food addictions.

Supplements for Maximum Pre-Conception Care:

1. Begin taking a quality prenatal vitamin/mineral formula with absorbable forms of the nutrients. Make certain this supplement has at least 400 - 800 mcg of folic acid 30 - 50 mg of iron and 20 - 35 mg of zinc. See appendix for sources.

2. Some women find wheat germ oil to be an excellent source of Vitamin E which is important for fertility.

3. A supplement supplying essential fatty acids is important for correct baby development. Good sources are flaxseed oil, evening primrose oil or black currant oil. I prefer flaxseed until the 34th week of pregnancy when I switch to Evening Primrose Oil (EPO).

4. An herbal source for minerals is an excellent choice to supply those macronutrients necessary for the functioning of the glandular system such as alfalfa, red clover blossoms, kelp, spirulina, red raspberry as well as other nutritive herbs.

5. If morning sickness was a problem during a previous pregnancy, milk thistle extract (standardized to contain at least 70% silymarin) is of great benefit to aid the liver's functions. Recommended amount: 280mg per day. Dandelion is a gentler liver stimulant if a milder liver tonic is desired.

6. A preparing for pregnancy whole body cleanse is of benefit to anyone especially those with toxic metal content, sluggish bowels, liver/gallbladder problems. A good cleanse will last at least two weeks to one month and will not be the type to keep you on the toilet constantly. Any cleanse performs its best when combined with a whole foods diet. An herbal cleanse should be done at least one month prior to conception.

Take care of any health problem not previously addressed.

MAXIMIZING FERTILITY POTENTIAL

As previously stated, it is the belief of this author that the Lord God opens and closes the womb. I do believe, however, that we often engage in activities or habits that are not favorable for conception. It is our responsibility to clean up our bodies and get them nutritionally ready for God to plant our husband's seed within us. Dads are responsible as well for getting nutritionally ready to supply healthy seed.

Steps a woman can take if she has been praying for pregnancy and hasn't been blessed with a baby yet are:

1. Follow the pre-conception care advice on previous pages.
2. Check thyroid and pituitary function through lab tests. I do hasten to add that these tests are often unreliable for those on the edge of what is considered normal. Mom may need to visit a good endocrinologist if she feels she does have a problem that lab tests are not indicating. I have a good friend with Hashimoto's disease whose lab tests do not indicate a thyroid deficiency, yet her endocrinologist is able to see the subtle problems indicated that her family physician completely missed.
3. Some women may need to gain five or ten pounds if they are under their ideal weight. Some women may need to lose weight if they are carrying excess weight due to the estrogen produced by our body fat.
4. Infertility due to scar tissue formation or endometriosis may require surgical intervention after careful weighing of risk/benefit ratio. An herbal therapy that may, or may not, help are castor oil packs. Soak a clean piece of flannel in 4 ounces of castor oil. Warm it in the oven (be careful not to start an oven fire) and apply to the abdomen for 20 minutes to 1 hour daily for two weeks or two to three times weekly for 6 weeks. Blue cohosh and black cohosh stimulate tissue health of scarred structures when taken internally.[10]
5. Aid the body's slightly acidic vaginal environment by avoiding foods contributing to a very alkaline environment: refined sugars, starches and alcohol. Sperm perform best in a slightly acidic environment.
6. Correct any deficiencies found in lab work. Herbal and vitamin supplements are a natural way to correct these deficiencies by "feeding" the glands the nutrients they need in a way that doesn't overstimulate them. The following herbs have been shown in preliminary scientific investigations to help normalize the production of hormones by normalizing glandular function:
   a) Chaste berry (Vitex agnus-castus) - German experiments and a German study showed that extracts of agnus-castus can stimulate the release of Leutenizing Hormone (LH) and inhibit the release of Follicle Stimulating Hormone

(FSH). One other study suggested that the volatile oil has a progesterone-like effect.[11]

b) False unicorn (Chamaelirium luteum) - Current pharmacology indicates that the steroidal saponins have adaptogenic effect on ovaries (normalizing function).[12]

c) Red raspberry (Rubus spp.) - Various species of red raspberry have been shown to induce ovulation as well as relax the uterus.[13]

d) Wild Yam (Dioscorea villosa) - Wild yam is utilized as the basis of commercial birth-control products sex hormone production (conversion of its steroid diosgenin to progesterone).[14] Although wild yam does not convert to progesterone in the human body, some herbalists believe it to be of benefit to those with low progesterone levels due to its effect on the adrenal glands as well as being beneficial for its antispasmodic effect on the uterus. Low progesterone levels in a woman's body do not allow the endometrial lining to build for the baby to implant and the pregnancy to be sustained.

e) Black Cohosh (Cimicifuga racemosa) - Black Cohosh has estrogenic effects meaning it acts like the female hormone estrogen which makes it useful for those women with low estrogen levels.[15] Do not take after pregnancy is confirmed.

f) Vitamin E deficiency is associated with low plasma levels of FSH and LH in pituitary tissue.[16]

Cycle Regulation

Richard Scalzo, in the *Protocol Journal of Botanical Medicine*, recommends the following:

Follicular phase, day 4-14 (Pre-ovulatory botanical compound):

Dong quai	20 drops
Shatavari *(asparagus racemosus)*	20 drops
Ashwaganda	20 drops
Helonias root	20 drops
Bupleurum root	20 drops
Oat seed	15 drops
Licorice root	10 drops
Ginger root	10 drops

Usage: Three time daily
Discussion: The botanicals, which include phytoestrogens, nutritives, tonics and antiinflammatory agents, serve to balance the estrogen/progesterone ratio. The formation of

luteinizing and follicle stimulating hormones are also balance, and inherent actions in the botanicals maintain blood pressure, smooth muscle contraction, and improve elimination, enabling the physiology to recover form and be prepared for the post-ovulatory phase.

Amanda McQuade Crawford recommends in her book, *Herbal Remedies for Women*, the following formula:

Follicular Phase:

Dong quai	3 oz
Panax ginseng root	1 oz
Siberian ginseng root	1 oz
Sarsaparilla root	2 oz
Damiana herb	3 oz
Rosemary herb	1 oz
Black cohosh root	1 oz

Take three capsules twice daily with meals and large glass of water or combine the above herbs in TincTract™ form into one combination TincTract™ and take 1 teaspoon three times daily with water.[17]

Women should choose one of the above formulas, not both.

Luteal Phase, Day 14-28 (Post-Ovulatory botanical compound):

Vitex agnus-castus	25 drops
Black cohosh	20 drops
Kava Kava	20 drops
Wild Yam root	15 drops
Saw Palmetto berry	15 drops
Oat Seed	10 drops
Black haw bark	10 drops
True Unicorn (*Aletris farinosa*)	10 drops
Ginger root	5 drops

Usage: Three times daily
Discussion: The botanicals in this compound are antiinflammatory, nervine, anodyne, and help to balance hormone levels.[18]

OR a women may choose…

Luteal Phase Formula 2:

Chasteberry	4 oz
Cramp bark	1 oz
Skullcap herb	3 oz
Siberian ginseng root	1/2 oz
Sarsaparilla root	2 oz
Rosemary herb	1 oz

Three capsules twice daily.

Lengthening the luteal phase (after ovulation until the bleeding begins)

Vitex, once again, is the herb most used for this purpose. Vitex has a normalizing effect on the pituitary which controls the length of the luteal phase. As with all normalizing herbs, vitex may need to be taken several months to achieve results. 1-2 capsules of a standardized extract of vitex each morning is the usual dosage for cycle regulation purposes.

Natural progesterone cream may be used from ovulation until the beginning of the new menstrual cycle. The brand I'm most familiar with and have used myself is the ProGest brand. Directions that come with the cream should be followed for dosage. I prefer to use changes in diet to reduce excess estrogen levels (see Part 7, PMS) and herbal intervention first before relying on a somewhat natural product.

Infertility Compound: For those who want one formula for full-month use.

False unicorn *(Helonias root)*	30 drops
Vitex agnus-castus	20 drops
Squaw vine	20 drops
True Unicorn *(Aletris farinosa)*	15 drops
Black haw	10 drops
Ginger root	10 drops

Usage: Three times daily.

Panax and/or Siberian ginseng may be used for their adaptogenic effects on the body. Panax ginseng is contraindicated for pregnancy; therefore, moms should not use panax ginseng during the luteal phase of the cycle when pregnancy may have already occurred. Sarsaparilla may also be used during the luteal phase for its purported progesteronic effect.

Steps a man can take when praying for pregnancy to maximize his fertility:

1. Follow the pre-conceptional care advice.
2. Wear loose underpants and trousers. Do not sit in one place for long periods.
3. Do not sit in hot tubs.
4. Get adequate rest and regular exercise.
5. Studies have shown that nutrients are beneficial for improving sperm count and normal sperm formation.[19] [20] [21] The following supplement recommendations are based on empirical information as well as available scientific literature:
   a) l-Arginine - 1.5 - 3g daily for 3 - 6 months
   b) Essential fatty acids provide the basis for prostaglandin production. Seminal fluid is rich in prostaglandins. Some men with low fertility of unknown origin have low levels of seminal prostaglandins.[22]
   c) Zinc - 50mg daily
   d) Chromium - 50 - 200 mcg daily
   e) Selenium - 50 - 100 mcg daily
   f) Vitamin E - 400 - 600 IU's daily for increased sperm motility and morbidity[23]
   g) Vitamin A - 7500 IU's daily
   h) B Vitamins - 25 - 100 mg daily
   i) Vitamin C - 500 mg daily
   j) Free-form amino acids - 500 mg twice daily
   k) l-Lysine - 500 mg daily
   l) L-acetyl-L-carnitine helps to increase sperm count and stimulate testosterone production[24]
   m) Glutathione, 600mg daily has shown significant benefits on sperm motility.[25]

Herbal Formula for Men 1:

Muira puama bark	1 oz
Panax ginseng root	3 oz
Siberian ginseng root	2 oz
Damiana herb	2 oz
Spearmint or Peppermint herb	6 oz

Take three capsules twice daily when wife is taking her formula six days weekly for at least 10-12 weeks.

Herbal Combination for Men 2:

Siberian Ginseng, Saw Palmetto, Gotu Kola, Damiana, Sarsaparilla, Horsetail, Ginkgo. Take three capsules twice daily.

Nettles, oatstraw and burdock may be added to men's daily routine for added nutrition. Astragalus increased sperm motility when administered 10mg invitro.[26]

Other Steps that May be Taken for Women:

1. Checking for ovulation by keeping a record of daily basal body temperature (BBT). The BBT is taken each morning at the same time before any activity takes place and the body is at complete rest. The normal, non-pregnant axillary (under arm) temperature ranges from 97.4 to 98.2 F (or 36.3 to 36.8 C).

2. Checking cervical mucous for changes signifying fertility. To best learn how to take both the basal body temperature and how to check cervical mucous, one should contact the local Couple to Couple League. They have instructors who teach classes on Natural Family Planning. While these classes often are attended by those wishing to prevent pregnancy, it is an excellent way for a woman to learn how her body works so she can recognize those fertile times.

3. It is also helpful to seek the counsel of an herbalist or nutritionist with experience and success in dealing with infertility.

When Baby Dies
Within the Womb

Miscarriage

Miscarriage is the loss of baby prior to 20 weeks gestation. The majority of miscarriages occur within the first twelve weeks of pregnancy. One study in which beta subunit hCG (level of pregnancy hormone) was measured in women in the latter end of the luteal phase of their cycles showed physical evidence of pregnancy. This study suggests that many miscarriages occur before a woman is even aware she was pregnant at all, occurring at the time of the menstrual cycle.[27]

There are many causes of miscarriage with some originating with baby, mom or dad. We will not be addressing the many possible causes of miscarriage here. Rather our attempt will be to prevent the occurrence of miscarriage (to the degree we are able) through sound nutrition and supplementation. Normal function of all endocrine glands is important for maintaining a healthy pregnancy; therefore it is prudent for moms, first of all, to provide their bodies with healthful food.

Symptoms of miscarriage are: vaginal bleeding or spotting and cramping. Bleeding may be bright red or pink (fresh) or dark brown (old). Two-thirds of moms who have bleeding unaccompanied by cramps carry their babies to term. If bleeding increases, cramps or back pain occur at regular intervals or a gush of fluid from the vagina occurs, mom should consult with a qualified health professional immediately.

Miscarriage is not just "missing getting to carry baby to term." Miscarriage is the loss of life, the life of a child. My own miscarriages have been a mixed bundle, so to speak. My first and my last were the most traumatic for me. Those in-between were not easy, but I did not experience the same amount of grief as the first and last, perhaps due to the fact that I knew I was pregnant longer with Sarah and Abel.

My husband and I chose to acknowledge the life of the children who died in the womb, even those very early miscarriages by:

1. Naming our children. For those documented (I know for certain I was pregnant) miscarriages, we felt it important to give those children a name. I was too early pregnant to really know whether our child was a boy or girl; so we prayed and chose a name based on who we felt the child to be (if we're wrong, it won't affect the eternal scheme of things). This has allowed us to call those children by name in remembrance as well as given a concrete validation of their life, which served the purpose for which God created them.

2. Having a family ceremony and burial. We did not do this with all of our miscarriages, but we did with the last, Abel. A dear friend of mine reminded me to save

the baby (or what we could retrieve) and keep in extreme cold until the ceremony as well as choose a biodegradable box for burial. Our other children chose to draw a picture or place in the box something special (we had already wrapped the baby in a blanket before allowing the children to do this). We had a short service consisting primarily of affirmation, through prayer, of God's sovereignty, mercy and comfort over, and for, our family. Together, we chose a special stone to mark the grave of our child. All families will not have the ability to do this due to home location.

3. Talked about the hopes and dreams we had for that child. With our first miscarriage, Sarah, Keith and I sat down together to talk about the disappointment we were feeling due to the loss of our child. I, in particular, had already begun buying little baby booties and clothes that I looked forward to dressing her in; dreaming of how it would feel to hold a sweet little girl in my arms. Keith and I were able to talk of our sadness while at the same time encouraging one another to trust in the Lord of All Creation's wisdom for our life.

4. Let others know our needs: physical, emotional, spiritual. We knew, particularly this last time, that a woman's body does not realize there's no baby to hold. The body does react to having been pregnant and having gone through labor the same way as with a term pregnancy. Mom has to take it easy for a week or two just as if she had her baby with her. We asked our church for help with meals and cleaning for a couple of weeks as well as letting them share in our grief and encourage us with prayer.

These are some of the steps we took as we dealt with our babies' deaths. All parents will not feel comfortable with all or maybe any of the above; however, all parents should know they have the ability to grieve just as any other parent who has lost a child. The pro-life movement would probably gain more ground were it to acknowledge the lives of children who die within the womb of natural causes as well as those taken forcibly by the abortionist's hand.

Lifestyle/Dietary Recommendations:

1. While there is no definitive evidence showing that bed rest has any effect on the outcome, many caregivers feel limiting activity has some physiologic benefit. I feel it certainly has emotional benefit in helping mom to feel she is doing everything possible to save her baby.

2. No intimate relations (sexual intercourse) with husband until all bleeding has ceased.

3. Continue high-quality whole food diet.

Nutritional Supplement Recommendations:

1. Black haw and crampbark are the two herbs most commonly used by European physicians, Native Americans and modern herbalists to calm the uterus. Prominent naturopaths in Europe even use black haw to counteract the effects of abortifacient drugs.[28] [29] [30] See combination below for dosage.

2. *Red raspberry has a long history of use in pregnancy for morning sickness, uterine irritability and threatened miscarriage.[31] Standard dosage: 2 capsules three times daily. Do not use red raspberry before reading the cautions about *Rubus idaeus* and prayerfully considering what God allows for your family.

3. False unicorn is prized by herbalists for its adaptogenic effect on the ovaries (normalizes function), and this has been confirmed by current pharmacology.[32] See combination below for dosage.

4. Wild yam (Dioscorea villosa) is the basis for commercial birth-control products created by converting Diosgenin (a steroid-like material contained in wild yam species) to progesterone.[33] This herb may benefit those women who are threatening miscarriage due to a stimulation to the adrenal glands of the body as well as the antispasmodic effects of the herb.

Combination "CarryOn" for Threatened Miscarriage:

A combination of black haw, false unicorn, and wild yam (Liquid Light™ or Mother's Choice™). While this combination relaxes the uterine muscle, it does not create a uterus that would prolong an inevitable miscarriage (if the baby had already died). It also helps the body to normalize hormone production. 1 teaspoon every 2 to 3 hours for several hours, then 1/4 - 1/2 teaspoon once the bleeding and contractions have lessened.

Mom may want to add either or both pasque flower *(Anemone pulsatilla)* herb and passionflower herb to the above combination.

Other nutrients vital to a healthy pregnancy: Essential Fatty Acids found in natural polyunsaturated (cold-processed) oils such as canola, safflower, soy and flaxseed oils, pumpkin seeds, sunflower seeds, Evening Primrose oil and Black Currant oil; zinc; magnesium; and vitamin E.

*There has been speculation that the cultivated variety of red raspberry (Rubus idaeus) may be of danger to pregnant women due to the presence of caffeic acid in the plant that has been shown in one test to inhibit chorionic gonadotropin activity in rats being injected.[34] Other studies clearly show uterine relaxation. The question is whether Rubus idaeus can cause miscarriage in women who are prone to miscarriages. The R. stringosus variety has been advocated as an alternative to R. idaeus. This advice has been based on the assumption that the wild variety (stringosus) has been safely used throughout history by women during pregnancy to add tone to flaccid uteri and relax irritable uteri.

There is no available research on R. stringosus so it is difficult to validate the claim that stringosus is safer than idaeus. It is also not known whether stringosus contains caffeic acid as does R. idaeus. One midwife in Madisonville, Louisiana, DeAnne Domnick, found that a client she was helping through a miscarriage had taken Rubus idaeus during her pregnancy. A couple of days later some naturopathic students came by and were saying "Only idiots use idaeus during pregnancy." Although she was unable to substantiate their crude remark, she felt cautious enough for her own clients to only recommend R. stringosus for pregnancy use.[35]

The Basic CARE Booklets from the Medical Training Institute of America also issue a caution about using R. idaeus as well as recommending R. stringosus for pregnancy. I was also unable to track down the source for this caution.

I feel it somewhat necessary to defend Rubus idaeus. It is the cultivated variety of red raspberry, and Rubus stringosus is wild variety. Since R. idaeus is the cultivated variety, it is the one found in most (almost all) herbal combinations and as a single herb in liquid or capsule form. It would seem that we would be seeing a great increase in miscarriages among women using red raspberry during pregnancy if R. idaeus is indeed a problem. I should also note that those concerned with women using R. idaeus during pregnancy feel it is only a problem for *women prone to miscarriage.*

I personally feel that moms who have had several miscarriages who are wanting to be very cautious should use R. stringosus. The problem with that is that it is not widely available. Most herb companies use R. idaeus and most caregivers educated in herbalism feel comfortable recommending it. I was branded a "habitual aborter" (woman who has had three or more miscarriages) prior to using herbs for healing. I have used the Rubus idaeus variety of red raspberry in my last three pregnancies, and my pregnancies keep getting better and better. I had absolutely no bleeding or spotting with my fourth child, Eliana.

For moms concerned about cultivated red raspberry (R. idaeus), it can most certainly be taken after the 16th week of pregnancy when hCG levels stabilize.

STILLBIRTH

Stillbirth is defined as a baby born dead after 20 weeks gestation. Just as with miscarriage, there are many reasons for this. Although there are no nutritional recommendations specific to stillbirth, with the exception of zinc as a preventive, the best thing mom can do is to follow a whole foods diet and abstain from harmful practices: alcohol, smoking, drugs, environmental teratagens, etc. I was able to find one study that related Vitamin E deficiency to intra-uterine growth retardation and prematurity.[36]

Some stillbirths are caused due to placental problems such as *placenta abruptio*, where the placenta detaches from the uterine wall while baby is still *in utero*, or from nutritional deficiencies evident by the health, or lack thereof, of the placenta. Placentas truly are a window into the environment of the womb. If a placenta does not look healthy or has anomalies, mom can purpose to work more diligently in the next pregnancy on her nutrition.

Certainly all stillbirths are not caused by lack of good nutrition, there are many cases that are simply unexplainable. I wish there were an answer that we could grab hold of to explain why we must go through such a painful experience. I know for me, even though my miscarriages were early, I was able to take great comfort in Psalm 139, knowing that God formed my baby just as He desired for His Divine purpose and numbered my baby's days before baby was even formed. God is good, and His work in me and my family is holy and just; therefore, as painful as is the death of a baby, God still redeems my baby's life for His good and holy purpose.

PART TWO

The Nutritional Needs of the Pregnant Woman

*"Oh, give thanks to the Lord, for He is good!...
Who gives food to all flesh, for His mercy endures forever." Psalm 136:1 & 25*

A BIBLICAL APPROACH
TO NUTRITION

Does what we eat matter to God? It would seem from a look at the Holy Word of God that there has not been a time in history that God did not explicitly give instructions as to what He considered good food for our bodies. Each covenant God made with man is coupled with nutritional guidelines (not always stated) that we may draw upon to design a healthful, "Biblical" diet for our families. We will examine here the guidelines that came with each of the covenants: Adamic, Noahic, Abrahamic, Mosaic, Davidic and the New Covenant through Jesus.

Our firm belief in the Parker family is that scripture supports gracious table fellowship with others, even those who do not share our same dietary convictions. Clearly, God wants us to love and honor Him above all else as well as loving others as we love ourselves, including extending gracious love to other's dietary habits as we would hope they would extend the same graciousness to our dietary habits. Following our own dietary convictions appears, in scripture, to be secondary to the command not to offend our brothers and sisters in Jesus.

In most fellowship settings, we can easily maintain our own dietary patterns without making an issue of our dietary beliefs. If one of us eats plants and not meat, would it be gracious to serve hamburgers if we know of their preferences? If we are not aware of their preferences, the gracious act of the vegetarian would be to nibble on the hamburger so as not to offend the host. The point is that our dietary choices are an issue of stewardship of the body created for us by God. Foolish we would be to consume a daily diet of hamburgers and french fries. These foods do not contain the necessary nutrients to maintain health or life for very long. A full complement of nutrients must be consumed through a variety of foods for the maintenance of health. Stewardship involves what we do each day to care for those areas God has entrusted us with. We are also responsible for stewardship of the Body of Christ in that we must give much thought to how we treat one another so that we care for one another rather than being thoughtless in our actions. Refusing a sister's or brother's hospitality because of our own dietary habits would be offensive and hurtful, therefore not edifying (building up) to the Body of Believers. Spiritual matters must come before physical matters.

We look now to the different Covenant periods of history to see how the Word can help us discern the most healthful dietary practices.

Adamic Covenant:

The first covenant God made with man is the one made with Adam, the covenant of works. It may be a "true" covenant was not made at this time, yet scripture relates God's promises to all mankind through Adam. God did at this time make provision of food a priority for Adam and Eve.

And God said, Behold, I have given you every herb bearing seed, which is on the face of all the earth, and every tree, in the which is the fruit of a tree yielding seed; to you it shall be for meat.
And to every beast of the earth, and to every fowl of the air, and to every thing that creepeth upon the earth, wherein there is life, I have given every green herb for meat: and it was so.

Genesis 1:29-30

We can surmise from this passage that God's dietary instruction was for Adam and Eve and their descendants to be vegetarians. The plants of the earth which God had created would provide daily nutrition. After man's (Adam and Eve's) sin, God cursed the ground and said that Adam would eat of it only with sorrow (etsev in Hebrew which means to labor, work, toil) and that it would bring forth thorns and thistles (Genesis 3:17). God still gives the "herb of the field" as man's food (Genesis 3:18-19).

Some believe that because of God's curse on Cain after he murdered Abel in the field, the earth (ground) would no longer yield all the nutrients to supply man's complete nutritional needs.

And now art thou [Cain] cursed from the earth, which hath opened her mouth to receive thy brother's blood from thy hand;
When thou tillest the ground, it shall not henceforth yield unto thee her strength; a fugitive and a vagabond shalt thou be in the earth.

Genesis 4:11 - 12

Those who believe this also believe that vegetarians need to supplement their diets with vitamins and minerals that the earth no longer provides. I do not know whether this is the correct interpretation of this passage or not. In reading this, it would only seem that this applies to Cain and his descendants, not to all men, because there is more to this curse than just the earth not yielding her strength. God also curses Cain with being a fugitive and vagabond, and all men have not become fugitives and vagabonds. What is interesting to know is that there are areas of our world that do not serve well for food production.

Noahic Covenant:

The Noahic Covenant is a promise from God. God vows to never again destroy the earth by a flood and gives the rainbow as a symbol of that promise. God explains the sacredness of life which is in the blood and gives the command not to eat blood or shed man's blood.

> *Every moving thing that liveth shall be meat for you; even as the green herb*
> *have I given you all things.*
> *But flesh with the life thereof; which is the blood thereof, shall ye not eat.*
>
> Genesis 9:3-4

This passage clearly shows that man is to view blood as the source of life, even animal blood, as his life-giving fluid. This certainly brings into question the view of animal rights' activists that eating animal flesh is a violation of the animal's sacredness. God only views the blood of the animal as unclean for food and gives permission to eat the blood-drained flesh.

The assumption many make in light of this passage is that Noah and his descendants could eat *any* animal because God did not specify clean and unclean here in Genesis 9. However, Noah *did* know which animals were clean and unclean because God had told him to bring "Of every *clean* beast thou shalt take to thee by seven, the male and his female: and of beasts that are not clean by two, the male and the female. Of fowls also of the air by sevens, the male and the female; to keep seed alive upon the face of all the earth" (Genesis 7:2-3) *emphasis mine*. While we cannot know if Noah ate animals that God had termed "unclean," it is clear Noah understood the difference. I somehow have a hard time believing that Noah ate the unclean animals, which were fewer in number, rather than the clean animals, which were more generously provided by God's direction t Noah. The most apparent issue in terms of food in this covenant is that God did give permission at this time to eat animal flesh that is drained of blood and as before to continue eating plant food. The prohibition was against the consumption of blood.

Abrahamic Covenant:

The Abrahamic Covenant is the promise of God to make a great nation of Abraham's Seed, through whom He, God, will bless the whole world. God at this time promises to Abraham's seed the land of Israel as its everlasting possession. This convenant with Abraham was made because of Abraham's faith in God. God promises to bless those who bless Israel and curse those who curse her. Israel, the nation of people, is to be an instrument of God. The sign of the Covenant is circumcision of males, which set God's people apart from the rest of the world. Since God did not give new guidelines for diet, those given to Noah still stand.

As previously stated, I have found the Scriptures to be illuminating for me when trying to decide whether the current "fad" diets are truth that we do well to follow or whether they are merely an outgrowth of the experiences of a minority of people that are then promoted to the majority. Food-combining has always seemed to me to be one of those practices that might be beneficial for some people who might have digestive difficulties yet unnecessary for most people. When studying the covenants, I noted with interest that when God appeared to Abraham in the form of three men, Abraham, upon recognizing that he was seeing God, served God bread, meat, milk, and butter (Genesis 18:1-8). This meal certainly breaks all the food-combining laws yet was obviously a fine meal since Abraham served these foods to God.

The Jewish prohibition of having dairy and meat together is obviously part of the rabbinical code, not the Old Testament law, since Abraham served both to God at the Genesis 18 meal.

Mosaic Covenant:

God gave this covenant through Moses. This covenant linked to the Abrahamic Covenant through the continuation of the covenant of grace, God's promise of the Seed of Abraham. In the Mosaic covenant, God shows his people their need of the Seed of Abraham, Jesus, through their inability to follow, to the letter, the law He gave to them through Moses. God promises to bless Israel for their obedience and curse their disobedience. The Mosaic covenant served as Israel's national constitution, containing instructions for Israel's socio-judicial system as well as personal and moral issues. The temple system, priesthood and sacrifices are shadows of Jesus who came as fulfillment of this system. Jesus serves as the perfect and complete sacrifice for the sins of God's people. We are allowed to come before the throne of God through Jesus as our Mediator, our Priest. Our bodies, as Believers, are now the temple of God. We present to Him as living sacrifices our bodies, our very lives.

Jesus, alone, fulfilled the law of God. Through His sacrifice, we can enjoy the grace of God, the gift of eternal life with Him. We cannot earn God's grace because we see clearly that the law is impossible to perfectly follow, thus our need for Jesus as atonement for our sins. As Believers under God's grace, we have the benefit of the Spirit of God, the Holy Spirit, which causes us to desire to follow God's law. We want to follow God's commands because they are His commands, created not just to show us our need for the Saviour, but for our doctrine, reproof, correction and instruction in righteousness (II Timothy 3:16).

We do not believe that one must follow the Mosaic dietary law for salvation. We believe that as the Mosaic law is clearly sound in its social, judicial and personal moral standards, so it is profitable for our physical bodies to follow the dietary law as *guidelines* for health. Scientific thought seems to be slowly catching up to the health-truth of the biblical dietary guidelines. Food fads come and go, yet the enduring truth remains that our bodies are healthier when given foods that God considered food for us, clean for us. Eggs were bad for awhile, now they are "good" again. Crustaceans, such as shrimp, crab, lobster, etc., are consumed liberally, yet those concerned about our health warn of the dangers inherent in eating these scavenger sea creatures that can be filled with toxic wastes from shorelines and contain a load of fat that contributes to a host of health problems.

Butter was a major "no-no" for a long time, now researchers realize that the imitation butters and margarines are doing major damage to the human body. Butter is now back "in" although moderation is encouraged. "Enriched" foods are still popular. How long will it take for us to realize that God created whole foods naturally "rich"?

The biblical dietary meat guidelines are found primarily in Leviticus 11 and Deuteronomy 14:2-21. The distinction between clean and unclean animals was basically:

Land Creatures: Any land animals that had cloven hooves *and* chewed their cud was clean and could be eaten. Any land animal that failed this test was considered unclean to eat or touch. Examples of clean animals would be: cattle, sheep, goat and venison. Examples of unclean animals would be: camel, squirrel, hare, swine (pigs), horse, etc. Also included in the unclean lists were animals that "goeth upon his paws (cats, dogs, bears, etc.) among all manner of beasts that go on all four;" "the creeping things that creep upon the earth; the weasel, and the mouse, and the tortoise after his kind, And the ferret, and the chameleon, and the lizard, and the snail, and the mole" (Leviticus 11:27-30); and "whatsoever goeth upon the belly (snakes), whatsoever goeth upon all four, or whatsoever hath more feel among all creeping things that creep upon the earth (spiders, centipedes, millipedes, caterpillars, etc…)" (Leviticus 11:42).

My children observed one day at the zoo that the giraffe was a clean animal because it had hooves and was chewing its cud. This means that in the event you find yourself on the African Savannah, the giraffe is a better food choice than a lion (a lot easier to catch too, I would think).

Water Creatures: "Whatsoever hath fins *and* scales in the waters, in the seas, and in the rivers, them shall ye eat" (Leviticus 11:9). Clean water creatures would be: salmon, red snapper, tuna, halibut, bream, perch, bass, etc. Unclean water creatures would be shrimp, lobster, crab, crawfish, squid, scallops, catfish, etc.

Fowls or Flying Creatures: God specifically gave a list of the unclean fowl. They are as follows: eagle, ossifrage, osprey, vulture, kite, raven, owl, night hawk, cuckoo, hawk, little owl, cormorant, great owl, swan, pelican, stork, heron, lapwing and the bat Leviticus 11:13-20.

Flying Insects: God said that the "flying creeping things that goeth upon all four, which have legs above their feet, to leap withal upon the earth" (Leviticus 11:21) were clean to eat. These include the locust, bald locust, beetle and grasshopper. All other creeping things which have four feet are unclean.

These dietary laws did not negate the earlier commands. God added more specific instruction. The other scriptural mandate concerning diet in Leviticus 3:17: "It shall be a perpetual statute for your generations throughout all your dwellings, that ye eat neither fat nor blood."

Davidic Covenant:

This covenant that God makes through the prophet Nathan for David, the King, is one in which God promises David that his throne will be established forever through his descendents (II Samuel 7). The dietary guidelines are not altered at this time. The Mosaic dietary law is still in effect for David and his descendants.

New Covenant in Jesus

Jesus is the New Covenant through His life, death and resurrection. Adam and Eve's sin brought spiritual death to all men born after him. "For all have sinned and come short of the glory of God" (Romans 3:23). "For the wages of sin is death; but the gift of God is eternal life through Jesus Christ our Lord" (Romans 6:23). God sent Jesus into the world to be the sacrifice for our sins. As we trust in the blood of Jesus' sacrifice, believing that He conquered death through His resurrection and die to our selfish, sinful ways and worship Him as Lord of our life, we are promised eternal salvation, everlasting spiritual life instead of everlasting spiritual death for those who do not believe (John 3:16-21, John 5:24, Romans 5:8-9, Ephesians 2:8-10).

God also promises to all believers in Jesus the indwelling of the Holy Spirit.

> *But ye are not in the flesh, but in the Spirit, if so be that the Spirit of God dwell in you. Now if any man have not the Spirit of Christ, he is none of his.*
> *And if Christ be in you, the body is dead because of sin; but the Spirit is life because of righteousness.*
> *But if the Spirit of him that raised up Jesus from the dead dwell in you, he that raised up Christ from the dead shall also quicken your mortal bodies by his Spirit that dwelleth in you.*
>
> Romans 8:9-11

Through Jesus, there was no longer a need for the temple system of priesthood and sacrifices. Jesus is now our door through which we walk into God's presence, the spiritual kingdom of God (John 3:5, John 10:1-18, John 14:6). Jesus said of the law, "Think not that I am come to destroy the law, or the prophets: I am not come to destroy, but to fulfil. For verily I say unto you, Till heaven and earth pass, one joy or one tittle shall in no wise pass from the law, till all be fulfilled. Whosoever therefore break one of these least commandments, and shall teach men so, he shall be called the least in the kingdom of heaven: but whosoever shall do and teach them, the same shall be called great in the kingdom of heaven" (Matthew 5:17-19).

As with the other covenants, the New Covenant includes dietary instructions. New Covenant dietary issues are an area of much disagreement among believers. Our purpose here is to share some possible interpretations of the New Covenant dietary guidelines. We fully believe the Holy Spirit is more than capable of convicting each believer as to what he or she should do concerning the consuming of food. I highly recommend the reading of Dr. Rex Russell's book, *What the Bible Says About Healthy Eating*, for a more thorough explanation of biblical dietary instruction.

Vegetarianism

As to why God decided to allow meat to be eaten after the flood, we could only speculate on world-wide climactic change and perhaps a change in the earth's ability to grow complete foods. Whatever we speculate, it would still be just that, speculation. The truth would remain that all nutrients currently recognized are available in a variety of plants. Complete vegetarianism is only spoken of before the flood and in the new earth, or New Jerusalem, when God's perfect will shall be enacted for us, His people.

Vegetarianism is also mentioned in I Timothy 4:1-5 in reference to the end times where there will be a turning away from the faith and people commanding to abstain from meats. The Word states that "every creature of God is good, and nothing to be refused, if it be received with thanksgiving: For it is sanctified by the word of God and prayer" (I Timothy 4:4-5). The word in that verse is "creature," not plant. There are many groups in the world now that hold an animal's life higher than man's life or needs. This is clearly a violation of scripture. An animal's blood is the part God considers significant, not the flesh of the animal. Jesus himself ate fish and bread when He went to the disciples at the sea of Tiberias (John 21:1-14). Jesus also fed the five thousand fish and loaves (Mark 6:30-44). Scripturally, the eating of blood-drained, animal flesh, is not wrong.

Certainly, there is nothing in Scripture that says only eating plant foods is wrong, either. In fact, Paul says in Romans 14:1-23, that some will eat only herbs (or plants) while others eat all things. His statement is that the "weaker brother" may eat only herbs. I find this to be interesting in that there are several illnesses that are definitely helped by converting to a vegetarian diet such as heart disease or allergies and asthma. Could this be a practical meaning of the "weaker brother?"

Are all things clean now or are the Leviticus guidelines still in effect today?

We see that God has led us from complete vegans (no animal foods at all) with Adam to "abstain from blood" with Noah to the complete dietary code with Moses. Now, in Jesus, where are we?

Certainly, we see that the law is not destroyed under the New Covenant, the law is fulfilled. If the law is still profitable for structuring our legal system and our moral standards and our child-training philosophies, can we not also see that our body profits from utilizing the dietary law as guidelines for ourselves and our families? I do not think it necessary for all of us to maintain the same dietary practices. God apparently did not believe so either since He allows us freedom in the area of diet. Freedom always comes with responsibility, and this instance is not different. We are definitely instructed to be stewards over creation.

Stewardship of our bodies includes recognizing that God's laws are always the best for us. For instance, the admonition in the Mosaic law to wash the hands with running water when touching anyone who is sick is practically applicable to prevent illness from spreading from person to person. Staying apart from others when there is a discharge from the body also prevents communicating disease to others. These practical applications of scripture may be applied in the area of our diet as well. Those foods God considered unclean are increasingly being considered unhealthy. For our own family, the simple fact that God created our bodies and knows what is the ideal food for us is enough to have us follow His dietary guidelines rather than some man or woman who is striving to figure out what is good for us. Our strivings will never come close to the wisdom of the Father in caring for His children.

The one admonition that we find in the New Testament that affirms the lasting covenant with Noah that we should abstain from things strangled and from blood.

> *Wherefore my sentence is, that we trouble not them, which from among the Gentiles are turned to God:*
> *But that we write unto them, that they abstain from pollutions of idols, and from fornication, and from things strangled and from blood.*
>
> Acts 15:19-20

> *For it seemed good to the Holy Ghost, and to us, to lay upon you no greater burden than these necessary things;*
> *That ye abstain from meats offered to idols, and from blood, and from things strangled, and from fornication: from which if ye keep yourselves, ye shall do well, Fare ye well.*
>
> Acts 10:28-29

> *As touching the Gentiles which believe, we have written and concluded that they observe no such thing, save only that they keep themselves from things offered to idols, and from blood, and from strangled, and from fornication.*
>
> Acts 21:25

The context of the above passages tells us that the Jewish believers wanted to have the Gentile converts observe the dietary law and Paul was trying to convey to them that this was overly burdensome to a people so unused to any dietary guidelines. Paul and the elders decided that the minimum requirements for the good of the Body of Christ would be the above guidelines. Some people today believe that even the "abstaining from blood" prohibition is null because our situation is not the same as it was in the early church. My concern is this: if we choose to avoid trying to follow some of the New Testament admonitions in addition to throwing out the Old Testament admonitions, where do we stop?

As Paul so aptly put it nearly 2,000 years ago, "For sin shall not have dominion over you: for ye are not under the law, but under grace. What then? Shall we sin, because we are not under the law, but under grace? God forbid. Know ye not, that to whom ye yield yourselves servants to obey, his servants ye are to whom ye obey; whether of sin unto death, or of obedience unto righteousness?" (Romans 6:14-17) Grace is not a license to disregard God's law. Grace is being out from under sin's dominion so we now *desire* God's laws. Our desire to follow the laws of God, both Old Testament and New Testament, come from a desire to yield ourselves unto our Master, the God of All Creation.

If the reason for having the early church Gentiles abstain from blood was only because it offended the Jews, why would we choose to offend them today and possibly keep them from the Gospel. The same can be applied to those Gentiles or Jews who are following dietary guidelines. Should we follow our dietary beliefs to the extent that we offend those who are not eating like us? I believe the answer lies in the beginning of this chapter: we do well to follow the dietary law as a guideline for healthy eating and as a sign of our submission to God's will for our bodies, yet if the issue comes up in our brotherly relations with other believers, we are not to allow the issue to be a fellowship-breaker or an offense to a brother or sister.

To some Believers, eating pork would be a sin against the dietary law to which they are not bound for salvation, but consider a sin of poor stewardship and/or lack of yielding to God's best. To others, not eating pork would be the sin of legalism, adding a burden that they feel God does not require. Still others simply don't care, they go about their lives totally unconcerned about any of their eating or living habits offending both of the other sides. Perhaps what we all need is a friendly splash of water to remind us of the important issues: allow the Holy Spirit to direct in this area that God has allowed some freedom, follow our convictions in our daily life, fellowship with one another in love, not giving offense by remaining rigid to the extent that we break fellowship with a brother or sister over an issue that is not a core doctrinal issue.

Our focus, then, may be on:

- Eating foods that God has so abundantly provided,
- Pursuing health through evaluating all lifestyle habits and foods to see if they qualify as good stewardship of our bodies,
- Thanking God for the provision of His Body of Believers whom we can fellowship with; His Grace which we do not deserve no matter how good we think we eat or behave; and His Mercy for not allowing us to become as ill as our dietary and lifestyle habits may warrant.

What are Whole Foods...
And How Do We Eat Them?

The *Naturally Healthy*™ approach to good nutrition results from our belief in eating "whole foods." Does this mean eating a whole apple or whole orange at one sitting? No. Our definition of "whole food" is a food that is in the closest state to which God created that food. For example, God created the grain, wheat, for our food. Is it more nutritious and healthful for our bodies to eat steamed, cracked wheat berries (the grains of wheat are called wheat berries) or is it healthier to eat white bread from wheat berries that have been stripped of their bran and germ, ground and bleached? The obvious answer is the steamed wheat berries.

Our daily food should be chosen from a well-rounded variety of whole foods. The key to obtaining maximum nutrition from our foods is variety in our food choices. If we decide to eat only pizza and burgers, we will be missing out on a large number of nutrients while increasing our need for those nutrients. When we choose "junk" food instead of nutrient-filled whole food, we cause our bodies to have to work very hard to protect us from the negative effects of "junk." If we want our body to function properly and be healthy, we need to "eat and live right."

This concept is similar to what my husband says about his work sometimes (he is a manager of software development): "I spend so much of my time putting out fires, taking care of all the little things that come up when the wrong data or function is fed to the computer, that I don't have time to do my regular work to keep the system running smoothly. As a result, sometimes, the entire system has to be shut down and re-booted (re-started) to solve the problems that have occurred because the day-to-day normal operations have been ignored." Our body functions much in the same way.

If we constantly eat or continue lifestyle habits to undermine our health, our body will expend all of its energy on "fighting fires" or trying to keep operations running in spite of being fed the "wrong data." This eventually will lead to body system breakdown because the normal day-to-day work or function of the body has been ignored as the energy was diverted to "fire-fighting." Nutrition is vital for "All systems are functioning within normal parameters." As we realize that the eating of whole foods is essential to our body systems, we also must examine *how* we are to eat these good foods.

How we eat or prepare whole foods is just as important as choosing them over their processed counterparts. Everyone has a different idea about how we should eat our foods: combined in a certain way, cooked at very low temperatures, totally raw, all fruit, all vegetables, any way and every way. The one abiding rule *we* follow is variety and moderation in all things!

The best way to eat most fruits and vegetables is raw with their peel intact (that is, if the peel is edible!). A good guideline would be eating at least 50%, with a goal of 75%, of our fruits and vegetables in their raw state. Some vegetables, the starchy veggies such as corn and potatoes, must be cooked to make them digestible. If we do want to cook our veggies, the most healthful methods are: lightly steaming, baking, grilling or sautéing (stir-frying). When stir-frying, a small amount of extra-virgin, cold-pressed olive oil is the healthiest choice. Butter may be used in small amounts as well as cold-pressed (expeller-pressed) canola or safflower oil. Cooking methods to avoid are boiling and frying. These same cooking methods are appropriate for cooking our meats as well. Raw meat is a definite "No-No" during pregnancy due to the risk of contracting toxoplasmosis, E. coli contamination or other parasites from undercooked meat. Quite frankly, I wonder about eating raw meat at all because of the inability to eat blood-less raw meat!

Grilling is a popular cooking method that has recently been attracting negative press for its carcinogenic (cancer-causing) potential. When foods are grilled to the point of being "blackened," cancer-causing substances are formed in the meat that are best avoided. If we do grill meat, we should not allow the fat from the meat to drip onto the coals, and we should not cook to the point of burning it or "blackening" the meat.

Microwaving foods has become an everyday cooking method for most American households. While microwaves do not emit or use gamma waves, daily microwave exposure is not recommended. Microwave ovens use pico waves that are significantly less toxic than gamma waves. Pico waves penetrate tissue deeply and rapidly and increase the vibrational rate of water and tissue molecules. The increased vibrational rate generates heat and cooks the food. There is great concern over the release of toxic chemicals in food from their microwave packaging, particularly those foods that are browned or made crispy in the microwave. Certainly, microwaves are convenient; however, their use should be limited in the *Naturally Healthy* home. When a microwave is in use, those in the home should be standing at least 5 feet away from the microwave oven, and a periodic check for leaks should be performed.

Vitamins and minerals are lost when foods are cooked quickly at very high temperatures. A loss of nutrients also occurs when fruits and vegetables are prepared in water. The cooking water, or broth, we end up with is more nutritious than the soggy vegetables contained within. My grandfather used to feed me "pot likker," the liquid left in the pot from cooked mustard/turnip greens. I loved it when I was a "little folk," and I still like it, especially in the winter since that's when greens grow so well! This brings us to another point; *it is best to eat foods when they are in season.*

Eating Seasonal Foods

Eating foods in season certainly ensures their freshness. The fresher the fruit, vegetable, grain, nut or seed, the more nutrients are present. The deterioration of the fruit or vegetable begins when it is removed from the plant. Chemicals are needed to provide long-term storage for the "fresh" fruits and vegetables we purchase in our grocery stores throughout the winter months. The measures taken to increase the food's shelf life also increase our health risk.

Spring is a time when I think "clean." Generally, as the earth quickens with spring renewal, I have an urge to clean my entire house (attic to darkest (over-cluttered) closet) as well as my body (impure thoughts and habits to impure colon). God, in His infinite wisdom, must motivate this desire. The foods that grow best in spring are those that are conducive to cleansing: abundant varieties of greens, citrus fruits, carrots, broccoli, cauliflower, apples. Legumes (beans and peas) begin their growing season in early spring along with the grains. We quite naturally desire fewer "heavy" foods such as thick, hearty soups, meat and cheese and begin to plan lighter meals. Another interesting aspect of spring that I have noticed in the last couple of years is that our family tends to "catch" some sort of respiratory illness that cleanses our respiratory tract. I think some of the "allergy" symptoms that many people today are experiencing may be some form of body response to the previous season's poor food habits. This opinion is just a theory of mine that may flesh out in a few more years' observation of families.

As the season changes into summer, the Lord's food blessings from the earth change to "lighter," juicier foods. Amazing, isn't it? It grows so hot (at least here in Texas), and our Father so graciously provides those big, juicy peaches, nectarines, watermelons, cantaloupes, grapefruit, grapes, berries and…Oh, I do love the foods of summer! These foods, being so juicy, provide much-needed natural water to keep us cool on those hot days while still providing abundant nutrients. Who could imagine wanting to eat chili in summer?

Fall brings harvest time. We finish off the last of the juicy fruits and begin to harvest the root vegetables and winter squash we will eat now as well as store for winter use. Some vegetables, such as potatoes and the winter squash varieties lend themselves well to storage in a cool, dark, dry area (attic, cellar). My grandparents had a little outbuilding with a cool, dirt floor that they used specifically for storing root vegetables. The cold season storage building was right next to my grandmother's "canning shed" where she stored all of her canned jams, jellies and some fruits and vegetables for those special treats in the winter months. Most of our fall food will be cooked since the root vegetables and hard winter squash need to be cooked for digestibility and nutrient-release. As we harvest grains, nuts and seeds, our protein food consumption increases as we prepare our homes and bodies for the coming indoor activities of winter. For a more thorough discussion of grains, see our publication, *Becoming Naturally Healthy*, available from *Naturally Healthy Publications*. Most legumes harvested in the fall may be prepared from the dried state. Those available fresh usually are limited to Green Beans (Snap Beans) and Peas. Dried legumes can be sprouted or cooked. Dried legumes need to be soaked prior to cooking to aid digestibility and to decrease the "gas" potential.

Winter brings the focus and activities indoors. Our winter foods are warm and hearty foods that provide much-needed fuel that provides for our warmth. A heavier consumption of meat is common in winter. In the time before refrigerators and freezers, families waited until the first freeze to butcher their animals so the meat could be preserved without spoiling. Families ate their meat over the winter and tapered off heavy meat consumption during the spring. Heavier meat and fat consumption tends to add a few pounds which helps to keep us warm. Complex carbohydrates, from grains, legumes, nuts, seeds and vegetables provide the mainstay of the winter menu.

Benefits of the Seasonal Food Diet:

- Lessens the amount of chemicals in our foods since foods are fresher
- Lowers the cost of our food since the supply is abundant
- Promotes whole food eating since we eat what God provides for that season (God did not mean for tomatoes to be chemically-preserved so they taste like cardboard)
- Increases our consumption of a variety of foods since growing seasons differ (the strawberry season fades into blueberry which fades into raspberry...)

Organic Food

Ideally, all of our food intake would be organic (food grown without using chemical pesticides or chemical fertilizers); however, in the day-to-day real world, the availability and cost of organic foods prohibits most of us from eating a 100% organic diet. Choosing as much organic food as possible is important and should be a priority in our home during pregnancy and our children's developmental years. To ease pressure on the family budget, we might begin purchasing 25% of our food organic, then increase to 50% to reach a realistic goal of 75% organics in our diet.

For beginners on the whole foods diet, some of this may seem overwhelming. Consuming healthful food does not have to put a strain on the family budget. Actually, whole foods are usually less expensive than prepared foods. The best method I have found to lower the overall food bill and put more nutritious offerings on my family's table is to buy in bulk quantities. This method of decreasing costs is not for large families only. Bulk-buying simply takes some advance planning as well as a commitment to use what has been purchased.

When the diet consists primarily of complex carbohydrates (as it should), advance buying as well as combining orders (co-operative buying) are the keys to economical health! Personally, I purchase the grains I do not use a large amount of through a buying group that purchases from a regional co-operative warehouse. Those grains I use in large quantities (for us, that's wheat, corn, oats, 7-grain mix, brown rice), I purchase in 50-lb. bags from a business that deals with large volumes of grains and kitchen equipment. For example, a 50-lb. bag of organic Golden 86 Wheat only costs me $16.00 when I buy in this manner. If I buy the wheat by the pallet (20 bags), my cost is considerably lower.

For those all-important fruits and vegetables, I also purchase these with friends from a source that allows 15% over wholesale cost for purchases in case quantities. This method of buying allows my family to enjoy the freshest of organic produce for less than the supermarket charges for chemically-laden produce. For those times when we run out of our organic produce, we try to avoid purchasing conventional produce that cannot be peeled or is a root vegetable. Our organic produce "staples" are: carrots, romaine and leafy lettuce and potatoes. We started out buying the "staples" from organic sources. We began to add to our organic shopping list each ordering time until a large percentage of our produce consumption was organic.

Tips on Buying the Freshest (and least expensive) Produce:

- Ask the supermarket manager what days the produce trucks deliver fresh produce to the store
- Shop at a local farmer's market (forming a co-op and buying in bulk can lower prices even more)
- Purchase from a friend with a garden
- Form a buying co-op and offer to buy in case quantities from health food stores for a certain percentage over wholesale cost (this is a great way to get organic produce and the stores benefit by getting us into the store to buy our other groceries and supplements)
- Buy from a co-operative warehouse
- Grow your own

Our family does eat meat. We try to use meat more as a side attraction to our meal rather than the focus of our meal. Meat is a food we definitely purchase from sources committed to natural farming. "Natural" meat is from animals raised without antibiotics or growth hormones. Even better is when we can find meat from animals raised on organic grasses and grains free from pesticides and chemical fertilizers. Once again, if we take the time to locate quality resources, our natural meat does not have to cost more than the meat from the grocery store. We have found that group-purchasing of "natural" meat can create prices competitive with the supermarket as well as personal bulk-buying of, for example, an entire beef at one time or a whole case of chickens. I do know that I do not want antibiotics or hormones coming into my own or my children's bodies unless it is medically necessary, certainly not through our food.

Juicing

Juicing is an excellent way to get concentrated, easily-digested nutrients. Juicing offers the ability to "disguise" or "hide" less tasty vegetables in the juice of more flavorful fruits. Fresh juices, as opposed to bottled or frozen, still have the necessary enzymes and vitamins and minerals from the fruit or vegetable. Frozen juices are next best in nutrient content with bottled coming in last. I believe juicing should be a *part* of a healthful diet as long as juices do not become the mainstay of everyday eating (or should I say drinking).

Juicing is of great benefit in pregnancy since the digestive process slows because of the hormone, progesterone. Since digestion is slower, heavy and large meals can be hard for the first trimester mom to handle. The cautions I have about large amounts of *fruit* juicing on a regular basis are as follows: juice supplies concentrated plant sugar that can precipitate a hypoglycemic response; juice does not contain all of the fiber of the plant or fruit and fiber is essential to good health; and juices promote a cleansing action in the body, and pregnancy is not the time to fast and detoxify. Vegetable juicing, on the other hand, functions as a superb avenue for obtaining the necessary amount of daily nutrients for pregnancy. A blend of carrot, beet and parsley (easy on the parsley as too much could possibly stimulate uterine contractions, may use up to 1 bunch of parsley in juice blend) provides a nutrient-rich juice that can substitute for several exchanges in the fruit and vegetable daily food plan without mom having to feel overloaded on food.

Whole Grains

Whole grains and wholegrain bread are an integral part of the whole foods diet. The simple addition of whole grains and whole grain bread to the diet confers to the body protection from a number of "Western" diseases, such as constipation, colon cancer, diabetes, diverticulitis, gallstones, etc. Grains have a protective outer coating called bran that prevents the grain from spoiling or "going rancid." Since wheat is one of the most popular grains for cereals and breads, I will use it to illustrate the healthfulness of whole grains.

The wheat kernel is a gold mine of nutrients. Once the wheat kernel is cracked or ground, the bran no longer is able to protect the grain from spoilage. The flour will begin to lose nutrients immediately after milling. In only seventy-two hours, flour that has been milled from whole grains will be rancid and most of the nutrients will be gone. Rancid flour has free radicals in it that have been shown to cause numerous health problems including an increase in cancer risk. The bran is extracted during the white flour refining process thus causing a loss of the following percentages of nutrients originally in whole wheat flour: 86% of the niacin, 73% of the pyridoxine, 50% of the pantothenic acid, 42% of the riboflavin, 33% of the thiamine and 19% of the protein.

The endosperm of the wheat kernel is the inner part of the kernel. It is primarily made up of starch and is the source for white flour. The endosperm contains the following percentages of nutrients: 42% of pantothenic acid, 32% of riboflavin, 12% of niacin, 6% of pyridoxine, 3% of thiamine and 70-75% of protein. While the endosperm still contains a large amount of protein, the endosperm alone (as in the case of white flour) is very deficient in the B vitamins as well as severely lacking in fiber

The germ or embryo portion of the wheat kernel is what causes the wheat to sprout and grow into a plant if allowed. Wheat germ contains essential oils which cause whole wheat flour to become rancid if not used within a few days. The germ is extracted from white flour because of the difficulty in preserving the flour's quality. The bitter taste in 100% whole wheat flour and bread purchased in food stores results from spoiled or rancid wheat germ. The nutrients lost when milling out the wheat germ are: 64% of the thiamine, 26% of the riboflavin, 21% of the pyridoxine, 7% of the pantothenic acid, 2% of the niacin and 8% of the protein.

Obviously, bread made from white flour is an inferior product. I would not even call it food since the word, food, implies a nutritive substance. Even bread made from flour milled more than 72 hours before baking is not healthful due to rancidity and the resulting free radical production. The best choice for health is to grind our own flour with a quality home grain mill and bake it fresh into bread immediately. Baking and grinding equipment are easily obtained in today's market and are a good investment in health.

Milk

Milk, a food promised to the children of Israel in the Promised Land, is either being constantly "improved" upon by removing key nutrients, homogenizing and/or pasteurizing, or boosting production through the use of hormones in the cows. Milk has come into disfavor, being forbidden by those who believe only animals should drink milk past infancy. Both of these scenarios are a problem. The milk that was so fit for Abraham to serve the Lord God Almighty when He came to visit is not the same substance currently being sold in our stores today. As is usually the case, when man begins to "improve" God's perfect design, problems develop.

Raw milk (unpasteurized, unhomogenized) is much maligned today as a carrier of disease. This *can* be true in cases of poor hygiene and health in a milk cow herd. In fact, listeria, a microbe responsible for stomach distress and possible teratogenic effects in pre-born babies, can be present in raw milk making the consumption of such a product a risk factor for pregnant women. However, the alternative of homogenized, pasteurized, hormone-laden milk from the corner supermarket is not such a grand alternative.

Pre-born babies may also be affected by their mothers' consumption of genetically-engineered rBGH (recombinant bovine growth hormone) milk. The pre-born may also be subjected to minute amounts of antibiotics in milk from cows injected with rBGH. This continual antibiotic usage may increase an individual's risk of antibiotic-resistant bacteria production in the body. As if all of that is not enough, an increased amount of IGF-1 (insulin-like growth factor I) is present in milk from cows treated with rBGH. How this hormone will affect coming generations is a question many of us concerned with adulteration in the food industry dread having answered in the coming years. Even the pasteurization and homogenization processes destroy nutrients and create chemical by-products strongly linked to disease in the human body.

So what's a body to do? The safety of drinking certified raw milk from disease-free cows milked in a clean environment is an alternative for most of us. Pregnant women *do* need to take extra precautions to ensure that there are no *listeria* organisms present in the milk (*listeria* may also be present on hot dogs, luncheon meats, raw meat and left-overs) since healthy cattle may harbor *listeria*. Mothers may want to find alternate sources for their calcium intake during pregnancy. Calcium is easily and prominently found in nuts and seeds, such as almonds, sunflower and sesame seeds; legumes such as soybeans and soybean curd, tofu; and vegetables such as broccoli and dark, leafy greens. Cheese made from either certified raw milk or from pasteurized milk (hard cheese is generally not made from homogenized milk) is also a good choice for moms during pregnancy and breastfeeding to ensure adequate calcium intake. As always, cultured milk products, such as yogurt made with live cultures, should be a part of the daily diet to prevent disease and provide quality nutrients.

Water

Since over 60% of our bodies are made up of water, we would be best served by making certain the water we ingest and bathe in is pure and clean. Over the past few years, the poor quality of tap water has become increasingly clear. Outbreaks of water-borne disease are on the rise. Health officials point to our water supply as a major factor in disease: gastrointestinal illnesses, skin problems, lead poisoning and even certain types of cancer.

When we fill our glass at the tap, we can be making for ourselves a chemical cocktail that could possibly contain any or all of the following contaminants: chlorine and chlorine-by-products such as trihalomethanes, a known cancer-causing agent; nitrates; radon; lead; flouride; microbes; toxic wastes from dump sites or merely lawn chemicals. Since we cannot function in health without water, what are our best choices?

Filtration systems are a consumer's best buy for good health. The very best systems filter the water in the entire home so that bathing and showering (where we absorb more than we drink in a day) water is as pure as purified drinking water. The primo filters are those which employ at least three filtration methods in one unit: reverse osmosis, sediment filters and activated carbon filtration. Mere carbon filtration, whether activated charcoal or silver-impregnated, is not very effective for the majority of contaminants and must be changed often. Frequent filter changes cause the relatively inexpensive purchase price to balloon into a costly venture over the long-term. Distillation is not the best option for families with small children and pregnant women due to the fact that distilled water can leach minerals from the body. Small children and pregnant women simply cannot afford to have minerals leached out at a time when they need a constant supply. Due to the fact that there are so many different filtration systems on the market today, a consumer's best choice would be to contact Fred Van Liew at Fred's Essential Water & Air, 1-800-964-4303, for complete information and guidelines for purchasing a home water treatment system.

Sweeteners

Who of us does not have a sweet-tooth craving now and then? The difficulty lies in trying to decide what sweetener is the best choice. Refined cane sugar (white, table sugar) is called "the natural choice" in the industry's ads and even natural foods magazines are telling us refined cane sugar is not all that bad for us. The truth is that no matter what the industry's ads say, refined cane sugar does decrease immune response by lowering white blood cells up to four hours after ingesting sugar. Even natural sugar from honey, maple syrup, date sugar, dried cane juice (Sucanat®) fructose or fruit juices can have this same immune system effect.

The benefit of using natural sources of sweeteners rather than refined cane sugar is natural sweeteners do not have the up/down effect on the blood sugar like refined cane sugar. Refined cane sugar is addictive and stimulating to the adrenal glands which over time can cause depletion of adrenal sufficiency. In addition, refined cane sugar is the harbinger of dental caries. In third world countries today, dental caries are not found in the inhabitants until refined cane sugar consumption becomes prevalent.

Artificial sweeteners such as aspartame (Nutrasweet), saccharin, sorbitol all carry some health risk to sensitive individuals. The best thing I can say about these artificial sweeteners is that they are not a whole food; therefore, we do not eat them.

Sugar Equivalents:
1c Sugar =

1/2c Raw Honey	2/3c Maple Syrup
2/3c NutriCane Sugar	1/2c - 1c Fructose
1c Date Sugar	1c Fruit Juice
1c Sucanat	
1/2c Frozen fruit juice concentrate	

Beginning a change in diet to reflect a greater interest in whole foods can seem a bit overwhelming. The whole foods diet is so simple that it does seem somewhat complex. In our fast-paced society, slowing down and planning ahead is required to achieve a healthful whole foods diet. A quieter life is what we are all to be seeking according to the Word of God. How much easier a quiet life is found when we take time to notice what our Wonderful Creator has provided for us each season and plan our family's meals around these healthful provisions. A summer grape tastes so much better after the long winter wait.

The main points to remember when embarking on a whole foods diet are:

- Go slowly - Integrate whole food choices into the family's diet over an extended period of time allowing everyone to get used to new tastes and textures. Slow changes also prevent mom's body from being "shocked" into major detoxification which would not be good for baby,

- Plan for variety - Don't get locked into only eating a few foods. Encourage the entire family to try new foods (over and over until they learn to like it!).

NUTRIENT NEEDS OF PREGNANCY

Nutrient	Pregnancy Need	Reasons for increased nutrient need in pregnancy	Safety*
Protein	80 - 100 grams An individual protein amount for pregnancy may be calculated by multiplying pregnant weight by 0.62.	Rapid fetal tissue growth Amniotic fluid Placenta growth and development Maternal tissue growth: uterus, breasts Increased maternal circulating blood volume: a. Hemoglobin increase b. Plasma protein increase Maternal storage reserves for labor, delivery and lactation	Excessive protein intake has been associated with an increase in the number of prematurely-born babies and neonatal deaths, as well as fetal growth retardation. The studies suggest supplementing with more than 20% of calories from protein, is associated with fetal growth retardation whereas supplying less than 20% of calories from protein, yields a boost in weight of babies. Data is limited; however, and the debate over protein continues.
Calories	2500	Increased basal metabolic rate (BMR), energy needs Protein sparing for tissue growth	Biggest concern is getting healthy calories as opposed to empty calories from processed junk food.
Minerals			
Calcium	1200mg	Fetal skeleton formation Fetal tooth bud formation Increased maternal calcium metabolism Promotes normal blood clotting after birth Essential to normal contraction-relaxation cycle in muscles, especially heart Required for proper functioning of central nervous system	Conservative long-term maximum is 1,500mg per P. Hausman, *The Right Dose*, New York: Ballantine Books

Phosphorus	1200mg	Fetal skeleton formation Fetal tooth bud formation Increased maternal phosphorus metabolism	Calcium and phosphorus exist in a constant ratio in the blood. An excess of either limits use of calcium. Upper limit is 1500mg as with calcium.
Iron	18 - 30 mg	Increased maternal circulating blood volume, increased hemoglobin Fetal liver iron storage High iron cost of pregnancy	30mg is safe maximum; however, the National Research Council (NRC) recommends a 30 - 60mg supplement daily to an 18mg food intake. Author's opinion is that over 30mg should come from plant sources unless a deficiency is apparent.
Iodine	175mcg	Increased BMR - increased thyroxine production	Doses greater than ten times the normal requirement result in no toxic effect per Robert H. Garrison, Jr. M.A.,R.Ph. & Elizabeth Somer, M.A.,R.D., *The Nutrition Desk Reference*, Connecticut: Keats Publishing
Magnesium	500-1,000mg	Coenzyme in energy and protein metabolism Enzyme activator Tissue growth, cell metabolism Muscle action Binds calcium to tooth enamel	Toxicity seems to only be associated with those persons with renal insufficiency since the kidneys are very efficient at excreting excesses of magnesium in healthy individuals.
Zinc	20 - 35mg	Component of insulin Important in growth of skeleton and nervous system Immune function	Excess zinc decreases copper. To produce toxic effects, more than 2g must be taken; however, in one study, decreased immune function occurred in

			men who took 150mg of zinc twice daily for 6 weeks. Drs. Michael Schmidt, Lendon Smith and Keith Sehnert believe that 25mg is sufficient in healthy individuals. In those with skin problems, recurring infections, loss of taste sensation, etc., they may need higher amounts until symptoms improve but no more than 75mg daily unless a consultation with a competent health professional has occurred.
Copper	2 - 3 mg	Catalyst in formation of hemoglobin Constituent of 11 oxidase enzymes Influences iron absorption and mobilization and other tissue stores	Toxic at high levels.
Manganese	10 mg	Cofactor for a number of enzymes Collagen formation Synthesis of fatty acids and cholesterol Aids in formation of prothrombin Digestion of proteins Protein synthesis (by stimulating RNA polymerase activity)	Excessive manganese interferes with iron absorption and can precipitate iron-deficiency anemia. Low toxicity although toxicity symptoms have been observed in miners who inhale large amounts of the mineral.
Sodium	from diet	Assists in maintaining dramatically expanded blood volume needed for placental circulation. Normal functioning of muscles Essential component of amniotic fluid Maintains acid-base and water balance Cell membrane permeability	High sodium intake correlates with elevated blood pressure and edema.

Chromium	150mcg - 200mcg	Necessary for glucose utilization Possible cofactor of insulin	Range of concentration at which chromium is effective is narrow. If exceeded, the function of chromium reverses to inhibit, rather than enhance, insulin activity.
Selenium	100 - 200mcg	Constituent of glutathione peroxidase Binds to heavy metals and possibly reduces toxicity from mercury contamination Inhibits lipid peroxidation	Excessive selenium intake impairs embryonic development, and bone and cartilage develop abnormally. 500mcg should be maximum intake - diet plus supplement per Marilyn Shannon, *Fertility Cycles and Nutrition*, Ohio: CCL International, Inc.
Vitamins			
Vitamin A	5,000 I.U.	Aids bone and tissue growth and cell development Essential in development of enamel-forming cells in gum tissue Helps maintain health of skin and mucous membrane Constituent of visual pigments	5,000 I.U. maximum for pregnancy. I personally prefer that half of my vitamin A allowance come from beta-carotene. There has been some evidence to support a lower vitamin A allowance for pregnancy nearer to 5,000 I.U. maximum.
Vitamin D	400 I.U.	Needed for absorption of calcium and phosphorus, and mineralization of bones and teeth	Most toxic vitamin. The threshold of toxicity is 500 - 600 mcg/kg of body weight per day.
Vitamin E	400 I.U.	Needed for tissue growth To stabilize membranes and to protect them against free radical damage To protect the lungs against oxidative damage from air pollutants	Considered safe for non-pregnant adults at 1000 I.U., even by its opponents. Some midwives have seen an association with a too-firmly attached

			placenta with overzealous vitamin E supplementation. Recommended amount should be sufficient.
Vitamin B 1 Thiamine	25-100mg	Needed to remove carbon dioxide To covert amino acids, fats and carbohydrates to energy	Toxicity is rare and only seems to associated with thiamine injections.
Vitamin B 2 Riboflavin	25-100 mg	Important in energy production Essential for fatty acid and amino acid synthesis Necessary for cellular growth	No known toxicity.
Vitamin B 3 Niacin	25-100mg	Needed for metabolism of fatty acids and amino acids Essential for formation of steroids and red blood cells Maintains integrity of all body cells	Nicotinic acid at 750mg can produce vasodilation and flushing and itching of the skin. Nicotinamide does not produce this effect. Only supplement with nicotinamide, not nicotinic acid.
Vitamin B 6 Pyridoxine	25-100mg	Builds amino acids - protein metabolism/nitrogen metabolism Synthesis of hemoglobin Conversion of glycogen to glucose	Reported toxicity begins at 500 mg. Nutritional counseling would be appropriate at 200mg.
Folic Acid Folacin	400 - 2000mcg	Amino acid conversion Biosynthesis of purines, choline, methionine, etc.	Large doses may increase need for zinc, masks B 12 deficiency in vegetarians and those with pernicious anemia. Relatively safe even at 4,000 - 5,000 mg. Several studies have shown a link with a decrease in neural tube defects in mothers who adequately supplemented their diets with folic acid.

Vitamin B 12	25 - 100 mg	Activates amino acids during protein formation Biosynthesis of purines, choline, methionine, fatty acids, etc. Proper DNA replication	No toxicity reported. May rarely mask folic acid deficiency.
Pantothenic Acid	25 - 100 mg	Oxidation of fatty acids, pyruvate, etc. Synthesis of fatty acids, citrate, phospholipids, and cholesterol Acetylation of choline	No known toxicity.
Biotin	25 - 100 mg	Changes amino acids into protein Synthesis of fatty acids Derives energy from glucose Converts folic acid to usable form Reduces symptoms of zinc deficiency	No toxicity reported.
Vitamin C	1000 - 2000 mg	Formation of collagen, the protein that forms the basis for connective tissue Prevents bruising by maintaining integrity of capillary walls Metabolism of tyrosine and folic acid; iron absorption	Chewing may increase tooth decay if teeth are not brushed afterward. May decrease copper levels. Relatively safe except in iron-overload diseases. Some infants of mothers who consumed extremely large doses of vitamin C regularly in pregnancy experienced a deficiency after birth.

The Naturally Healthy Daily Food Plan

Daily Food Plan for Pregnancy: Protein, Vitamins, Minerals and Energy

Foods for Protein	Daily Amounts	Suggested Uses
Eggs - "Free-Range," "Fertile"	2	Breakfast use, whole boiled for snack, chopped or sliced hard-boiled for salads, in sandwiches.

Dairy Products - As close to the natural as possible, "Certified Raw Milk Cheese," "Yogurt with live cultures - unsweetened," cultured dairy is best
1 cup milk, skim - 7.9g
1 cup milk, whole - 8.6g
1 cup yogurt, plain - 9.45g
1 cup goat's milk - 5.4g
1 cup sheep's milk - 14.6g
Cheeses (1 1/4 oz.):
  Brie - 6.4g
  Camembert - 6.9g
  Cheddar - 8.5 g
  Cottage, plain - 4.6 g
  Cream - 1g
  Danish blue - 6.7g
  Farmer - 8.6g
  Feta, sheep/goat - 5.2g
  Goat's milk, soft - 4.4g
  Gouda - 8g
  Mozzarella - 8.4g
  Parmesan - 13.13g
  Ricotta - 3.13g
1 cup sour cream - 7.8g
1/2 cup dried milk , skim - 40.8g
1/2 cup dried milk, whole - 29.7g
	1 choice daily if you wish to have dairy products.	Beverage, in cooking, snacks, salads.
		*Soft cheeses and raw milk products may carry the bacteria *listeria* which is associated with miscarriage and stillbirth.

Meat - Organically-raised, Kosher if possible:
1 oz. lean beef - 8.3g*,
  lamb - 7 g,
  venison - 11.66 g, goat,
	1 choices daily from a selection of meats	Main dish, sandwich, salad, snack

1 oz. chicken, dk meat, wing - 4.6g
1 oz. turkey - 9.6g
1 oz. deep-sea fish with fins &
  scales:
  red snapper - 6g,
  tuna. - 11.6g (canned/water)
  haddock - 7.6g
  halibut - 7.6g
  orange roughy
  carp
  trout
  perch		

Legumes & Lentils: (1/2 cup) Blackeye pea - 9.2g Butter bean - 8g Green bean - 8.7g Lima bean - 8.6g Navy bean - 8.7g Pinto - 8.5g Red kidney bean - 8.8g Soya bean - 11.8g Chickpea/garbanzo - 9g Lentils - 8.6g Peas - 7.8g Split pea - 9.4g	2 for meat-eaters 5 for vegetarians	Cooked and served alone or in combination with grains, cheese, or meat; soups, salads; main dishes, peanuts as snacks or natural peanut butter in sandwich.
Grains & Flour: (1/2 cup) Amaranth - 3.9g Barley, pearled - 9g Barley - 10.8g Wheat, cracked - 10.45g Wheat bran - 15.9g Whole wheat bread - 10.4g Millet - 11.2g Oatmeal - 14g Brown rice - 2.9g Wild rice - 15.9g Quinoa - 14.7g Popcorn - 3.4g Rye bread - 9.4g Buckwheat - 9.2g Corn tortillas - 7.45g Cornmeal - 10.6g Hominy/grits - 9.8g	10 choices daily	Grains can be cooked whole, cracked or rolled, made into granola or cereal, made into bread to be eaten plain, for toast, croutons, pizza, sandwiches, cinnamon rolls, etc. Grains are very versatile and should be used liberally for they are not only an excellent source of protein but high in dietary fiber, calcium, iron, magnesium, manganese, and folic acid. If using the flour of the grains, try to obtain the freshest available (home

Flour - buckwheat - 6.8g
   carob - 4.5g
   rye - 9.3g
   soya - 41.6g
   wholewheat - 14.4g
   millet - 6.5g
   brown rice - 5.6g
		grinding is best). After several days the oils that are in the grain will oxidize after the grain is milled.

Vegetables & Fruit of worthy mention for protein: (1/2 cup) Soya bean sprouts - 7g Gherkins, pickled - 6.8g Olives, in brine - 12.4g Spinach, boiled - 5.7g Sweetcorn, cob - 4.6g Apricot, dried - 5.4g Avocado - 4.7g Banana chips, dried - 5g Coconut, creamed - 4.8g	1 choice daily	Can be eaten for snacks, salads, accompaniment to meals.
Nutritional Food Supplements: (1 oz.) Alfalfa Leaf Concentrate: 8.4g Brewer's Yeast - 11.4g Nori - 6.7g Spirulina - 17.3g	1 of these choices may be substituted for a vegetable & fruit choice	If used for protein purposes, one should use the powdered herb alone or in a smoothie drink. It takes 44 capsules of Spirulina to make an ounce of herb.
Nuts & Seeds: (1/2 cup) Almond - 21g Brazil - 15.8g Cashew - 17.3g Hickory - 13.2g Peanut - 29.5g Peanut Butter - 25.5g Pine nut - 11.3g Pistachio - 21.5g Walnut, black - 28.25g Walnut, English - 15.8g Linseed - 26g Melon - 28.25g Poppy - 20.4g Pumpkin - 28.25g Sesame - 28.25g Sunflower - 23.7g Tahini(sesame butter) - 27g	5 choices daily	Snacks, nut butters, in cooked or baked dishes.

Calcium-Rich Foods		
Dairy Products: 1 cup Milk, skim - 324mg 1 cup Milk, whole - 310.5mg 1 cup Goat's milk - 270mg 1 oz. Milk, dried skim - 387mg 1 oz. Milk, dried whole - 319.1mg 1/2 cup Sour cream - 105.1mg 1/2 cup yogurt, Goat's milk - 135.6mg 1/2 cup yogurt, Cow's milk - 155mg Cheeses: (1/2 cup or 1 lrg slice) Brie - 610mg Camembert - 395.5mg Cheddar - 813.6mg Cottage, plain - 82.5mg Cream - 110.7mg Danish blue - 565mg Edam - 870.1mg Farmer - 779.7mg Feta, Goat/Sheep - 406.8mg Goat's Milk, soft - 406.8mg Gouda - 386.2mg Mozzarella - 667mg Parmesan - 1356mg Ricotta - 271.2mg Rocquefort - 598.9mg	1 choice daily - If you chose a dairy product for one of your protein choices, eliminate this category for the day.	Beverage, snacks, in cooked foods, sandwiches.
Soya Products: (1/2 cup) Cheese - 508.5 mg Tofu - 572.9mg 1 cup Tofu Milk - 250mg 1 cup Soy Milk - 35.1mg	You may choose this instead of the 1 dairy above.	As stated above.
Grains, & Flours (1/2 cup) Amaranth - 301.7mg Corn Tortillas - 158.2mg Carob - 315.3mg Soya - 254mg Wholewheat croutons - 138mg Wheat Bran - 124.3mg	2 choices daily.	Whole or cracked alone or in baked goods, salads, as an addition to cooked foods.

Nuts & Seeds: (1 oz. = 1 sm. handful)
   Almond - 70.6mg
   Brazil - 56.6mg
   Cashew - 13.6mg
   Hazel (Filberts) - 63.6mg
   Peanut - 22.7mg
   Pistachio - 39.4mg
   Walnuts - 30mg
   Poppy - 438.78mg
   Sesame - 351.5mg
   Sunflower - 36.4mg
Herbs & Spices are very high in calcium—for instance, cinnamon contains 184.4mg per 1/2 oz.
	You may choose from this category as a substitute for the Protein nuts & seeds category.	Snacks, baked goods, in cooked dishes, as nut or seed butters, salads.

Vegetables & Fruits: (1/2 cup) Alfalfa Sprouts - 37.3 mg Soya Bean Sprouts - 54mg Beetroot tops - 134.5mg Bok Choy - 175mg Borage - 105.1mg Broccoli - 124.3mg Collard greens - 87mg Dandelion leaves - 158.2mg Gherkins, pickled - 150.3mg Kale - 282mg Romaine lettuce - 75.7mg Mustard greens - 85mg Spinach - 687mg Turnip Green - 150mg Watercress - 248.6mg 1 oz. Kelp - 289.4mg 1 oz. Alfalfa Leaf Conc. - 254mg Apple Juice Conc. - 508.5mg Apricot, Dried - 104mg Blackberry, raw - 71mg	1 choice daily.	As stated above.
Dried Fruits Black Currant, dried - 107.35mg Date, dried - 77mg Fig, dried - 316.4mg Fig, dried, stewed - 180.8mg Orange (1 whole) - 70mg Olives, green - 118.65mg Raisin - 69mg Rhubarb, stewed - 105mg	As stated above.	Snacks, in baked foods.

Iron-Rich Foods		
Legumes, Nuts, Seeds, Grains & Whole-Grain Breads generally have an iron content from 3 - 7 mg.	4 - 5 choices daily	As stated above under Legumes, Grains & Flours
Egg Yolk - 6.1mg	2 daily - If you already chose 2 eggs in the protein category, you have met your daily egg requirement.	As stated above under Eggs.
Green, leafy vegetables and other dark green vegetables average 3mg of iron per 1/2 cup serving—these should be organic since you are eating the part that gets sprayed. Highest mg sources: Spinach Greens: collard, turnip, mustard, kale, beetroot tops, dandelion, alfalfa leaf, kelp Broccoli Peas Leaf & Romaine lettuce Endive Asparagus Sprouts	3 choices daily.	As stated above.
Iodine-Rich Foods		
Iodized Sea Salt Kelp, Nori, Spirulina, Kombu, Wakame - Sea Vegetables Seafood	Season food to taste with sea salt or kelp and other herbs. May choose 1 - 2 servings of seafood per week	Main dish, salad, sandwiches, in other cooked dishes.
Vitamin-Rich Foods		
Vitamin A 1 tbsp. Butter - 268.48mcg 1 oz. Cheeses - 106mcg 1 tbsp. Mayonnaise - 162mcg 1/2 cup Beetroot tops - 689.3mcg 1/2 cup Borage - 474.6mcg 1/2 cup Carrots (1 lrg) - 2260mcg 1/2 cup Dandelion leaves - 1582mcg 1/2 cup Kale - 1130mcg 1/2 cup Spinach - 915.3mcg	3 choices daily	In cooking or on foods, salads, cooked dishes, snacks

1/2 cup Sweet Potato - 1951.5mcg 1/2 cup Turnip Greens - 678mcg 1/2 cup Watercress - 565mcg 1/2 cup Romaine lettuce - 213.6mcg 1/2 cup Apricot, dried - 678mcg 1/2 cup Mango - 439.6mcg 1/2 cup Cantaloupe - 376.3mcg 1/2 cup Papaya - 227mcg 1/2 cup Prune, dried - 225mcg		
Vitamin C Foods Rose Hips(Ascerola) - 1204.6mg Black Currant (1/2 c)- 198mg Guava (1/2)- 207mg Kiwifruit(1 whole) - 110.7mg Orange, Whole - 80mg Grapefruit (1/2)- 43mg Lemon (1 avg) - 39.5mg Cantaloupe (1/2)- 66mg Papaya (1/2)- 84mg Mango (1 whole) - 84mg Strawberry (1/2 c)- 66mg Watermelon (1/2" sl.) - 42mg Apricots (1/2 cup) - 11.3mg Orange Juice 1 cup) - 124mg Broccoli (4 oz = 1 c) - 133mg Brussel Sprouts - 102mg Green Pepper (1 lrg) - 110mg Red Pepper (1 lrg) - 204mg	3 choices daily Make an additional choice out of the Vitamin A and C foods for one choice of a yellow or orange vegetable or fruit.	Snacks, salads, cooked, juices are the last choice since you miss out on the fiber and get instead a concentrated fruit sugar source.
Folic Acid Foods (the 4 oz values are approximately 1 cup) Asparagus (4 oz.) - 110.8mcg Broccoli (4 oz.) - 98.3mcg Endive (4 oz.) - 372.9mcg Okra (4 oz.) - 113mcg Peas (1/2 c) - 88mcg Spinach, cook (1/2 c) - 158mcg Avocado (1/2) - 74.6mcg Egg yolk - 59mcg Wheat Bran (1/2 c) - 293.8mcg Soy Flour (1/2 c) - 389.85mcg WW Flour (1/2 c) - 64.4mcg	1 serving daily.	Cooked as main dish or soups, snacks, in salads, breads.

Peanut Butter (1 oz.) - 16mcg Beans: Navy, Kidney, Pinto, Garbanzo, Black (1 c) - 60- 100mcg Beets (4 oz.) - 126mcg Lettuce, Leaf, Romaine (1 c) - 98mcg Spinach (1 c) - 106mcg		
Fats & Oils 1 tbsp. butter 1 tbsp. mayonnaise 1 tbsp. olive or canola oil 1/4 avocado 1 tbsp. peanut or almond butter 1 tbsp. tahini Small Handfull of Nuts: Almonds, Brazil, Cashews, Hazel/Filberts, Hickory, Macadamia, Peanuts, Pecans, Pine, Pistachio, Walnut	3 choices - If you have chosen any of these as your vitamin A foods, reduce these choices accordingly.	In cooking or on foods, snacks

Information in this food plan was compiled from the following sources: *Nutrition in Pregnancy and Lactation* by Bonnie Worthington-Roberts and Sue Rodwell Williams, Times Mirror/Mosby College Publishing: St. Louis, Missouri; *Eating for Two* by Issaac Cronin and Gail Sforza Brewer, Bantam books, Inc.:New York, New York What; *Every Pregnant Woman Should Know* by Gail Sforza Brewer with Tom Brewer, M.D., Penguin Books: New York, New York; *The Nutrition Desk Reference* by Robert H., Garrison, Jr., M.A., R.Ph. and Elizabeth Somer, M.A., R.D., Keats Publishing: New Canaan, Connecticut.

MAKING THE CHANGE TO WHOLE FOODS

The following is a list compiled to give an idea to the beginner of "whole food" eating what they can substitute for their usual processed ingredients.

Whole Food	Imitation/Processed Version
Freshly ground whole grain flour	Packaged white, wheat, rye, barley, oat flour
Purified water	Soda pop, Coke, Dr. Pepper, Kool-aid, etc.
Unsweetened fruit juices - fresh squeezed is best, frozen better, bottled okay	Juice "cocktails" or "drinks," powdered, artificial-flavored drinks
Herbal teas (no caffeine); green tea (caffeine)	Black tea, contains caffeine, coffee
Whole wheat pasta, spelt pasta, sesame pasta, etc.	White pasta of any shape
Brown rice, buckwheat, millet, barley, rye, oats, etc.	White rice, refined grains
Whole grains - whole, freshly cracked or rolled	Boxed cereals, processed grains
Whole grain toasted bread crumbs	Boxed croutons
Whole grain crackers	White flour crackers
Unrefined oils - cold-pressed or extra virgin olive oil	Hydrogenated fats and shortenings, refined oils
Butter	Margarines, spreads
Goat milk, Tofu milk, Certified raw milk	Homogenized, pasteurized milk
Certified raw milk cheese - "It's naturally white."	Dyed, added-to, homogenized, pasteurized cheeses
Plain yogurt with live cultures	Sweetened varieties or frozen varieties
Cultured dairy products	Uncultured, sweet dairy products
Unfiltered, unpasteurized apple cider vinegar	Distilled vinegar
Baking powder without aluminum or yeast	Baking powder containing aluminum
Low sodium baking powder (aluminum-free)	Baking soda
Carob powder	Cocoa, chocolate
Uncooked, unfiltered "Raw" honey - 1/2 c = 1 c sugar; Grade A Pure Maple syrup	White sugars (sucrose, dextrose, glucose, "raw" sugar, corn syrup)

Unsulphured molasses, fruit juices/purees, dried raw cane juice, fructose in small amounts	Brown sugar
Baked chips, popcorn, dried unsulphured fruits, raw nuts, granola	Fried chips, sulphured dried fruits, candy, snack items with added sugars, dyes, preservatives, other additives.
Organic fruits, vegetables and grains	Conventional fruits, vegetables and grains
Unhydrogenated peanut butter made with 100% peanuts without added sugar (or salt, if preferred), sesame butter (tahini), cashew butter, almond butter	Commercial peanut butter and other nut butters
Raw, lightly steamed, grilled vegetables	Boiled, fried vegetables
Raw fruits	Canned or frozen fruits with added sugars.
Clean (Leviticus 11) animals that can be completely bled - common ones we eat: chicken, turkey, deer, beef (in moderation)	Commercially raised animals fed grains/hay treated with chemicals and given chemicals to keep them "healthy"?
Beans, peas, lentils, whole grains, etc.	Eat less meat - Majority of protein should be from vegetable source for maximum health.

PART THREE

Discomforts and Health Variations Possible in the Childbearing Years

"What time I am afraid, I will trust in thee. In God I will praise His word, in God I have put my trust; I will not fear what flesh can do to me." Psalm 56:3-4

A BIBLICAL PRESCRIPTION
FOR HEALTH

The natural health and natural birth movements are full of diverse beliefs and practices. Many of these are blatantly anti-biblical and overtly occultic. Others seem to be toddling right on the edge ready to fall one way or another according to the handling of the specific practice. Even among practices obviously rooted in the Bible and exampled in the Bible, there are great extremes: "I'll use natural remedies only. We never go to doctors. They and their drugs are evil;" "I would never use herbs or have a home birth. It is unsafe and rooted in the occult;" "We depend totally on the Lord for healing and birth. To use herbs, doctors or even birth equipment is to depend on the arm of man, not God."

The following study is not meant to decide for you which belief, if any, is right; rather, this chapter is an entreaty for you to search the Word of God for answers to family health questions. We believe the Word contains all the answers for us, and that we need to test each movement, practice, book or idea by the Word of our unchanging Lord for validity in our lives.

Through study of healing in God's Word, my husband and I discovered that God used a variety of healing methods. We also have a clear understanding that *no matter what means used in the Word, He, our Lord God Creator, is always the Healer.* Before looking at methods of healing, we first must look to the causes of sickness or disease. We found many different causes, yet they all seem to fit into three categories:

1. Chastening
   - Sin of all - Man's original sin brought death and disease (Genesis 2:16-17, 3:16-24)
   - Sin from personal actions (2 Kings 5:27 and II Chronicles 21:12-19, Micah 6:13)
   - Satan's afflictions (Luke 13:16)
   - Judgment of God (II Chronicles 21:14-19)
2. Sickness Unto Death: This category could fit into either of the other two.
   - Accidents (II Kings 1:2)
   - Approaching death (Genesis 48:1)
   - Despair or Hopelessness (Proverbs 13:12)
3. God's Sovereign Power: Show God's strength (John 11:4, John 9:1-3, I Thessalonians)

As we have included this study in this pregnancy book, we want it to be clearly understood that *we do not believe pregnancy is in itself a diseased condition.* God spoke of pregnancy (Genesis 1:28) before the fall of man which brought sickness and death. There are instances in which discomforts and variations of health arise during pregnancy or birth, and these conditions are what we are addressing in this chapter.

Those healing methods that are demonstrated in the Bible are: Natural Means, Physician's Medicine for Healing, and Divine Healing.

Natural Means

Those practices which we all use to some degree in our everyday life no matter what belief in healing.

A. **Rest** - Rest is an important admonition for us from the Lord. Even He, our wonderful Creator, rested on the seventh day from all His work, and He instituted the Sabbath as a blessing of rest and renewal for us (Genesis 2:2-3). The Word speaks of rest as in: relaxing or ceasing from work (Genesis 2:2-3, 18:4, Exodus 20:10,11), sleep (John 11:13, Mark 6:31), being confident in the day of trouble (Habbukuk 3:16-19, Psalm 55:6), rest of salvation (Hebrews 4), rest in death (Job 3:13,17, Revelation 14:13). I know that as a mother of young ones, I find it imperative to my functioning in my daily duties (and absolutely necessary for the working of a gentle spirit) that I get to bed early and take a short nap with my little ones when possible. We, as a family, set aside one day per week just to enjoy the day that the Lord has given us with no work.

B. **Sleep** - Restful sleep is renewing to our body, soul and spirit. "I will both lay me down in peace, and sleep: for thou, Lord, only makest me to dwell in safety" (Psalm 4:8). The Word says that God desires to give His beloved sleep (Psalm 127:2), and it is vain (of no lasting benefit) to stay up late, get up early and be sorrowful of heart. From the following passages in scripture, we see that sleep is beneficial for us when we are trusting in the Lord, obeying the instructions and commands of our parents, following wisdom, working hard, doing our duty first and dreaming or dwelling on good things (Psalm 3:5, Psalm 127:2, Proverbs 6:20-22, Ecclesiastes 5:12, Psalm 132:1-5, Jeremiah 31:23-26). I am grateful for the "early to bed, early to rise" admonition of my grandparents and parents which obviously came from God's abiding Word. When I do not get adequate sleep, my head aches and my tummy is queasy until I get the needed restoration of sleep.

C. **Cleanliness** - Cleanliness is a necessary part of health and healing. We all know what happens when wounds are left unattended, unwashed and filled with filth. God gave specific instructions on hygiene practices (Deuteronomy 23:10-14). His instructions include cleansing and purifying with running water (Numbers 19:13,18, Exodus 30:18,19, Leviticus 8:6, 15:13) and cover or disposing of waste which is issued from us. Handwashing after eliminating; wiping noses; body washing; dish/utensil/food washing and covering or flushing excrement are examples of cleanliness. Disposable tissues are an example of following a hygiene practice from the Word since the Lord recommended that His people dispose of cloth items that had come into contact with bodily discharges. Cleansing inside is also important for health. Running (drinking) water through our bodies for inside cleansing is a necessity.

D. **Isolation during illness with discharge from body** - The instruction about issue of flesh whether it be running or stopped up is very clear: it is unclean and needs to be washed in water and kept away from others (Leviticus 15). We find this to be the area most often ignored by families, yet one that could benefit families the most. If we choose not to isolate ourselves during an illness and continue our regular outside activities, we will neglect other areas such as rest, sleep, merry heart and cleanliness. Staying home when ill, even with the "common cold" (is it common because we pass it around freely?), allows us to rest, get adequate sleep, be merrier because we are not traipsing around town when we do not feel great and gives us instant access to water to wash with which is not available in town (or is located in unclean public restrooms).

E. **Merry Heart** - "A merry heart doeth good like a medicine, but a broken spirit drieth the bones" (Proverbs 17:22, Proverbs 15:13, 15, 30, James 5:13, Proverbs 14:13, Proverbs 16:24, Proverbs 18:14). Having a merry heart and being able to rejoice even through afflictions as Paul did and James recommends is indeed good medicine. Our hope in the Lord and knowledge that His strength is made strong in our weakness enables us to persevere through the roughest of times. It is when we despair, without hope and reject His almighty comfort that our spirits break which can cause illness, even death (Proverbs 13:12).

F. **Herbal Medicine** - Herbal medicine, as discussed in the introduction to this book, is the use of plants in concentrated or standardized doses to create a medicinal action. Herbal medicine also includes the eating of healthy whole foods: plants, fruit of the vine, nuts and seeds. Fresh food creates healthy bodies. There are several direct referrals to the use of herbal (plant) medicine in the Word (Isaiah 38:21, Ezekial 47:12, I Timothy 5:23). God gave us plants to use for food in Genesis 29:30. Also indicated in scripture is that He intended herbs for medicine as well. The "art of the apothecary" as it is referred to in the Word is an art that used herbs and spices for healing. God's instruction for making the holy anointing oil and incense for the priests and temple is "make after the art of the apothecary" or make in the way the apothecary makes his oils and incense (Exodus 30:25, 35). In the new Jerusalem described in Revelation, John speaks of being shown the tree of life whose leaves "were for the healing of the nations" (Revelation 22:2).

Physician's Medicine for Healing

A doctor's or physician's job is primarily to treat disease or sickness, rather than in the prevention of illness. The apothecary has been replaced by pharmacists, and they supplement a physician's work by supplying the chemicals (drugs) most physicians use in treating patients. Does God view all modern medicine: physicians, surgery, medicines (drugs) as evil? We do not believe so. We find it incomprehensible that our Lord would liken Himself to a physician come to heal the sick if He felt all physicians were evil.

God called Luke, a Gentile physician, to write the most complete account of the life of our Lord as well as the book of Acts. Paul referred to Luke, his companion, twice as "the beloved physician" (Colossians 4:14, Philemon 24). Perhaps it was from Luke that Paul learned of "using a little wine for thy stomach's sake and thine often infirmities" (I Timothy 5:23). If God felt all physicians were evil, would He call a still-practicing-evil man (because the Word does not indicate that Luke abandoned his physician's work) to write His Holy Word? In addition, if the Word is valid for us today and God, All-Knowing or Omniscient, knew how the medical establishment would be, would he have had the writers of His Holy Word make it plain that some physician's services were utilized during biblical times? We are not saying the Lord condones the evil practices that go on in the medical establishment today, such as euthanasia, abortion, stealing parental rights, etc.

Three important factors in employing a physician in the healing process:

1. You must be sick. It might be supposed from looking at those who sought physicians in the Word that one must be very sick with an affliction one has not been able to care for naturally. The cost of running to the doctor every time there is a self-limiting problem might be avoided if we first made certain that we are following the natural principles given by God. If we are not following God's basic principles instituted to give us health, we need to attend to those areas first. In our family, we have a limit of time and degree of illness or injury that we abide by before turning to a physician for other options. There are situations where we would seek medical assistance immediately, such as meningitis or a broken bone.
2. It is wrong to seek *only* physicians. King Asa was greatly diseased in his feet and sought only the physicians, not the Lord (II Chronicles 16:12). The use of the word *only* implies that seeking the physician is not wrong for "greatly diseased feet" but failing to also seek the Lord, "who kills and makes alive, wounds and heals and holds us in the palm of His hand" (Deuteronomy 32:29) is wrong. One wonders if King Asa might have benefited from the natural means God had provided as well.
3. Physicians are servants, not M.Deitys (Genesis 50:2). We must keep up with our personal responsibility to follow the natural means provided by God for health and

seek Him for spiritual renewal and restoration. Failing to do these two, and then seeking physicians for all is grossly wrong, sounds a bit like King Asa who died for this sin. How much better to find a servant of God in the practice of medicine who shares a partnership with you in restoring family health than one who finds personal satisfaction (pride?) in *his* healing of the family. God's position as ultimate healer even through the means He has provided us must not be usurped by well-meaning physicians or even by ourselves being prideful in our use of natural measures. God *is* the healer. When a drug works, praise God. When diet works, praise God. When herbs, rest, repentance, anointing and prayer deliver, praise God.

Pharmaceuticals are not a direct creation of God. They are man-made which means they are fallible and may cause problems as well as helping with certain problems. Pharmaceuticals are intended to "improve" on that which our Mighty Creator gave us; however, this logic applies to motor vehicles as well. Automobiles are man-made and are meant to improve on the ability and speed of our feet to carry us from one place to another. We believe that we may utilize pharmaceuticals when necessary in acute illness situations. Intense personal seeking of God's will for a medical situation is vital. Could what we are speaking about be a similar situation to "the eating of all things or only eating herbs" illustration Paul used in Romans 14:2-8? Let us not judge one another according to the convictions God has placed on our hearts concerning these issues. Let us instead focus on encouraging those around us to seek the Lord and His Word so that the Holy Spirit may bring about in them their own personal convictions in this non-doctrinal matter.

Any time there is a health care situation in our household, we, first and foremost pray for healing and, even more, pray that God would use the situation as He wills to search out our hearts, to cleanse us and grow us spiritually. We use natural measures the majority of the time while praying. Pharmaceuticals are rarely used in our family due to much study in natural healing. When we do use them, we limit pharmaceutical use to crisis situations while we are getting the rest of our lives back in line with God's principles of health and holiness.

While the statement that "all physicians are not evil" is true, I could not say that all are practicing under God's direction and principles. We *must* be discerning about when to seek medical assistance, whom to seek and what practices they advocate. The same discernment is absolutely necessary when dealing with natural health care providers. We must ascertain whether health care providers, their practices and beliefs follow the Word of God and flee from those who do not meet the Word Test:

- Does scripture support the practice or belief? Even if not directly referred to in the Word, have we made certain there is not a prohibition about the practice?

- Is it physiologically sound? Does the body really work this way, or did someone have this "revealed" to them from "higher powers"? Revelations must agree with the Word.
- Does it build and maintain the body and its natural functions, or is it self-destructive in some way? We are to take care of the "temple of God," our bodies, not destroy it.

Divine Healing

Divine healing *is* real. In John 4:46-53, the nobleman believed Jesus' word that his son lived. He returned to his home, found that indeed his son was healed at the very hour Jesus had spoken. This caused his entire household to believe. Jesus gave this gift of healing to His disciples who then proceeded in their ministry to heal (Matthew 10: 1-8). He provided in the gifts of the Spirit the gift of healing so that those blessed with this gift might minister to others in the body in this way (I Corinthians 12:9).

James' instructions for healing by faith are:

1. Pray. Beseech the Lord (James 5:13).
2. Call for the church elders. Have the elders pray over the afflicted anointing with oil in the name of Jesus (James 5:14,15).
3. Confess faults one to another and pray one for another that ye may be healed (James 5:16). This last implies an ongoing confession one to another in the faith and an ongoing praying for one another.

Others in the Word were healed simply by praying and believing in Jesus.

We must recognize that the physical affliction may have a spiritual source, sin. As stated before, man's original sin brought into the world death and disease (Genesis 3:16-19). Man's continuing actions of sinfulness also can bring disease (Luke 13:16, II Kings 5:27, II Chronicles 21: 12-19). An example may be of one who commits adultery only to find that the partner in adultery carried a sexually-transmitted disease. The result of that sin is physical, yet the root is immorality. The "cure" requires repentance and restoration with the Lord as well as treatment of the physical ill. We are wise to recognize when a physical problem is just physical. Personal or family sin is not at the root of every ailment (John 9:1-3). Disease or affliction may come so that the works of God may be made manifest in us, meaning that God does use affliction to bring about spiritual growth in us and others through our response to the affliction.

Spiritual health includes accepting God's sovereign will, even when He chooses not to deliver us from afflictions. Paul had an affliction that he besought the Lord to deliver him from three times. The Lord's answer was, each time, "My grace is sufficient for thee, for my strength is made perfect in weakness" (II Corinthians 12:8-10). Therefore, Paul gloried in his infirmities that Christ's power may rest upon him for when he is weak, he is strong in the Lord. Some might argue that Paul was not experiencing a bodily affliction. Instead of spending time in disagreement, can we instead agree that the Word does not exclude sickness or disease from the affliction category?

Jesus said of Lazarus' sickness that "This sickness is not unto death, but for the glory of God, that the Son of God might be glorified thereby" (John 11:4). While Jesus did raise Lazarus from the dead, Lazarus and his family did have to suffer while waiting on the Lord. Jesus delivered Lazarus from death in *His* perfect timing in order that He, the Lord, might be glorified through the incident. These are other instances in the Bible where faithful men of God suffered for long periods in order for the Lord's eternal plan to be fulfilled such as Joseph's bondage in Egypt. Joseph remained faithful to the Lord throughout years of slavery and imprisonment. This led ultimately to God miraculously leading His people out of Egypt into the Promised Land.

The key factors for healing are to beseech the Lord for healing, wait for His timing and not despair or have our faith weakened because of a continuing affliction (I Thessalonians 3:3, II Timothy 4:5). Instead of believing we are to be free from all suffering, including physical affliction, we might want to look more closely at those scriptures assuring us of suffering for Jesus' sake as Lazarus did (Matthew 24:9, Mark 4:17, I Thessalonians 1:6, II Timothy 3:11). The Word also says that afflictions are but for a moment in the eternal plan (II Corinthians 4:17). The personal suffering and the comfort we receive from the Lord enable us to help and comfort others (II Corinthians 1:3-11).

The Lord does promise deliverance from all afflictions in Psalm 34, verse 19; however, it is not for us to presume when or how He does this. Sometimes the deliverance may take place only at our death, not delivered in life from the affliction. Should we stomp our feet before God demanding immediate healing from all afflictions in every situation at every time we want it? We think not. We may humble ourselves before Him, cry out for healing, hope it will be quick while accepting His Sovereignty and comfort, respond with a willingness to let God use the situation for growth (James 1:2-4), know by faith that nothing can separate us from Him (Romans 8:33-39). Yes. As Shadrach, Meshach and Abednego so eloquently put it "Our God is able to deliver us, but if He does not choose to, He is still the one true God" (Daniel 3:17-18).

We came to see as we studied healing in the Bible that God *is* the Healer. We came to see that the Word recommends the use of natural means for health and healing and condones the use of physicians when necessary. Above all, we clearly see that seeking the Lord, praying, crying out to and trusting Him is the foundation for any healing program.

Divine healing is the root, the foundation. The use of other means is just that, a means God uses to accomplish His will. We believe our responsibility lies in being careful about our caregiver choice as well as choosing natural alternatives in self-limiting illnesses. If a practice does not pass the "Word Test," then we do not use that practice in our home. As our dear friend, Vivian Mock, said of our "using available techniques and practices, preferably natural," of approaching family health: "If you were in an airplane on its way to crashing and were told you had to jump, would you jump without the parachute provided and just pray and expect God to miraculously deliver you? That would seem foolish and presumptuous. You, of course, would put on that parachute (the means at your disposal) because you *have* to jump, and you would pray all the way down that your parachute would open or that God *would* miraculously provide a cushy landing if it did not."

During the childbearing year, most of the discomforts mom may experience will not create an illness in mom's body. Pregnancy is not an illness. Birthing a baby is not an illness. We do well to take that important factor into consideration when choosing a caregiver. Our choice needs to reflect our own attitude toward pregnancy and birth, a natural process God designed for women.

BODY SYSTEM CHANGES DURING PREGNANCY

Circulatory System

Blood and plasma volume expand by 50% to 60% to meet the needs of the growing baby and the placenta by which the baby receives nourishment. Expansion of blood volume peaks at 28 - 30 weeks. Anne Frye states in her book *Understanding Lab Work in the Childbearing Year*, "For a woman whose pre-pregnant weight was 130 lbs, blood volume increases about 2.1 quarts (from 3.5 to a total of 5.6 quarts)." This additional blood volume necessitates at least a two quart water and juice intake by mom to keep up with additional fluid stores which perfuse the placenta and help protect mom in case of hemorrhage during birth.

What gets in mom's bloodstream enters the baby. Baby is what mom eats, drinks, inhales or absorbs through her skin. The placenta is not a barrier that prevents harmful substances from getting to baby. It is instead like a sieve through which passes nutrients or terotagens (harmful substances) through the umbilical cord to baby. Placental function begins in the early weeks of pregnancy. The placenta transfers nutrients and oxygen to the baby and returns the baby's waste products back to mom's bloodstream for cleansing (detoxifying).

The placenta implants into the uterine wall (endometrium) by burrowing into the capillary supply. A "lake of maternal blood" is formed by blood pooling beneath the placental surface. The circulatory mechanism is know as an Arterial-Venous (A-V) shunt, as there is no capillary connection involved. The better the nutrients and the lower the toxins in mom, the more firmly an implantation will occur. A firm implantation will lower the risk of placental abruption later in the pregnancy.

Due to the expanded blood volume in pregnancy, some women experience dilutional anemia (low level of hemoglobin, oxygen-carrying red blood cells). This condition is most common in the seventh month of pregnancy when blood volume peaks. Increased circulatory demand can lead to varicosities (bulging veins) in women who have a family history of such or in those women whose venous walls are weakened from too much pressure.

General Recommendations for Circulatory System Support:

1. Drink at least two (2) quarts of water or diluted, unsweetened juice each day.
2. Include plenty of garlic, onions and fiber foods in diet.
3. Maintain good pregnancy posture (explained under Structural System) and avoid standing for long periods of time without resting with feet elevated.
4. Practice deep-breathing for fifteen (15) minutes each day.

Glandular System
Liver

The liver is our body's detoxifying organ; however, this is not its only function. If the liver is not doing its job properly, the whole body will suffer because the release of toxins into the bloodstream means the circulatory system will carry them to the entire body. A heavier burden is placed on the liver during pregnancy because more substances, natural to our body, are circulating.

The liver is responsible for the regulation and release of hormones in the blood, maintaining blood sugar (glucose) levels and detoxifying the blood of toxins that are released in the early portion of pregnancy. Our bodies naturally begin this detox in early pregnancy. I feel this is our Creator's way of creating a clean, pure place for our babies to grow. It is important to aid the liver's function at least during the first trimester. This is especially true for those who were unable to cleanse or detoxify the body prior to conceiving and for the woman who has a history of morning sickness. Pregnancy is the wrong time to consider a cleanse as the liver has enough to process already.

General Recommendations for Liver Support:
1. Eat bitter foods because they stimulate and support the liver. These foods include: spinach, beet root, romaine lettuce (most dark, leafy greens), and dandelion greens.
2. Drink water with a wedge of lemon squeezed in it several times each day. This supports the gallbladder as well.
3. Fermented foods are also beneficial: yogurt, sauerkraut, tamari, etc.
4. Milk thistle (containing at least 70% silymarin) is the best supportive supplement in my opinion. Recommended amount: 3 tablets per day.

Pancreas

The pancreas is an exocrine gland (exocrine glands secrete into the intestine, not the blood) that produces insulin, which is a glucose-regulating hormone. Its function depends largely on the liver (liver functions poorly, pancreas functions poorly). The placenta produces hormones that suppress insulin and allow extra glucose for circulation in Mom for use by baby and placenta. Glucose in foods is a fuel immediately available for use in the body. Excess glucose is converted to glycogen and stored in the liver until needed; then it is converted back to glucose for use. A larger demand for glucose (fuel) in pregnancy does not mean one should fill up on sweets and refined carbohydrates. It does indicate a need for complex carbohydrates which slowly release glucose into the bloodstream.

Too many refined carbohydrates place a greater demand on the pancreas. The pancreas then overproduces insulin to control the up/down blood sugar variations. Blood sugar rises; the pancreas produces an insulin surge. This creates a hypoglycemic reaction/abuse syndrome. Abusing the pancreas in this way can and does produce diabetes if the pancreas is weakened by the up/down variations, family history, alcohol, smoking, stress, obesity and/or lack of exercise.

General Recommendations for Pancreatic Support:
1. Eat complex carbohydrates, high protein whole grains and whole foods.
2. Support the pancreas by first supporting the liver.

Pituitary

The pituitary has a special function in pregnancy because it produces hormones that are essential to the pregnancy and childbirth process. The pituitary acts as a director for the hormone production of other glands in the body. It works in connection with the hypothalamus which produces: oxytocin - controls labor and breastfeeding, ADH (anti-diuretic hormone) - oversees the body's water balance mechanism.

The pituitary produces: *melanocyte-stimulating hormone* which increases skin pigmentation, *thyroid stimulating hormone* (TSH), *adrenocorticotropic hormone* (ACTH) which stimulates the adrenals to produce cortisone, *prolactin* which regulates milk production, *growth hormone* which controls the body's growth, *follicle-stimulating hormone* (FSH) which stimulates ovum production and *luteinizing hormone* (LH) which induces ovulation and helps maintain early pregnancy.

General Recommendations for Pituitary Support:
1. Include alfalfa in diet through supplements or organic alfalfa sprouts. Alfalfa can cause a problem similar to *Lupus* in some individuals.
2. For low-pituitary function, supplementation very early pregnancy as well as labor and birth may need to include some herbs with hormone precursors to stimulate pituitary function. See Herbs To Use Caution With During Pregnancy.

Thyroid

The thyroid is an endocrine gland that is responsible for the regulation of oxygen use, the rate at which various organs function, the metabolism of food and the growth and development of bone and muscle. All body systems are affected if function of the thyroid is abnormal.

Hormones produced by the thyroid: *thyroxine* (T 4) and triiodothyronine (T 3). T 4 increases early in the first trimester because of an increase in thyroxine-binding globulin (TBG) which is caused by high estrogen levels.

General Recommendations for Thyroid Support:
1. Insure adequate iodine intake by eating sea vegetables, deep sea fish or iodized sea salt.
2. Supplement with extra vitamin C and E.
3. For hypothyroid, organic thyroid glandular supplements from cattle or sheep may be beneficial. Recommended amount: 1 per day.

Parathyroid

The parathyroid is responsible for the regulation of calcium in the body. Parathyroid hormone (PTH) increases as calcium levels fall, prompting release of calcium from bones to raise blood levels. Serum calcium decreases by 10% in pregnancy which corresponds with a PTH rise at twenty (20) weeks. Phosphorus levels are unaffected.

General Recommendations for Parathyroid Support:
1. Lower food intake of high-phosphorus foods.
2. Increase calcium foods (dairy is high phosphorus).

Adrenals

The adrenals increase in size and activity during pregnancy. The classes of hormones produced by the cortex (outer layer) are: *mineralocorticoids* - control water and mineral balance, *glucocorticoids* - regulate normal metabolism and resistance to stress and *gonadocorticoids* (sex hormones) - supplement hormones produced by gonads. The medulla, inner layer, produces *adrenalin* and *noradrenalin* (norepinephrine) to regulate blood pressure.

Overstimulation of the adrenals is a concern whether one is pregnant or not. Highly processed foods, sugar, caffeine, stress and smoking overwork the adrenal gland until function is diminished without getting a "fix" from above-mentioned stimulants.

General Recommendations for Adrenal Support:
1. Consume a whole foods diet.
2. No smoking or caffeine drinking.
3. If adrenals are already overstimulated, supplement with additional B vitamins.

Uterus

The uterus is a muscular organ that before conception produces (in well-nourished women) a thick, spongy endometrial lining where the baby will implant and be nourished until placental function takes over. In one who is not pregnant, the uterus generally weighs several ounces, and at term, it weighs about two pounds. The amount and rate of growth as well as the integrity of the uterine tissue is dependent upon the nutritional health of Mom.

General Recommendations for Uterine Support:
1. Eat plenty of whole grains, nuts and seeds which contain a high amount of natural vitamin E. Do not overdo vitamin E supplementation; it can cause a placenta to implant too deeply into uterine wall.
2. Maintain good nutrition prior to and during pregnancy .
3. Mom may consider wheat germ oil supplementation if uterine tissue integrity is in question.

Digestive/Intestinal System

Circulating hormones in mom's bloodstream cause muscles all over the body to relax. These relaxed muscles include those in the digestive and intestinal system. This means that foods are not processed or digested as quickly as before pregnancy. Bile discharge is sluggish which increases the risk of gallstone formation. Peristalsis of the intestines slows down so elimination and defecation may not be as frequent as before pregnancy. This longer elimination time increases the likelihood of constipation and reabsorption of toxic waste from the intestines back into the bloodstream.

General Recommendations for Digestive and Intestinal Support:
1. Stay active in pregnancy - walk, swim, chase toddlers, etc.
2. Eat small meals throughout the day instead of three (3) large ones.
3. Don't lie down or slump in a chair immediately after eating.
4. Cut down on fats, sugar and refined foods. These are not good for you (except a small amount of natural fat; ex. butter, avocado, nuts or seeds). Sugar represses the production of stomach acid so not only will mom feel miserable, absorption of nutrients will be lowered. Refined foods do not contain the God-given fiber available in whole foods. Fiber naturally increases peristalsis and regular intestinal waste evacuation.

Structural System

The hormones that cause muscles to relax in the digestive and intestinal tract also allow for more swaying and flexible movements of joints. While this is beneficial for mom in adjusting to rapid addition of weight in the middle and during the childbirth process, aches can begin in the back and legs unless mom is taught good pregnancy posture. The center of gravity for mom changes as baby grows. Mom can counteract the ill effects of this change by following the general recommendations below.

General Recommendations for Structural System Support:

1. Keep head up. Rub baby; don't gaze down at him or her constantly.
2. Relax shoulders. The "throw your shoulder back, breasts out" posture strains the lower back.
3. Don't exaggerate the belly expansion by throwing baby out in the swayback posture. You'll be bigger than you want to be soon enough.
4. Tuck "hine-y" (buttocks) in, tilt pelvis forward and pull in those tummy muscles. It may be that you deserve to let it all hang out, but do you deserve the backache that comes with it?
5. Relax knees and let feet be comfortably, shoulder-width, apart. Rigidity has got to go.

Urinary System

The urinary system is one of the waste-management sites of the body. Just as the toilet in the bathroom requires a certain amount of water, so the body needs an adequate and proper liquid intake in order to flush waste and excess. The kidneys form urine, which is primarily made up of water, urea and sodium chloride. One liter of urine is the result of 1000 liters of blood filtration. The kidneys can regulate the concentration of the urine according to the body's current needs.

Hormonal changes relax the tone of the ureter and slow peristalsis. The bladder's position is changed due to uterine growth. These factors can increase the likelihood of stagnant urine being held in the bladder which provides a prime environment for bacterial growth.

General Recommendations for Urinary System Support:

1. Drink a minimum of two (2) quarts of water daily. Juices should be minimal and diluted. Water can be made tastier and even healthier for Mom by of squeezing a lemon wedge into the glass.
2. Empty bladder completely when voiding.
3. Avoid the start-stop method of urinating; just let it come. When Mom feels she holds no more, she can bear down and push those last drops out.
4. Make certain calcium supplements are assimilable. Stone formation is possible and certainly desirable to be avoided during pregnancy. Some 85% - 90% of stones are made up of calcium. I prefer total herbal sources for additional calcium supplementation since I have had stone experiences before - WHEW! My herbal supplement of choice for highly absorbable minerals in the colloidal, plant, form is Blue-Green Minerals by Mother's Choice. Calcium tablets should be in a chelated form of calcium rather than bone meal, oyster shell or a carbonate form that is difficult for the body to absorb.

**As a side note on kidney stones, mom should understand most doctors recommend limiting calcium intake in stone-formers (people with a history of stone formation); however, research indicates that it is a lack of dietary calcium that may cause these stones to form. Supplementing with an absorbable form of calcium is a major factor in preventing kidney stones. If a mom with a history of kidney stones ever drinks tea or eats dark green leafy vegetables containing oxalates, she should take her calcium supplement at the time of ingesting these foods or drink since calcium helps to bind the oxalates preventing their absorption which does increase kidney stone risk.

Nervous System

Autonomic nervous system changes include changes in blood vessels (blushing), glands (crying) and smooth or cardiac muscle (diarrhea, palpitations). The sympathetic nervous system can show changes such as heart and respiratory rate rises, sphincters tighten and visceral activity slows with emotions such as fright. With pleasant emotions, the reverse would occur. The "nesting" phenomena is thought to be an action of the nervous system during pregnancy. Nesting occurs when mother's activity focuses more on preparing for the birth and care of her baby. She becomes more passive and dependent on support figures as well. At least 50% of mothers experience lability of mood.

The "couvade" syndrome that some 20% of fathers experience is a nervous system response. Fathers experiencing couvade symptoms relate symptoms similar to their wives during pregnancy; some may even gain weight with her.

Most of the change in the nervous system changes occur in the first trimester and the puerperium when major endocrine and metabolic changes take place.

General Recommendations:

1. Relax. Enjoy the "nesting" instinct. Nurture your baby by nurturing yourself nutritionally and physically.
2. Emphasize complex carbohydrates in the diet which are an excellent source of B vitamins which are necessary to the function of the nervous system.
3. Get to know, bond, with your baby now by talking to baby, praying for baby, and helping your other little ones participate in loving and taking care of mom and baby.

Immune System

The organs primarily involved in producing the specialized cells of the immune system are the thymus, spleen and lymphatic system. T cells are derived from thymus and B cells are derived from bone marrow. T cells are responsible for cell-mediated immunity - they attack foreign material "in person." The B cells secrete antibodies which attach to material and mark it for destruction.

The foreign material is usually a protein called an antigen. The antibodies which are produced in response to its presence are specific to that antigen. Antibodies are in 4 main groups - immunoglobulins A, G, M and E (IgA, IgG, IgM, and IgE, for short). Only IgG antibodies cross the placenta. The IgG passes from mom to baby especially in the last 6 - 8 weeks of pregnancy. They protect the baby until its own antibody production reaches satisfactory levels in the first few months after birth.

Mom does have some general depression of maternal immunity during pregnancy because of the production of a special protein which may partly block lymphocytes (lymphocyte depressing factor - LDF) and because of an increase in adrenal cortical activity. Drugs which suppress immune function may accentuate this immune depression.

Some have claimed that preeclampsia may have an immunological basis, because it is more common in unrelated matings than in consanguineous matings. It is also more common in primigravidas (first time mothers) or when pregnancy is the result of a different father. More will be discussed on preeclampsia in a later chapter.

General Recommendations:

1. The best thing one can do for the immune system is to follow a natural whole foods diet, get adequate exercise and worry not. The Lord is well able to take care of those things which concern us if we turn those concerns over to Him.

2. For those who entered pregnancy with an illness or contract an illness early in pregnancy, follow the Strenthen Immune Function instructions located in a later chapter of Part 3.

3. Rest. This can single-handedly make all the difference for a mom in the healing process. A body has to have time to heal.

Respiratory System

The respiration rate is changed little by pregnancy, but the tidal volume, minute ventilatory volume and minute oxygen uptake increase appreciably as pregnancy advances. The residual air in the lungs decreases due to the diaphragm being raised while total pulmonary resistance due to progesterone and, perhaps, relaxin is reduced, and airway conductance is increased. At term, oxygen consumption has increased by nearly 20%. Diseases of the respiratory tract may possibly be more serious during pregnancy due to increased oxygen requirements.

Swelling of the mucosal tissue is common because of the increased progesterone levels in the body which can make mom feel as though she cannot breathe as efficiently as prior to pregnancy. This resolves within days of giving birth.

General Recommendations:
1. Practice deep-breathing at least 5 - 10 minutes each day.
2. Keep air in the home from drying out by using a humidifier is necessary. Dry air makes for a dry throat and nostrils which make for a prime environment for pathogens.
3. Remember to take daily prenatal supplements.
4. Follow recommendations for specific respiratory concerns in this section of book.

Bibliography of Source Material for *System Changes in Pregnancy*

Beischer, Norman A. and Eric V. Mackay. *Obstetrics and the Newborn.* 2nd Ed. Artarmon, NSW: CBS Publishing Australia Pty Limited, 1986.

Cunningham, F. Gary, MacDonald, Paul C., & Gant, Norman F. *Williams Obstetrics.* Norwalk, CT: Appleton & Lange, 1989.

Frye, Anne. *Understanding Lab Work in the Childbearing Year.* 5th Ed. New Haven, Connecticut: Labrys Press, 1994.

Scott, James R., DeSaia, Philip J., Hammond, Charles B. & Spellacy, William M. *Danforth's Obstetrics and Gynecology.* Philadelphia, PA: J.B. Lippincott Co., 1990.

Varney, Helen. *Nurse-Midwifery.* 2nd Ed. Boston, Massachusetts: Blackwell Scientific Publications, 1987.

HERBS TO USE CAUTION WITH
OR AVOID DURING PREGNANCY

All herbs that are used medicinally during pregnancy should be treated as medicines. Medicinal herb use should be limited to situations of necessity for a limited time period. Care must definitely be exercised in the first trimester since this is such a crucial time for the developing baby. We have so few studies on the effect of mom's ingestion of herbs during pregnancy that care and caution must be exercised, particularly in the first trimester. The German Commission E monographs, published by the American Botanical Council, (see Resources, Part 8) is an excellent place to start to find information about the safety of specific herbs during pregnancy. Some of the herbs listed in the following categories may be used during pregnancy with professional guidance if a health condition requires their use and if mom and dad are aware of the risks involved. Our own family experience of using herbs during pregnancy has been that there are certain herbs we choose not to use during pregnancy; however, there may be certain health conditions that arise that would necessitate the use of botanicals or pharmaceuticals. In these situations, we pray and make ourselves aware of the benefits and risks of both and usually choose to use the botanicals. There are some herbs that I would never use in the first or perhaps even in the second trimester, yet I would definitely use them at the end of pregnancy if the need arose.

Some herbs to avoid unless there is a physiologic imbalance necessitating their use are commonly called "hormonal" herbs. Even many herbalists use the term "hormonal" herbs. This can be misleading to the person unfamiliar with the way herbs function in the body. These herbs do not contain hormones; rather, they contain compounds which bind to hormone-receptor sites in the body and produce effects similar to hormones. We call the chemicals in these herbs, phytohormones or plant hormones. Phytohormones may exhibit estrogenic activity or progesterone activity.

As an herbalist who has worked with pregnant women, I prefer not to use herbs exhibiting hormonal activity during pregnancy unless there is a need to do so. An example of when the use of phytoestrogens might be recommended would be a woman who does not "kick into" labor naturally. This woman may need a boost from an herb to aid the pituitary gland in directing the production of the needed hormone release. Another instance when use may be indicated would be a woman who has repeated miscarriages, she may need some hormone-balancing support by using a combination of herbs with progesterone activity. Of course, these herbs are very beneficial for the woman trying to become pregnant to supplement the body's estrogen surge during ovum production and release. Phyto-estrogens, herbs with estrogenic activity, combined with a balancing herb with progesterone activity, can also benefit the menopausal woman wishing to go through "the change" naturally.

As always, moms must be aware of all that is involved in using the "hormonal" herbs. The use of these herbs is manipulation of an intricate and delicate process designed by our Creator. The risk of upsetting normal hormone balance must be weighed against the benefit one might derive from use of these herbs. In a mom who has a known hormone imbalance, these herbs may prove invaluable by providing the right food for an organ to function in its designated way. Moms who are not experiencing a hormone imbalance would best "leave well enough alone."

Herbs that Exhibit Estrogenic Activity:

Aletris farinosa (Blazing star or True Unicorn)
*Alfalfa (weak)
Angelica (Dong Quai)
*Anise
Black Cohosh
*Clovers
Daucus carota (Wild carrot or Queen Anne's Lace)
False Unicorn
*Fennel
*Garlic
Rheum rhaponticum (Golden rhubarb)
*Hops
*Licorice
Panax ginseng
*Pomegranate
Sage
*Soybeans
Vitex agnus-castus (Chaste tree)

* These herbs or foods may be eaten during pregnancy. Remember, it is long-term daily excess that can reap undesirable effects.

Herbs that Exhibit Progesterone Activity:

Licorice
Sarsaparilla
Wild Yam
Vitex Agnus-Castus (Chaste tree)

Herbs that May Have Contraceptive Effects, abortifacient in that they may inhibit implantation

Queen Anne's Lace or Wild carrot *(Daucus carota)* seeds; Solomon's Seal *(Polygonatum multiflora)* has been said to cause permanent sterility if used continuously over a period of a week; Alexandrium gum, alum, and Turmeric leaves combined. Given this information, these herbs would best not be used on a daily basis, certainly not the *Daucus* or *Polygontatum multiflora.* Turmeric may be okay to use on an as needed basis as the source, a book on Talmudic medicine, did not indicate which part of the formula was contraceptive.

Herbs of Which Small Amounts May Stimulate Contractions:

Blue cohosh
Celery seed
Cottonroot
Feverfew
Gentian
Golden Root or Golden Rod, Groundsel, Life Root, Wild Valerian (Senecio aureus)
Golden Seal
Greater Celandine
Motherwort
Pennyroyal
Rue
Shepherd's Purse
Spanish fly
Tansy
Uva Ursi
Wormwood

Herbs that May Stimulate Contractions in Large Amounts:

The herbs not marked with an asterisk generally may be safely used in cooking during pregnancy. They are included in this list because the internal use of their essential oil is definitely contraindicated during pregnancy

Bay
Blue Vervain
Celery
Cinnamon
Elecampane
**Ephedra

Myrrh
Saffron
Thyme

**Chemical constituent, ephedrine, has been linked with some birth defects.

Purgative Herbs that May Stimulate Contractions:

Purgative herbs are those herbs which stimulate peristalsis (the "worm-like" movement) of the intestines. They are called purgatives because they "purge" the body of waste products in the bowel. Those listed below are quite stimulating, as anyone who has used them can testify. Anyone taking these herbs should be aware that they contain a chemical called anthraquinone (this is what stimulates peristalsis). Dependence upon these anthraquinone-containing herbs is possible. This dependence is termed "lazy-bowel syndrome" and can begin in as little as three days continuous use.

Buckthorn
Butternut
Cascara Sagrada - small amounts in a combination product may be tolerated by some.
Turkey Rhubarb
Senna - I would never use senna during pregnancy. It is very strong.

Herbs That Are Contraindicated During Pregnancy:

The herbs in the following list (with the exception of the true emmenagogues) may be indicated for certain health conditions. These herbs should not be mom's or mom's care provider first line of defense, and they should only be used under the competent direction of a professional skilled in botanical medicine. Any use of these herbs constitute a risk to mom and baby; therefore, the decision to utilize these botanicals should not be entered into uninformed. The herbs listed below do not constitute an exhaustive list; rather, it is a sampling of commonly-known herbs that fit these particular categories.

True emmenagogues or abortifacients (herbs which induce menstruation, not to be confused with uterine tonics which may through tonifying or balancing the reproductive system allow menstruation to become regular) - Pennyroyal *(Hedeoma pulegoides)*, Tansy *(Tanacetum vulgare)*, Rue *(Ruta graveolens L)*, Cotton root *(Gossypium spp)*, Queen Anne's Lace or Wild Carrot *(Daucus carota L.)*, Golden Rod or Root *(Senecio aureus L)*, Wormwood *(Artemisia absinthium)*, Dittany *(Origanum dictamnus)*, Celery seed. These are to be completely avoided during pregnancy.

Antihistamines - Ephedra, Osha root
Alkaloids - Goldenseal, Barberry, Comfrey

Diuretics (those herbal diuretics that irritate the kidney which could also irritate surrounding tissue, namely the uterus) - Juniper berry, Buchu, Parsley, Uva ursi

Laxatives (purgative herbs as listed above)

Volatile Oils (herbs that *contain* volatile oils may be used for a few days or perhaps a
week but should not be used on a daily basis during pregnancy. The essential oils
of these herbs should definitely not be used internally during pregnancy at all) -
Rosemary, Thyme

Herbs Specifically Used for Miscarriage Prevention:

The following herbs are those which relax the uterine muscle thereby preventing
contractions. I have not seen this muscular relaxation be a problem in hemorrhage or
tissue retention for those women in whom miscarriage was unavoidable.

Black Haw/ Cramp Bark
Catnip
Chamomile
False Unicorn
Passionflower
Red Raspberry - Please see Part 1, section on miscarriage
Wild Yam

Acne

Many women experience a problem with acne during the first trimester of pregnancy due to liver's response to circulating hormones in the bloodstream. Although there are two types of acne: acne vulgaris which affects the hair follicles and oil-secreting glands and is manifested as blackheads, whiteheads and inflammation and acne conglombata which causes deep cyst formation with scarring. The most common form during pregnancy is acne vulgaris. The male sex hormone testosterone is the major hormonal factor in acne, causing sebaceous (sebum-producing) glands to enlarge and produce more sebum. The skin of patients with acne shows increased activity of an enzyme (5-alpha-reductase) that converts testosterone to dihydrotestosterone (a more potent form of testosterone).

Lifestyle/Dietary Recommendations:
1. Wash pillowcase in a natural, liquid laundry detergent.
2. Switch to a water-based, make-up foundation and other oil-free cosmetics.
3. Wash face twice daily to remove excess oil and sebum with a non-soap cleanser.
4. Follow the whole foods diet. Eliminate sugar, foods containing trans-fatty acids such as milk, milk products, margarine, shortening and synthetically-hydrogenated vegetable oils, fried foods and chocolate. Add anti-acne foods: butternut, sunflower seeds, Brazil nuts, pumpkin, soybeans, cashews, pistachios, avocados, breadfruit, black currant, asparagus, chickpea, black beans, lettuce, strawberries, kale.[37]

Nutritional Supplement Recommendations:
1. Quality pre-natal formula providing: Zinc - 30-45 mg daily, Vitamin A - 10,000 IU's daily, Vitamin E - 200 - 400 IU daily, B 6 - 150mg daily in combination with other B vitamins. If pre-natal formula does not supply all of these nutrients, add single vitamins and minerals to satisfy these requirements.
2. Apply Australian Tea Tree Oil topically. A study conducted at the Royal Prince Hospital in New South Wales, Australia, a 5-percent tea tree oil solution demonstrated beneficial effects similar to those of 5% benzoyl peroxide but with substantially fewer side effects.[38][39]
3. Pantothenic acid supplementation showed complete cure of acne vulgaris if given liberally.[40] Please see upper limits during pregnancy in Part 2, Nutrient Needs....
4. A topical extract of Hawthorn to be effective in the treatment of acne.[41]
5. Since allopathic treatment commonly employs antibiotics to successfully treat acne, a natural alternative might utilize the herbs echinacea, 1,000mg daily and Burdock, 1,000-2,000mg daily to stimulate immune activity since they both exhibit actions on the skin as well as showing antibacterial actions.

Allergy/Asthma

An allergic reaction begins when a foreign substance is attacked and bound by an IgE antibody. The substance bound to the allergic antibody is called an "antigen" or "allergen." This IgE-antigen complex then binds to specialized white cells known as "mast cells" and "basophils." This binding causes the release of substances such as histamine which cause swelling and inflammation. Allergy may manifest as sinus congestion, asthma, hives, eczema, arthritis, intestinal inflammation and headaches.

Asthma is an allergic disorder characterized by spasm of the bronchial tubes and excessive excretion of a viscous mucous in the lungs which can lead to difficulty in breathing. It can be mild wheezing and/or coughing or a life-threatening inability to breathe. The allergic compounds that trigger asthma are derived from arachidonic acid - a fatty acid found only in animal foods.

A recent study of 706 Japanese factory workers demonstrated that a healthful lifestyle reduced IgE levels while unhealthful lifestyles elevated IgE. Those unhealthful practices which elevated IgE levels were: poor dietary habits, alcohol consumption, cigarette smoking, and increased feelings of stress.[42]

Lifestyle/Dietary Recommendations:
1. Eliminate carpets, rugs, upholstered furniture and other surfaces where allergens can collect. Pets should definitely not be indoors.
2. Encase bed mattress in allergen-proof material; wash sheets, blankets, pillowcases and mattress pads each week; toss pillow into clothes dryer for 10 minutes each week; use bedding made from Ventflex - a special hypoallergenic synthetic material; install air purifier. The best air purifiers utilize HEPA (high-efficiency particulate-arresting) filters, which can be attached to central heating/air-conditioning units. Portable HEPA units may be more effective than whole house systems unless the house system is of very high quality. Electrostatic filters maintain effectiveness only if washed weekly. Air purifiers that create ozone may be used as well. See Part 8 for companies selling allergy control products.
3. If rugs and upholstery are in house, use a vacuum with efficient filtering system (traps dust, bacteria, and some viruses in HEPA filters). See Part 8 for Resources.
4. Eliminate food additives tartrazine (yellow dye #5), colorings (azo dyes), flavorings (salicylates, aspartame), preservatives (benzoates, nitrites, sorbic acid), synthetic antioxidants (hydroxytoluene, sulfite, gallate) and emulsifiers/stabilizers (polysorbates, vegetable gums). All of these have been shown to produce allergies and play a role in asthma.[43]
5. Decrease intake of animal fats while increasing consumption of omega-3 oils found in flaxseed oil and cold water fish such as mackerel, herring, sardines and salmon.
6. A vegan diet, followed for one year, proved helpful in 92% of 25 patients in a long-term trial.[44]

Nutritional Supplement Recommendations:

1. Vitamin C - 1000mg daily,[45] Vitamin E, Selenium, Flavonoids especially Quercetin which has to be combined with Bromelain to increase absorption - 250 - 500 mg of Quercetin with 1,000mg of Bromelain taken thirty minutes before meals.[46][47]

2. Vitamin B12 supplementation in one clinical trial provided definite improvement in asthmatic patients who took weekly intramuscular (IM) injections of 1,000 micrograms.[48] The B12 injections are particularly effective in sulfite-sensitive individuals by forming sulfite-cobalamin complex which blocks sulfite's effect.[49] According to Michael T. Murray in *Natural Prescriptions to Over-the-Counter and Prescription Drugs*, oral supplementation with 1 - 3 mg B12 may provide similar benefit to the injectable form.

3. Vitamin B6 supplementation of 50mg twice daily has been shown in double-blind clinical studies to benefit asthmatic patients because it corrects the defect in tryptophan metabolism commonly found in asthmatics. Tryptophan is converted to serotonin, a known broncho-constricting agent.[50] Milk and dark turkey meats are natural food sources for tryptophan.

4. See **NOTE** The herb Ephedra, also known as Ma Huang, combined with herbs exhibiting expectorant qualities, such as lobelia, licorice and grindelia, have been found to be helpful for many people with allergies and asthma. Synthetic ephedrine is a common ingredient in over-the-counter and prescription medications for colds, allergies and asthma. The crude plant (the herb) not only contains a natural amount of ephedrine but other antiinflammatory and antiallergy compounds as well.[51]

    * The FDA advisory review panel on nonprescription drugs recommends that ephedrine not be taken by patients with heart disease, high blood pressure, thyroid disease, diabetes or difficulty with urination due to enlargement of the prostate gland, nor should ephedrine be used by patients on antihypertensive or antidepressant drugs.

    For use with allergies, the ephedrine content of ephedra preparations should be 12.5 - 25.0 mg taken two to three times daily. For the crude herb, an equivalent dose would be 500 - 1000mg taken three times daily. If ephedra is taken alone over a long period of time, the effects may diminish due to overstimulation of the adrenal gland. Combining ephedra with the expectorant herbs that are also adrenal-supporting herbs should prevent this from occurring.

    ** NOTE: An issue of *Herbalgram*, a publication of the Herb Research Foundation, reported that ephedrine may be linked to some birth defects. Because of this and ephedra's stimulant effects (similar to caffeine in tea, coffee and colas), ephedra or ma huang should not be used during pregnancy unless mom does so under the supervision of a professional health provider.

5. Dr. Andrew Weil, M.D., author of *Natural Health, Natural Medicine,* recommends a lobelia - cayenne mixture for asthma attacks:
   - 3 parts tincture lobelia (I prefer the use of TincTract[TM]s by Tri-Light/Mother's Choice[TM])
   - 1 part capsicum
   - Take 20 drops of mixture in water at start of bronchial constriction and repeat every thirty minutes for a total of 3 - 4 doses.[52]

6. Ginkgo biloba herb has received scientific attention as well for its anti-allergic, anti-asthma agent, platelet activating factor (PAF). One study concluded that Ginkgolide B is the most active PAF antagonist found in this class of ginkgolides. It appears that Ginkgo relieves bronchoconstriction because of its PAF antagonist activity. Another randomized, double-blind, placebo-controlled crossover study of 8 atopic asthmatic patients showed that Ginkgo achieved significant inhibition of the bronchial allergen challenge compared to placebo.[53] The therapeutic dose used would be equivalent to 40 mg three times daily of the standardized extract containing 24% ginkgo heterosides.

7. Another herb that may be beneficial is coltsfoot, used extensively in Chinese medicine. Two studies show the leaves of the plant to contain substances that can soothe inflamed mucous membranes and suppress asthma attacks (not relieve acute attacks).[54] [55] Coltsfoot, just like comfrey and borage, contains pyrrolizidine alkaloids (PAs). These alkaloids may cause a liver disease known as hepatic veno-occlusive disease (HVOD). Different PAs possess different levels of toxicity, and current studies have concentrated on isolated compounds or extremely large doses on rats. The risk to humans has not been firmly established. Although empirical (historical) use implies safe internal consumption, it would seem wise for the pregnant mom would be wise to either avoid using these herbs internally until safety is established. I personally use a liquid combination containing coltsfoot for my daughter, Eryn, who has been having difficulties with asthma. We have seen no toxicity problem in Eryn by using this combination and only use it as needed for the cough, not as an every day herb. 1/2 - 1 teaspoon of Lungs Plus or RespirAid TincTract[TM] containing coltsfoot as needed for cough and congestion is what we have personally found to be effective for Eryn. If we allow her to get to the point of attack, this combination does not relieve the attack itself. We have to begin using it prior to the acute stage.

8. Mullein and marshmallow root are both herbs with a very high mucilage (protective gel that forms when the herb comes in contact with water) content. This demulcent effect is very soothing for mucous membranes. The herbs are used, not their oils. 500 mg two to three times daily may be helpful for soothing inflamed mucous membranes in the respiratory tract.

Anemia

Anemia is a condition in which the blood does not contain an adequate amount of red blood cells or hemoglobin (iron-containing) portion of the red blood cells. The function of the red blood cell (RBC) is to transport oxygen from the lungs to the tissues of the body and to exchange it there for carbon dioxide. There are many different types of anemia with the most common ones associated with a deficiency of iron, folic acid and B12. These are the types we will address.

Iron-deficiency anemia - A woman with low hemoglobin levels usually experiences symptoms such as fatigue, pale fingernail beds and eyes (under lids), and pica (the desire to eat ice, corn starch or clay). Anemia is assumed to be a natural part of pregnancy, and according to Anne Frye in her book *Understanding Diagnostic Tests in the Childbearing Year*, it is, in a way. Frye states that because of the physiologic dilution of red blood cells caused by increasing plasma volume, it looks like iron or hemoglobin levels are falling.[56] Actually what takes place is that during the first twenty-eight weeks of pregnancy, a woman's total blood volume expands to meet the needs of baby. The plasma volume (a part of total blood volume) rises to 50% while the red cells only increase about 30% commonly creating a reduction in hemoglobin of two grams by 28 to 30 weeks. This is a good sign that the blood volume is expanding properly. Dietary intervention as well as supplementation should occur at 12 weeks if the hemoglobin level is below thirteen so mom does not get to the end of her pregnancy in the 10 or below hemoglobin range.

Folic acid-deficiency or Megaloblastic anemia - This type of anemia is most common in those who eat few or no fresh green vegetables. The most noticeable symptom is the "mask of pregnancy" (brown spots on face) as well as other pigment changes. It may also cause vomiting and loss of appetite. Since folic acid has been found to be instrumental in preventing neural tube defects, supplementation of this nutrient ideally should begin three months before pregnancy.

B12-deficiency, also Megaloblastic anemia - B12 is a water-soluble vitamin. It is the only vitamin produced only by bacteria, and this only occurs is there is adequate cobalt available. B12 is a cobalt-containing substance that is necessary for normal functioning of the nervous system and contributes to protein, fat, and carbohydrate metabolism.

Dietary absorption of B12 is highly dependent on the source and how well an individual body assimilates it. Several factors may contribute to impaired B12 absorption:

a) Insufficient hydrochloric acid in the stomach. Corrected by stimulating acid-formation with herbs: peppermint, cayenne, papaya, bromelain or supplementing with hydrochloric acid. Adequate salt intake is necessary for acid production.

b) Compromised pancreatic function. Corrected by balanced calcium supplementation.

c) Pancreas-related malabsorption problem stemming from inhibition of the proteases (protein digesting enzymes). Corrected with enzyme trypsin.

d) High heat in cooking destroys B12.

e) Diet high in fat, excess mucous-forming foods, and refined foods.

f) Exposure to cigarette smoke, alcohol, birth control pills, nitrous oxide (dental anesthetic gas or auto emissions), mercury amalgam dental fillings, and certain antibiotics (such as Neomycin).

g) Pectin and vitamin C can both destroy B12, while cellulose (dietary fiber) enhances absorption.[57]

h) Food sources that are low in B12. While it has been assumed that meat-eaters have no risk of B12 deficiency, research in the past years has uncovered a decrease in B12 from foods normally rich in B12 (cheese and liver) possibly due to soil low in cobalt creating cobalt-deficient plants that the animals graze on creating B12 deficient animals. They can't give what they don't have. Vegetarians need to insure adequate B12 intake as well since plant sources may be cobalt-deficient.

Since some believe that only consumed, not stored, B12 crosses the placenta and gets to baby, it is extremely important that mom has a diet rich in B12 source foods and supplements her diet with additional B12 as well.

Lifestyle/Dietary Recommendations for all three types of anemia:
1. Cook with iron skillets.
2. Follow the whole foods diet.
3. Add the following foods to diet : prunes, apricots, black cherries, dark, leafy greens (particularly organic dandelion greens), sea vegetables, fermented foods (soy sauce, miso, tamari, etc.), molasses, grapes, almonds, beets, organ meats (absolutely only from certified organic sources - I personally have my doubts about eating even organic liver!). If you do eat liver, make certain it is certified organic calf liver and eat no more than 4 ounces per week.

Nutritional Supplement Recommendations:
1. Nettle leaf, Red Raspberry and Oatstraw infusion - Make by steeping one ounce of each herb in two quarts of boiled water for at least four hours (this makes a strong infusion). Drink 1/2 to 1 cup several times daily. For those who do not wish to drink an infusion, these herbs may be purchased in capsules singly or in a combination and taken 300 - 500 mg 2 to 3 times daily. All of these herbs are high in iron

and vitamin C which aids the absorption of iron. They are also a good source of chlorophyll. For those who like anise, 1 teaspoon of seeds may be added to the infusion. A 1990 study showed that anise enhances iron absorption.[58]

2. Taking a vitamin C and bioflavonoid supplement when taking iron supplements aid absorption.

3. Vitamin E supplementation at 600 IU daily for 30 days may reverse anemia due to vitamin E's ability to reduce the fragility of red blood cells.[59]

4. Alfalfa leaves, Kelp powder and Dandelion herb are also high in iron and chlorophyll as well as a wealth of other minerals. Alfalfa is an excellent source of vitamins A and D as well as a rich source of K. It has been used in medicine for blood clotting. I personally recommend this combination to all women during pregnancy because it is rich in all the minerals and vitamins necessary for health and dandelion is mildly stimulating and supporting of the liver which needs assistance at least during the first trimester.

5. Spirulina and chlorella both contain high amounts of protein and B vitamins, especially folic acid. Spirulina is the best vegetable source of B12. The powder, although not the tastiest thing in the world, is the best way of taking these nutritive foods. Nutritive amount: 2 - 4 T daily of the powder or 6 - 12 tablets or capsules daily.

6. The liquid TincTract™ **called Tri-Iron by Mother's Choice™** by Tri-Light contains the herbs: Yellow Dock, Dandelion, Raspberry, Nettles and Anise. These herbs both supply excellent levels of iron with herbs added to enhance absorption.

7. Yellow Dock in combination with other herbs mentioned above or alone can be helpful for anemia that is unresponsive to other measures. The dock plant family does contain anthraquinones (chemical constituents that stimulate intestinal peristalsis), just as cascara sagrada does, so one would not want to overdo the dosage. One 450 mg capsule may be taken two to three times daily. If diarrhea occurs, reduce dosage by one capsule.

8. Chlorophyll, in capsule or liquid form, has been used by herbalists to encourage a quick hemoglobin rise for those women close to due dates. Some midwives have used chlorophyll capsules for the four weeks prior to due date and have found a reduced amount of bleeding in those women utilizing this supplement. 2 - 3 capsules daily or 1/2 to 1 cup of the liquid daily.

9. The prenatal supplement should contain adequate iron, folic acid and B12 levels in absorbable forms (Iron - citrate, gluconate or fumarate, Folic acid - folacin, B12 - cobalamin).

10. Herbal combination in capsules I have used personally throughout my (healthy) pregnancies to prevent anemia: Red beet root, yellow dock root, red raspberry leaves, chickweed herb, burdock root, nettle herb and mullein leaves.

11. Many midwives have found the supplement called Floridix with iron or Liquid Herbal Iron, a mix of fruit and herb concentrates, to reverse anemia in the pregnant woman.

12. Some moms will have to try several different therapies to achieve positive results or even use several at one time. Exercising daily or at least three times per week helps increase the oxygen supply to the body which will help raise hemoglobin levels.

13. For moms with very low B12 levels, one 1000mcg injection may make all the difference in the world for her.

Bronchitis

Bronchitis is the term used for inflammation of the bronchial tubes. When these tubes become irritated, they produce mucous which stimulates a cough in an effort to clear the air passages. The main symptom is a cough that hasn't gone away after an illness (eliminate allergies as the source of the cough) that produces thick yellow or green sputum. A low-grade fever (below 101 degrees F) may also be present.

Since it is imperative that mom's airways be clear to breathe in oxygen for her and baby, aggressive preventive measures should accompany coughs from colds or flu. If mom's bronchitis does not improve within 48 hours, she coughs blood or temperature rises above 101 degrees F, medical attention should be sought immediately.

Lifestyle/Dietary Recommendations:

1. Keep air in the home moist with a humidifier as necessary. If a humidifier is used, it must be disinfected regularly to prevent mold and mildew from growing which could create a worse environment than dry air.
2. Stay away from cigarette smoke - personal and second-hand.
3. Garnish foods liberally with garlic.
4. Identify food allergies and avoid those foods.
5. Eliminate dairy products until condition has resolved and cut down on meat while increasing complex carbohydrates.

Nutritional Supplement Recommendations:

1. Treat colds, flu, sinusitis, chronic post-nasal drip with immuno-stimulant and demulcent herbs such as: Echinacea, Garlic, Myrrh, Thyme, Mullein, and Licorice.[60]
2. Common plantain showed a quick turnaround on subjective complaints and offered objective benefits to 80% of patients with bronchitis in a 1982 study. Treatment lasted for 25-30 days.[61]
3. The bioflavonoid quercitin combined with bromelain is used because of quercitin's ability to aid the immune system's response to respiratory viruses and bromelain's antiinflammatory actions. This combination must be taken 30 minutes before meals for the anti-inflammatory effect.

Carpal Tunnel Syndrome

Carpal tunnel syndrome is a disorder caused by compression of the median nerve as it passes between the bones and ligaments of the wrist. Common symptoms are: weakness in the hand, pain, numbness, tingling and aching that can radiate up into the arm and shoulder and is particularly troublesome at night.

This syndrome may appear during pregnancy due to the change in hormonal levels that encourages fluid build-up, and thus, swelling in the wrists.

Lifestyle/Dietary Recommendations:

1. If mom works at a computer keyboard often, she should stop at regular intervals to give her wrists a break. She should make small circles in the air with her hands to help restore circulation and ease pressure.
2. Warm, moist heat may help relieve pain.
3. Tartrazine (FD&C yellow #5) and excessive protein both are B6 antagonists thus should be avoided.
4. Fresh pineapple juice which contains the anti-inflammatory enzyme bromelain can be added to the diet.

Nutritional Supplement Recommendations:

1. A curcumin (from tumeric) preparation can be rubbed on wrist during painful episodes. Curcumin is nature's most potent anti-inflammatory agent.[62] Enzymatic Therapy has some excellent ointments and preparations designed for anti- inflammatory effect. See resource section for more information.
2. Bromelain tablets are anti-inflammatory and should have at least 1200 clotting units and may be taken 200 - 500 mg thirty minutes before meals for an anti-inflammatory effect.
3. Vitamin B6: 100-200 mg daily has been demonstrated in several clinical studies to relieve all symptoms of carpal tunnel syndrome in patients with low B6 levels.[63 64 65 66 67] Pregnant women should limit their intake to no more than 100mg daily.

Chlamydia trachomatis

Chlamydia is recognized as the most prevalent sexually-transmitted disease and a major cause of infertility. While we will not be discussing all STDs, I have included this one because of its prevalence and the infertility factor. Many women are not aware they have this disease until it is too late. It is often asymptomatic until symptoms have become severe enough to cause pelvic inflammatory disease (PID). PID leaves 15 - 20% of those affected infertile. The symptoms of PID include: lower abdominal and pelvic organ pain especially on moving the cervix, chills and fever or urethral infection. Four to ten percent of pregnant women have vaginal chlamydia. At highest risk are those women with a history of gonorrhea or multiple sexual partners; however, increasing numbers of monogamous women are testing positive for chlamydia as well.[68]

In pregnancy, vaginal infection can lead to prematurity, stillbirth and neonatal infection. Blood tests cannot distinguish between past infections and current infections. Cultures may be done if chlamydia is suspected.

Lifestyle/Dietary Recommendations:

1. Eye prophylaxis for baby with erythromycin is a must at the birth for moms currently chlamydia-positive.
2. For acute symptoms, echinacea douches or sitz baths may be done twice daily. As douching during pregnancy can be hazardous, please see Douching Instructions for Pregnancy on page 140.

Nutritional Supplement Recommendations:

1. Echinacea (E. purpurea, angustifolia, and/or pallida) should be taken at 1000 mg twice daily by both mom and dad.
2. Anti-inflammatory herbs may be used if PID is present: Curcumin in the herb tumeric at a dosage of 400mg 3 times daily, bromelain from pineapple at a dosage of 250 - 750mg 3 times daily, de-glyzirrhinated licorice at a dosage of 250 - 500mg or 4 - 6ml Tinctract 3 times daily.[69]

Cholesterol

Cholesterol, carried in blood plasma by lipoproteins, is certainly a "buzz" word these days. Cholesterol is often referred to in terms of "good" or "bad." The "good" cholesterol is the high-density lipoprotein (HDL). HDL transports cholesterol to the liver for metabolism and excretion and actually protects against heart disease. Low-density lipoprotein (LDL) transports cholesterol to tissue and is the "bad" cholesterol which increases a person's risk of heart disease. The table below shows recommended values for cholesterol in pregnant and non-pregnant moms.

Type	Non-Pregnant Level	Pregnant Level-Late Pregnancy
Total Cholesterol	less than 200mg/dl	200 - 325 mg/dl
LDL	less than 130mg/dl	200 - 220 mg/dl
HDL	greater than 35 mg/dl	30 - 80 mg/dl
Triglycerides	50 - 150 mg/dl	200 - 300 mg/dl

Sources: Murray, Michael T., N.D. *The Healing Power of Foods.* Rocklin, CA: Prima Publishing, 1993. Frye, Anne. *Understanding Lab Work in the Childbearing Year.* New Haven: CT: Labrys Press, 1990.

The level of cholesterol in mom's blood begins to rise after the first trimester, peaking in the last month. This process may be due to cholesterol providing increased amounts of precursors for the formation of placental hormones. The increased cholesterol levels may be the precipitating factor in the increase in mom's risk for gallstones during pregnancy.

Lifestyle/Dietary Recommendations:

1. Saturated fats (milk and other animal fats) must be reduced. They tell the liver (which manufactures the majority of cholesterol in the body) to produce more cholesterol. Unsaturated fats tell the liver to produce less.

2. Not all fats are bad, in fact, essential fatty acids (EFAs) are great for us. EFAs are found in marine fish oils (Omega-3), cold-pressed safflower, sunflower, canola, Evening Primrose, Black Currant and Borage oils. These EFAs actually provide the building blocks for the chemical regulators known as prostaglandins which, in pregnancy, help prepare the body for birth.

3. Nuts and seeds should be eaten. They do have a high oil content; however, a study of 26, 473 Americans found that the people who consumed the most nuts were the least obese. This study also demonstrated higher nut consumption was associated with protective effects against heart attacks.[70] Nuts are best purchased in shells free

from splits, cracks, stains, holes or other surface problems. They should be stored in a cool, dry environment. Hulled nuts and seeds should be stored in airtight containers in the refrigerator or freezer.

4. Margarines have "gotta" go. Butter may be used in limited quantities. Oils for cooking should be canola and olive oils.

5. A whole food diet is essential for lowering cholesterol levels: high in fruits, veggies, whole grains and legumes. A whole food diet is naturally a high-fiber diet. Fiber absorbs bile which contains cholesterol and moves it along the intestines for excretion. Lack of fiber means the bile and cholesterol will be reabsorbed.

Nutritional Supplement Recommendations:

1. Gugulipid, from guggal or mukul myrrh tree, extracts standardized to contain 25mg of gugulipid per tablet taken three times daily have been shown in clinical studies to be effective in lowering cholesterol or triglyceride levels.[71][72]

2. Garlic and onions, those wonderfully odiferous vegetables, have been shown in numerous studies to lower LDL cholesterol and triglycerides while raising HDL cholesterol. The equivalent of 1 clove of garlic and/or half an onion per day is necessary to get a 10 - 15% reduction in total cholesterol.[73][74][75]

3. Another nutrient that has been evaluated for effectiveness in lowering cholesterol and triglycerides is pantethine, the active form of pantothenic acid; however, it is a fairly expensive nutritional supplement. The standard dosage for efficacy is 900mg daily. This should be saved for elevated triglyceride levels.[76][77]

Other nutrients recommended for elevated cholesterol and triglyceride levels are chromium and vitamin C.[78]

Chorioamnionitis

This infection primarily arises in the vagina affecting the membranes and amniotic fluid which then can infect the baby and placenta. It is defined as inflammation of the chorionic and amniotic membranes. The greatest risk factor is premature rupture of membranes (PROM), especially pre-term. This condition can occur postpartum as a uterine infection due to unclean delivery techniques, retained tissue, blood loss or trauma due to instrumental deliveries. The placental site becomes infected first spreading to surrounding tissue. This infection is listed as one of several possible cesarean complications (5 - 10% of elective, 10 - 30% of emergency).[79]

Signs of infection are: elevated temperature, tachychardia in baby, tender uterus, vaginal walls unusually warm (hot) to touch, foul-smelling, and/or purulent amniotic fluids. With the onset of chorioamnionitis, delivery needs to be quick, within 6 - 8 hours. Allopaths most commonly treat the infection with IV antibiotics, commonly Ampicillin.[80] Medical intervention must not be delayed once the signs of infection begin. Delaying treatment and delivery could mean serious compromise of baby's health and life. My recommendations here are for preventive measures only.

Lifestyle/Dietary Recommendations:

1. If membranes have ruptured, precautions should include: no sexual intercourse, no vaginal exams, bed rest, avoid public toilets, check temperature twice daily, wipe from front to back (wash with a peri-bottle before and after eliminating), no tub baths until active labor has begun, no sanitary pads or change pads very frequently if they are a must. Mom's caregiver will probably draw white blood counts every other day with a baseline at the onset of PROM. A study by Dr. Lewis Mehl found that the risk of infection increases after the fourth day of PROM in most cases. Mom should try to stimulate labor if she is at least 37 weeks pregnant.[81]
2. Increase complex carbohydrates to prepare body for labor.
3. Check baby's heart tones daily and check for normal baby movements.

Nutritional Supplement Recommendations:

1. Vitamin C - 1000 mg every 2 hours. Vitamin C and beta-carotene intake may act together to prevent premature rupture of membranes (PROM) in high-risk women.[82]
2. Echinacea (E. purpurea, angustifolia, pallida) - 500 - 1000 mg every 2 hours. Echinacea may elevate lymphocytes on blood count.
3. Garlic - 4 cloves, or the equivalent, should be taken 3 times daily.

Colds

Colds are caused by viruses in the upper respiratory tract. Allergies may decrease resistance and allow the virus to infect. The best course of action is to boost the immune system to prevent secondary infections and reduce length and severity of symptoms. These aggravating symptoms include: stuffy nose; sneezing; dry, sore throat; slight temperature with fatigue and headache. Antihistamines are useless for colds and are actually detrimental as they dry out mucous membranes that need to be kept moist with thin secretions.[83]

Lifestyle/Dietary Recommendations:
1. Rest and wash hands frequently.
2. Increase liquid intake to keep nasal secretions thin. A dry throat and nose allow viruses to attack. Herbal teas and water with lemon juice added are best.

Nutritional Supplement Recommendations:
1. Vitamin C with bioflavonoids - 500 - 1000 mg every 1 - 2 hours.
2. Zinc lozenges containing 23 mg elemental zinc taken every 2 hours have been shown to reduce the duration of the common cold. They should not be taken at this dosage for more than one (1) week.[84]
3. Echinacea (E. purpurea, angustifolia, pallida) taken three times daily in the following amounts have been shown to decrease length of colds and flu: Dried root (or as tea) - 0.5 to 1 g; Freeze-dried plant, 325 - 650 mg; Juice of E. purpurea stabilized in 22% ethanol - 1 - 2 ml (1/4 - 1/2 t); Tincture (1:5) - 2 - 4 ml; Solid (dry, powdered) extract (6.5:1 or 3.5% echinacoside) - 100 - 250 mg.[85]
4. Other beneficial herbs are licorice, especially for scratchy or hoarse throats, and astragalus.[86] [87]

Constipation

Constipation is characterized by infrequent bowel movements that often result in a hard-to-pass stool. This condition is caused by an inappropriate diet, inadequate exercise and can even be caused by laxative and/or enema abuse. The ideal frequency of bowel movements is two to three times daily. Elimination should correspond to the number of times one eats a meal each day. Mild, infrequent constipation usually responds well to a high-fiber diet, plenty of fluids and exercise. If the situation has become chronic, a "re-training" of the bowels may need to occur.

Lifestyle/Dietary Recommendations:

1. Eliminate known causes such as certain foods or poor dietary habits.
2. Never repress the urge to defecate. "Go when ya gotta go."
3. Focus on a high-fiber diet - the whole foods diet is naturally high-fiber.
4. Drink at least two quarts of water daily. Some of this can be fresh juices.
5. Begin a bathroom routine. Sit on the toilet at the same time every day (even when the urge is not there). The best times are after breakfast and exercise.
6. Exercise at least 20 minutes three times weekly.

Nutritional Supplement Recommendations:

1. For mild constipation, psyllium hulls provide bulk to make the stool more fibrous and soft, making passage more comfortable and regular.
2. Take no laxatives or enemas except as outlined below in bowel "re-training."
3. Week 1: Take Yellow Dock before bed (lowest amount necessary to ensure bowel movement in the morning - probably 2 - 4 capsules).
4. Week 2 - 6: Decrease dosage by 1/2 each week. If constipation recurs, take previous week's dosage. Decrease if diarrhea occurs.
5. For non-pregnant moms, cascara sagrada may be used instead of yellow dock.

Coughs

This is one discomfort that needs no explanation. We all have had a cough at one time or another. Coughs may be the result of inhaling irritating substances (cigarette smoke, environmental pollution), allergy, colds or dry air. If the cough persists past one of these problems, a more serious infection may be present.

Generally, it is better not to suppress a cough. A cough is the body's way of getting irritating mucous up and out. The exception to the "not suppress" rule would be a dry, irritating cough at night that prevents rest or a spasmodic cough that is painful or leads to gagging.

Lifestyle/Dietary Recommendations:
1. Drink extra amounts of liquids, preferably sipping on warm herbal teas or chicken soup throughout the day to loosen and thin secretions.
2. Eliminate irritating factors such as cigarette smoke, perfumes, dry air, etc.

Nutritional Supplement Recommendations:
1. For dry, irritating coughs, wild cherry bark is well-known for its ability to quiet a harsh cough. I particularly like a combination that contains: White Pine, Wild Cherry, Spikenard Root, Whole Elder Berries, Cinnamon Chips, Licorice Root (available from Tri-Light and Mother's Choice™).
2. For coughs that sound wet or loose, I like a combination containing: Mullein, Wild Cherry Bark, Chestnut, Astragalus Root, Peppermint, Coltsfoot, Plantain, Chickweed, Pleurisy Root, Elecampane Root, Horehound (also available from Tri-Light and Mother's Choice™). Moms will want to be careful (or avoid) with this combination due to its content of coltsfoot.
3. Marshmallow root (Althaea officinalis) is very soothing to respiratory membranes because of the high amount of mucilage in the plant. It is best combined with other expectorants and used as a tea. A tea may be made combining licorice, marshmallow and plantain with small amount of thyme.

Cramps, Muscle

Muscle cramps (a sudden, involuntary, and painful tightening of a muscle) may occur after strenuous work, after sitting or standing uncomfortably for a long period or after a huge meal. All of these may cause muscles to be temporarily nutrient-deprived or prevent the muscles from properly disposing of waste. While most people immediately think of calcium deficiency when experiencing leg cramps at night, magnesium-deficiency is much more likely. Magnesium-deficiency may be the result of ensuring adequate calcium intake without simultaneously getting in adequate magnesium. Severely low calcium intake may also cause muscle cramps.[88]

Leg cramps during pregnancy may also be the result of inadequate salt intake. If leg cramps accompany swelling and a slight rise in blood pressure, increase salt intake to maintain expanding blood volume needs.[89]

Lifestyle/Dietary Recommendations:
1. Stretch and massage cramped muscle. Pull foot toward body instead of pointing toes downward. This will relieve most leg cramps immediately.
2. Apply pressure to the upper lip, 2/3 of the way up from the upper lip to the nose. This works very well for any type of cramp.

Nutritional Supplement Recommendations:
1. Make certain mom's prenatal contains at least 1000mg of Calcium and at least 500mg of Magnesium.
2. An additional 400 - 500mg of Magnesium may be necessary if mom's diet is high in dairy products.
3. ContractEase Formula by Mother's Choice™ for after-birth pains can also help relieve muscle cramps. The formula contains: Black Haw, Valerian, Skullcap, Hops, Chamomile, Fennel and Catnip. This is one of the Midwife's Formulas that I gave (I do not receive monies from sales of any of their products) to them for processing. I like the Mother's Choice™ formulas because they are glycerin-based TincTract™s (not standard glycerites) that moms can use without having to be concerned about alcohol like most alcohol-based tinctures.

Diabetes

Diabetes is a chronic disorder of carbohydrate, fat and protein metabolism characterized by elevations of blood sugar (glucose) levels. Diabetes greatly increases the risk of heart disease, stroke, kidney disease, blindness and loss of nerve function. This disease can occur when the pancreas does not secrete enough insulin or if the cells of the body become resistant to insulin. Insulin is a hormone that promotes uptake of blood sugar by the cells of the body.

Type I - Insulin-Dependent Diabetes Mellitus (IDDM) occurs most often in children and adolescents. Complete destruction of beta cells of the pancreas which make insulin is usual with IDDM. Lifelong insulin-therapy is necessary for glucose control. Moms with Type I diabetes need medical supervision in their prenatal care to help them in controlling their insulin/glucose ratio. These moms still need to follow the whole foods diet while adding protein to equal 1 gram of protein for each pound of their body weight. Exercise is extremely important. Mom's weight gain and salt intake do not need to be restricted as this can cause additional problems such as metabolic toxemia of late pregnancy. The best plan is to have diabetes under control six to twelve months prior to conception. This will insure that mom is improving her lifestyle and diet; therefore, she will be in best possible shape for providing for baby's needs.

Type II - Non-Insulin Dependent Diabetes Mellitus (NIDDM). The onset of this disease is usually after the age of 40. Insulin levels may be low, normal, or elevated. Lack of sensitivity to insulin by cells of the body is a major characteristic. Obesity is a major contributor (90% of all Type II diabetics are obese). In this form of diabetes, diet is of primary importance. Over 75% of Type II diabetics can control their disease by diet alone. Diabetes is very rare in cultures with diets rich in whole plant foods. Our Western diet and lifestyle is an overwhelming causative factor.[90] Generally, there are few complications during pregnancy in moms with NIDDM *if* they are diligent to follow a whole foods diet and exercise regularly.

During pregnancy, the placenta produces insulin-suppressing hormones that allow more glucose to circulate in mom's circulatory system for the baby and the placenta to use. This is referred to as a "diabetogenic" state. Sometimes a transient form of diabetes occurs only during pregnancy. We refer to this as Gestational Diabetes or Gestational Carbohydrate Intolerance/Type III diabetes. This condition has been questioned by some in the maternal care community as to whether it truly exists and whether the normal body mechanisms of pregnancy are clearly understood. Beyond the controversy, the item to keep in mind for women exhibiting diabetic symptoms for the first time during a pregnancy is to maintain a healthful diet, exercise and eliminate dairy products which can aggravate the glucose values due to all that milk fat (yes, even the 2% has fat).

Lifestyle/Dietary Recommendations:

1. The best diet for diabetics is the high-complex-carbohydrate, high-fiber diet (HCF) popularized by Dr. James Anderson and supported by scientific literature.[91] The HCF diet's positive effects are: reduced elevations in blood sugar levels after meals, increased tissue sensitivity to insulin, reduced cholesterol and triglyceride levels with increased HDL levels, and progressive weight reduction. If the conventional American Diabetic Association (ADA) diet is resumed, insulin requirements return. The HCF diet is as follows: Carbohydrate calories - 70 to 75%; Protein calories - 15 to 20%; Fat calories - 5 to 10%.

2. Legumes should be encouraged in addition to other factors in diet as they have been shown to be helpful in diabetes control.[92][93] Fiber supplements only reduce insulin dosages by 2/3 whereas dietary changes led to total discontinuation of insulin in 60% of type II diabetics and reduced doses in the other 40% in one study.[94]

3. Maintain ideal body weight. (This does not mean trying to lose weight during pregnancy. That would be a very bad idea.)

4. Exercise enhances insulin sensitivity, improves glucose tolerance and reduces total serum cholesterol and triglycerides.[95]

Nutritional Supplement Recommendations:

There is an increased need for nutrients in addition to a healthful diet. These additional nutrients may help prevent or improve major diabetic complications. The supplement recommendations that follow are adapted from Michael T. Murray, N.D.'s book *Natural Alternatives to Over-the-Counter & Prescription Drugs.*[96] These are the most well-researched (and clinically-experienced in natural medicine) recommendations I have found. This book is a must for the family bookshelf.

1. Chromium picolinate or polynicotinate (bound to several niacin molecules) - 200 - 400 mcg daily.

2. Manganese is a co-factor in key enzymes of glucose metabolism. Diabetics have been shown to have only 1/2 of the manganese of healthy people (30mg daily).

3. Magnesium is involved in glucose metabolism. It is best derived from the diet: tofu, legumes, seeds, nuts, whole grains and green leafy vegetables. Supplementation needs to be 300 - 500mg daily, with 50mg of B6 needed for the magnesium to get inside of cells.

4. Zinc because diabetics tend to excrete too much zinc in their urine (30mg daily).

5. Biotin enhances insulin action by increasing enzyme glucokinase which is responsible for the first step in glucose utilization by the liver. One study revealed 16mg of biotin daily resulted in significant improvements in blood glucose control in diabetics.

6. Bitter melon (Momordica charantia) (looks like an ugly cucumber) has been used extensively in folk medicine for diabetes. Studies have confirmed its blood-sugar lowering action. Clinical trials show that 2 oz of the fresh juice result in lower insulin requirements. The juice tastes very bitter. Not recommended for use during pregnancy.

7. Onions and garlic both lower blood sugar. The active principles are believed to be sulfur-containing compounds, allyl propyl disulphide (APDS) and diallyl disulphide oxide (allicin) respectively. Flavonoids may also play some role. APDS given in doses of 125mg per kg of body weight to fasting humans caused a marked fall in blood glucose levels and increase in serum insulin. Allicin at 100mg per kg of body weight produced similar effects. Raw & cooked onions are effective in amounts of one to seven ounces.

8. The herbal extract of Gymnema sylvestre, given to 27 patients with type I diabetes on insulin, reduced insulin requirements and fasting blood sugar levels and improved control. It enhances insulin action and may possibly regenerate or revitalize beta cells of pancreas. One study shown that gymnema sylvestre given with oral hypoglycemic drugs improved blood sugar control in Type II diabetics. Twenty-one out of twenty-two reduced drug dosage; five discontinued medications and controlled diabetes with gymnema extract alone. Dosage was 400mg daily of extract. No side effects were reported, and it does not produce hypoglycemic effects in healthy individuals.

9. Other beneficial nutrients: Vitamin C - 3 - 8 g daily, Vitamin E - 400-600 IU daily, B12 - 1000mcg daily, and Selenium - 200mcg daily.

Many of these nutrients will probably be supplied in a quality prenatal formula. Mom should keep this in mind as she figures up total daily intake.

Diarrhea

Diarrhea is characterized by loose, possibly watery, frequent bowel movements. Most people experience some degree of cramping prior to and during bowel movements. Diarrhea may be caused by excessive fruit consumption (we call this "fruit poop"), diet sodas, bacteria-laden food, intestinal "flu" virus or stress. Diarrhea contracted while traveling abroad is called "traveler's diarrhea" and may be caused by a parasitic infection (see Protozoa Disease). Chronic diarrhea is most commonly caused by: lactose intolerance, inflammatory bowel disease (IBD), food allergy, gluten sensitivity, parasitic infections or benign/malignant tumors. Any diarrhea that lasts for more than a couple of days or includes pain, rectal bleeding, fever or chills, and/or extreme lethargy should be discussed with your professional health care provider.

Lifestyle/Dietary Recommendations:

1. Stay near the toilet. This means rest.
2. If diarrhea episode came after eating half a cantaloupe by oneself, cut back on cantaloupe consumption.
3. Do not go on clear, sugary liquid diet. "Sugar passes right through you and draws water and salts out of the body, leading to vomiting," says Dr. William B. Greenough, III, M.D., Johns Hopkins University.[97]
4. Do eat starchy foods such as bananas, rice, potatoes, corn, wheat, peas, carrots in thick soup or drink form.
5. Blueberry soup made from 1/3 oz. dried blueberries or black currant extract from dried black currants both have proved effective in human tests to combat gastrointestinal infections especially *Escherichia coli*, a bacteria responsible for many cases of diarrhea (at least half of all cases of traveler's diarrhea).[98] Pour 1 pint cold water over 3 heaping teaspoons of dried blueberries. Bring to a boil; let simmer for 15 minutes. Let cool; strain. Pour into bottle and drink 1 - 2 tablespoons several times daily (up to 10).
6. Avoid milk or clear broth. Add yogurt with live cultures. Research at the University of Minnesota found that various strains of *E. coli* thrived in milk and broth but died or did not grow in yogurt cultures. A special strain of friendly bacteria, *Lactobacillus GG*, in a new yogurt developed by professors Sherwood Gorbach and Barry Goldin of Tufts University produces an antimicrobial substance that acts like an antibiotic.[99] In fact, yogurt eaten daily (6 oz.) can actually prevent diarrhea according to studies at the University of California at Davis.[100]

Nutritional Supplement Recommendations:

1. Two - three capsules of fenugreek seeds with water three times daily often produces quick and "marked" relief, usually after the second dose according to Dr.

Krishna C. Srivastava at Odense University in Denmark.[101] While fenugreek does contain saponins and sapogenins which are starters for steroidal hormonal drugs, the use of fenugreek seeds for a short period of time has produced no ill-effect for pregnant women.[102] There is a possibility of uterine stimulation due to the saponin content; however, diarrhea itself produces uterine stimulation. Risk of short-term stimulation versus the benefit of a shortened diarrhea attack must be weighed.

2. Berberine, a chemical constituent of barberry, goldenseal, and Oregon grape has been found in studies around the world to kill microorganisms such as *Staphylococci, Streptococci, Salmonella, Shigella, Entamoeba histolytica, Vibrio cholerae, Giardia lamblia, Escherichia coli* and *Candida albicans.*[103] These are impressive results from some potent herbs. Berberine is a uterine stimulate; therefore, pregnant women should exercise caution when using herbs containing this chemical. Oregon grape appears to be the safest of the three to choose during pregnancy; however *women should not use berberine-containing herbs without consultation with a herbal professional.* 1 - 2, 250mg capsules three times daily for bacterial or protozoan diarrhea.

3. Inner Strength™ (or Probioplex™ available from Ethical Nutrients or Metagenics) is a product containing "Active Immunoglobulin Concentrate" (AIC). It is derived from raw milk whey product shown to be effective in increasing the production of friendly bacteria. The effect is enhanced when combined with a probiotic supplement such as *Lactobacillus acidophilus* or *Bifidobacterium infantis* (also available from Ethical Nutrients or Metagenics or Progressive Labs/Kordial Products). 1/3 t. Inner Strength to 1/8 to 1/4 t. of a probiotic taken three to four times daily can increase beneficial bacteria and decrease pathogenic bacteria.

4. Another product I like is AntiDiaTribe (available from Mother's Choice™). It contains herbs commonly used to support the normalization of bowel movements: Peppermint, Catnip, Nettle, Chamomile, Slippery Elm, Blackberry, Raspberry, Bayberry, Pau D'Arco, Cinnamon, Gentian, White Oak Bark and Clove. 1/2 t. for adults with every bowel movement or three to four times daily.

Dizziness/Fainting

Dizziness (vertigo) or feeling "faint" occurs most often in the early months of pregnancy and near the end of pregnancy. This may be due to the effects of estrogen on a woman's body. Some moms see black spots or actually see everything "go black" upon rising too quickly from a reclining position. This "blacking out" may be due to a change in blood flow to the brain when mom quickly stands up.

Lifestyle/Dietary Recommendations:
1. Rise slowly from seated position.
2. Do not stand for long periods of time without moving around.
3. Drink adequate (at least 2 quarts daily) amounts of water daily to keep up with expanding blood volume.
4. If mom feels as though she is going to faint, have her put her head below the rest of her body for several minutes until she feels better.
5. Loosen any restrictive clothing so circulation can be adequately maintained.
6. Inhale the scent of rosemary oil with the essential oil of camphor or just rosemary oil.

Nutritional Supplement Recommendations:
1. Ginger has been shown to relieve dizziness (vertigo).[104] One gram (1000mg) as needed.
2. One study of people with chronic dizziness showed a significant improvement or alleviation of their symptom when treated with ginkgo extract.[105] Ginkgo stimulates a positive circulatory response in the body which makes it a beneficial herb for improving blood flow in pregnancy. One 450mg capsule 2 - 3 times daily.

Ear Infections (Otitis Media)

This condition occurs primarily because of swelling and blockage of the eustachian tube. This swelling allows fluid to accumulate which provides an environment for bacteria and viruses to grow. Common symptoms include: earache, redness or bulging of the eardrum, and fever with chills. Most ear infections may be prevented through adequate hydration (drinking water) during respiratory infections. A lack of good water intake causes the secretions to thicken leading to a prime environment for bacterial overgrowth and increasing pressure.

Lifestyle/Dietary Recommendations:

1. Take steps to open eustachian tubes: yawn and chew gum.
2. Drink warm chamomile tea.
3. Massage area around ear. Pull earlobe down gently, stroke neck and rub temple. These actions encourage drainage and increase blood flow.
4. Eliminate dairy products from diet until condition clears. Dairy products cause the body to produce mucous which further clogs eustachian tube.
5. Raise the head of the bed to help tubes drain.
6. Drink plenty of water to encourage thinning of mucous.
7. Eliminate foods to which mom is allergic. In one study of children with frequent, severe ear infections presented to the American College of Allergy and Immunology, 78% were found to have specific food allergies. After eliminating the offending food from the diet for 11 weeks, 70 out of 81 experienced improvement. This is important for baby because foods eaten during pregnancy to which mom is sensitive are likely to cause allergies in baby.[106]
8. Avoid foods with simple sugars: sucrose (white table sugar), candies, cookies, ice cream, sodas, maple syrup, honey, dried fruits, fruit juices. Yes, even the more healthful sweeteners (honey, fruit juice, maple syrup) can provide enough sugar to feed bacteria or viruses during illness.

Nutritional Supplement Recommendations:

1. Apply warm (not hot) drops of herbal ear drops containing Mullein, Echinacea or Goldenseal, Garlic, etc. to ear canal once daily. This is not to be done if the eardrum is perforated. I particularly like a combination called HearDrops™ that contains: Mullein, Skullcap, Goldenseal, Black Cohosh, Blue Cohosh, Yarrow, Rosemary with the essential oils of garlic, tea tree and peppermint in a base of extra virgin olive oil (Mother's Choice™). Before using drops, dry ear first with a few drops of a vinegar/alcohol mixture. This prevents the oil from sealing in excess moisture which could make the problem worse. Remember that oil "drives in the herbs," while glycerin "draws" fluid out of the ear. Whatever the product used,

flushing the ear with hydrogen peroxide the following morning after treatment will allow mom to regain her equilibrium that may be lost due to fluid in the ear canal.

2. German researchers have found the herb Echinacea to kill a broad range of disease-causing bacteria, viruses, fungi and protozoa. The herb contains a natural antibiotic, echinacoside, that compares to penicillin in its broad-spectrum activity. It also contains echinacein that counteracts germs' tissue-dissolving enzyme, hyluronidase, preventing the germs from getting into body tissues. Other studies show increased macrophage (germ-eaters) activity and increased T-cell (T-lymphocytes) activity up to 30% more than immune-boosting drugs.[107] 500 - 1000mg every 2 hours in the acute crisis stage, tapering off to at least 1,000mg for 7 to 10 days after improvement.

3. ViraMune™(Mother's Choice™) contains Red Root, Echinacea, Yarrow, Myrrh, Red Clover, and Oregon Grape Root. These herbs are immunostimulants that increase lymphatic drainage which should be encouraged during an ear infection.

4. Essential fatty acids are very important for those who experience repeated ear infections. These may be found in foods such as nuts and seeds, deep-sea fish such as herring or mackerel, and in Evening Primrose Oil, Flax Seed Oil and Black Currant Oil.

5. N-acetylcysteine local application decreases inflammation of the middle-ear mucosa and prevents long-term fibrotic changes in patients suffering from secretory otitis media.[108]

Eczema, Psoriasis

Eczema (atopic dermatitis) and psoriasis are both considered an allergic disease characterized by intense itching and red, dry skin primarily located on the face, wrists, insides of elbows and knees.

Lifestyle/Dietary Recommendations:

1. Since food allergy is a major cause of these conditions, eliminating common allergens to see if improvement occurs would seem a wise move. Most common foods causing dermatitis are: cow's milk, eggs, tomatoes, artificial colors and food preservatives.
2. Those people with eczema and psoriasis appear to have an essential fatty acid (EFA) deficiency. EFAs synthesize anti-inflammatory prostaglandins; therefore, a deficiency would allow inflammation to occur. Foods high in EFAs are: fatty fish (such as mackerel, herring and salmon), nuts and seeds.
3. Be sure to get plenty of sunlight.
4. Eliminate bath oils, lotions, etc.

Nutritional Supplementation Recommendations:

1. Treatment with Evening Primrose Oil has shown a normalizing effect in essential fatty acid abnormalities and relieved eczema in many patients. 500 - 1000 mg three times daily.[109] Borage oil may also be used for beneficial effects.[110]
2. Licorice extracts contain a compound that when applied to skin exerts an effect similar to that of cortisone in treatment of eczema, contact or allergic dermatitis, and psoriasis. The compound 18-beta-glycyrrhetinic acid acts like cortisone but does not exhibit negative side effects. Several studies show glycyrrhetinic acid to be superior to cortisone especially in chronic cases. One study showed 93% of eczema patients treated with glycyrrhetinic acid improved, compared with 83% of those treated with cortisone.[111]
3. Chamomile extracts. The flavonoid and essential-oil components of chamomile possess significant anti-inflammatory and anti-allergy activity.[112]
4. Allantoin-compounds isolated from comfrey root which has a long history of use in skin-care have been shown to soften, protect and stimulate normal cell growth.[113] It is particularly useful in eczema and psoriasis. It is safe, non-allergenic and non-irritating for external use. The roots have twice the allantoin content as the leaves.[114]
5. Zinc is important in fatty acid metabolism in which eczema and psoriasis sufferers are deficient. 30 mg daily.[115]
6. Another supplement which has been recommended for psoriasis is milk thistle extract which improves liver function, inhibits inflammation and reduces excessive cellular proliferation. 70 - 210mg three times daily.[116]

Epstein-Barr Virus

The Epstein-Barr Virus is a member of the herpes family of viruses. It replicates in the B-lymphocytes and remains for life. Like other herpes viruses, it lies dormant until something triggers an outbreak. Incubation in primary infection is 30 to 50 days. The symptoms are fatigue, swollen glands, fever, sore throat and increased white blood count.[117] The virus is transmitted by saliva/respiratory droplet secretions contact. Clinical episodes are generally expressed as infectious mononucleosis. The virus if reactivated during pregnancy does not seem to correlate with congenital birth defects.[118] Any initial episode of infectious mononucleosis in mom should have lab tests to rule out Cytomegalovirus infection.

Lifestyle/Dietary Recommendations:

1. During the episode, Dr. Richard S. Griffith, M.D., professor emeritus of medicine at Indiana School of Medicine and an infectious disease specialist, recommends avoiding high arginine foods such as: almonds, Brazil nuts, cashews, hazelnuts, peanuts, pecans, walnuts, chocolate and gelatin; restricting coconut, barley, oats, corn, wheat, pasta and brussel sprouts; and adding 1 - 2, 500mg, lysine tablets daily during infection.[119]

2. Eating foods high in Quercetin and other bioflavonoids such as: buckwheat, onions, green peppers and tomatoes may decrease the infectiousness of RNA and DNA viruses, such as herpes, polio and Epstein-Barr, by inhibiting their replication.[120]

3. As always with any infection, limit or eliminate sugar intake, stick to simple foods: fruits and veggies, and rest.

Nutritional Supplement Recommendations:

1. Glycyrrhizin, a saponin present in licorice root demonstrated inhibition of Epstein-Barr Virus (EBV), cytomegalovirus (CMV) and hepatitis B virus in a 1979 study.[121]

2. Organo-germanium sesquioxide (marketed primarily as Ge-132) appears to be helpful in the treatment of viral diseases such as Epstein-Barr. 50 - 100 mg daily minimum for treatment. To induce interferon synthesis in humans, a daily intake of 50 - 75 mg/kg of body weight is necessary. It seems to be without any significant toxic effects.[122]

3. Lapacho or Pau D'Arco may be effective against Epstein-Barr virus due to its inhibiting effects on the synthesis of DNA and RNA of the virus in the cell. No significant toxicity in humans is apparent,[123] although use during pregnancy is not advised.

Excess Mucous (Phlegm)

This condition is quite common during pregnancy. Due to circulating hormones, mucous membranes increase their secretions all over the body. This includes those membranes in the respiratory passage. There may be mild swelling of nasal membranes creating a stuffy nose. Signs of excess mucous in the body are: increased vaginal discharge, oily hair, shiny nose, possibly a blocked nose, postnasal drip, or phlegm collecting in the throat.

Lifestyle/Dietary Recommendations:

1. Certain foods tend to increase the formation of mucous in the body. The table below lists those that are mucous-forming and those that are mucous-reducing.

Mucous-Forming Foods	Mucous-Reducing Foods
All meat, milk, cheese	Fruits and vegetables especially raw (exceptions on other list)
Chocolate, cocoa	Whole grains - oats, wheat, rice, barley, rye, etc.
Tofu (soybean curd)	Whole grain bread (except for sensitive people)
Eggs	Onions
Most nuts, especially peanuts	Garlic
Yams	Watercress, mustard greens and seeds
Bananas, oranges (in excess)	Horseradish
Oily or greasy foods	Hot peppers
Alcohol	

Most people can cope with the mucous-forming foods because of strong digestive systems. It would be prudent to avoid those foods during periods of illness, weak digestion (first months of pregnancy) or if mom is having a problem with postnasal drip and phlegm in her throat during the night or upon waking.

Nutritional Supplement Recommendations:

1. Elder berries and flowers reduce phlegm as well as act as an anti-inflammatory and expectorant. A very useful combination is one of elder, yarrow and peppermint (Yummy Yarrow & Elderberry by Mother's Choice™). These are best taken in a liquid so that the herbs come in contact with the mucous membranes and phlegm.

2. A combination containing herbs such as Horseradish root, Mullein leaves, Fenugreek seeds, Fennel, and Boneset herb is helpful in liquefying and moving mucous secretions out of the body.

3. Freeze-dried Nettle leaves (available from Eclectic Institute) have been shown to be effective in reducing hay-fever symptoms in allergic persons. I personally have found these to be quite helpful during those times in my pregnancy when I wake up with phlegm in my throat. I take 2 capsules before bedtime and 2 upon rising.

4. Quercitin with bromelain, 200-500 mg taken 30 minutes before each meal.

Fever

An elevated body temperature, fever, is the body's mechanism for mobilizing the immune system to defend against invading organisms. Most of the time, we want to allow the fever to do its work in the body; however, in pregnancy an elevated temperature of 101 F , or above, in mom can cause developmental problems for baby (mostly in early pregnancy). It is advisable then to work to lower the temperature naturally and, if the temperature continues to rise even while utilizing natural measures, to consult with a maternal care provider about other treatment options (see box below).

While acetaminophen is the "safest" pharmaceutical analgesic/antipyretic to use during pregnancy, it does carry some risks. Acetaminophen does place a heavier burden on the liver to process this drug. It is my practice to always use the herb milk thistle which contains silymarin while using acetaminophen. One study found that milk thistle may offer some protection against the toxic side effects of acetaminophen.[124] Herbal extracts or tinctures containing alcohol should not be used in combination with acetaminophen due to possible lethal effects.

Lifestyle/Dietary Recommendations:

1. During a fever, the only foods consumed should be fruits and vegetables which can be easily digested so energy is not diverted from the immune response to digest heavy foods.
2. Liquid intake (water with lemon) should be increased to one cup per hour to keep the body well-hydrated.
3. Rest is an important part of healing. Fever is a symptom of an illness, and when we are ill, we need to be in bed — not doing errands. Moms should call on friends and family for help with other children or household chores.
4. Bathing in lukewarm water may help lower the fever. Adding essential oils of chamomile or lavender to bath water is soothing and calming.
5. Fresh star fruit should be eaten twice daily as well as cucumber, cantaloupe and water chestnuts.
6. A tea recommended in *The Healing Power of Foods* by Michael T. Murray, N.D. to promote perspiration thereby lowering temperature is:
   Cinnamon-Ginger Tea
   > 1 inch slice of fresh ginger
   > 1/4 t. cinnamon
   > 1/4 lemon
   > 1 c. hot water
   > Juice or grind ginger - juice lemon - add to water and cinnamon.

Nutritional Supplement Recommendations:

1. The herbs white willow and meadowsweet contain salicin which is converted to salicylic acid in the body. The structural formulas for Acetylsalicylic acid (Aspirin) and salicylic acid are very similar; therefore, a very cautious herbal healing approach should be used when ingesting plant products containing salicin as when using aspirin. Salicin in plants does not cause gastric or intestinal upset or bleeding because it bypasses the stomach or intestine. It does have prostaglandin blocking (PGE2) effects when it reaches the liver where the acetyl-group is metabolically picked up.[125] The plant product containing salicin has not been associated with increased birth defects or Reye's syndrome as aspirin has, but willow is not advised for use during pregnancy.[126]

2. A TincTract™ (glycerin-based liquid herbs processed in 3-stages) of peppermint, yarrow and elder (Mother's Choice™ as Yummy Yarrow & Elderberry) is beneficial in increasing perspiration and lowering the body temperature.

3. Since fever is only a symptom of an infection, immuno-stimulants should be used to combat the underlying infection. Echinacea - 500 - 1000mg every 2 hours; Garlic - Fresh garlic, 1 - 2 cloves, or Garlic tablets - 3 - 6 daily; Oregon grape root (not during pregnancy without consultation with herbal professional) if dealing with a bacterial infection - 500mg three times daily.

4. Keep the bowels open with plenty of fruit, liquids and mild bowel stimulants if necessary - Yellow Dock plant is okay for mild bowel stimulation.

5. Capsaicin, a compound in capsicum or cayenne pepper, has been shown to lower body temperature through stimulation of the cooling center of the hypothalamus in the brain.[127]

Flu (Influenza)

Flu or influenza is a respiratory infection that affects the nose, throat and chest. While colds are upper respiratory infections, influenza infects the lower respiratory tract also. It affects the whole body causing muscle aches, fever and extreme lethargy. Contrary to popular belief, there is no "intestinal or stomach flu." These conditions are gastrointestinal viruses or bacteria unrelated to influenza. Adults very rarely experience gastrointestinal upset during influenza although children may have stomach upset during a bout of the flu.

Lifestyle/Dietary Recommendations:

1. Bed rest is a necessity during the flu — most people find themselves unable to do much else besides crawl into the bed and stay there.
2. Appetites generally are not hearty during the flu. Foods should be limited to fruits, vegetables and plenty of liquids.
3. Warm chamomile or lemon balm tea can be very soothing and healing.

Nutritional Supplement Recommendations:

1. Vitamin C (buffered powder or Ester-C powder) should be taken at 1000mg every 2 hours at the beginning of symptoms and continued until symptoms subside. Moms in their first trimester should limit their daily intake of Vitamin C to 3000mg.
2. A product containing ginger root, capsicum fruit, goldenseal root and licorice root may be taken at 2 capsules every 2 - 4 hours. This combination should not be used by moms prone to miscarriage because this amount of goldenseal could stimulate uterine contractions. This combination is particularly effective in combating the flu virus especially if begun at initial onset of symptoms.[128]
3. A liquid favorite of ours to take at bedtime when fighting the flu is Flew Away (available from Tri-Light) which contains: Boneset, Osha root, Mullein, Shavegrass, St. John's Wort, Peppermint, Capsicum, Clove. The major constituent, boneset, is prescribed currently in Germany by physicians for patients with colds and flu.[129] Moms should exercise caution due to the Osha root content unless flu is severe and benefit outweighs the risk of using Osha root which contains alkaloids that may be difficult for the liver to process.
4. The herb Astragalus has been found in studies to boost macrophage production and induce interferon production which prevents viruses from settling in to homestead in the respiratory tract.[130] This is a preventive-use herb, not one for crisis situations.

5. Echinacea is always the herb of choice for any type of infection —especially upper and lower respiratory viruses. Echinacea's effects on boosting immune response is well-documented.[131]
6. Bee Propolis extract given when exposed to influenza may lead to a reduction in HA titer and reduction in mortality and increased survival time.[132]

Gallstones

Gallstones are formed in the gallbladder when the bile crystallizes into hard pellets that can be as small as grains of sand or as big as an inch in diameter. Most of the time (80%), the stones are harmless, but sometimes when the gallbladder contracts to release bile, a stone or stones are forced out and plug the opening of the duct leading to the liver and small intestine. This leads to a gallstone attack characterized by pain that may radiate from the upper right chest. Some people describe the pain as extending up over the shoulder and down the back. Attacks can last minutes or hours. Nausea and vomiting sometimes accompany the painful attack.

Diet is an important preventive and treatment measure for gallstones. Gallstones tend to run in families and occur more frequently in women than men. Pregnancy itself is conducive to stone formation. Many women who have gallstone attacks experience them while pregnant or immediately postpartum.[133]

Lifestyle/Dietary Recommendations:
1. Eat more vegetables. A study in England found vegetarian women to be half as likely to form gallstones as meat-eating women.[134] Another recent study at Harvard found that women who ate specifically the most nuts, beans, lentils, peas, lima beans and oranges were resistant to gallbladder attacks.[135]
2. Avoid sugar, white flour and white rice. One British test revealed an increase in cholesterol content in bile (super-saturated bile produces stones) in the test group consuming sugar, white rice and white flour.[136]
3. Avoid coffee. Coffee with *or without* caffeine (and as little as one cup) can stimulate the gallbladder to contract which could lead to a gallbladder attack in those with gallstones according to Bruce R. Douglas and colleagues at the University Hospital in Leiden, the Netherlands.[137]
4. Don't skip breakfast. In a ten-year study by James Everhart, M.D., a scientist at the National Institute of Diabetes and Digestive and Kidney Disease, women who fasted overnight (fourteen hours or more) had the highest rate of gallstones.[138]

Nutritional Supplement Recommendations:
1. For gallstones accompanied by fatigue with sore liver and a tendency toward constipation, Christopher Hobbs in his book, *Foundations of Health - The Liver and Digestive Herbal*, recommends the following combination of herbs: Buplureum (6 parts), scutellaria (3) paeonia (3), ginger (4), unripe orange peel (2), jujube (3), rhubarb (1) and pinellia (3).
2. For gallstones accompanied by gallbladder inflammation and loss of appetite due to intestinal discomfort, Hobbs recommends a combination of: Buplureum (5 parts), pinellia (4), licorice (1.5), paeonia (2.5), jujube (2), and ginger (1).[139]

3. Dandelion has performed well in studies in both humans and laboratory animals to enhance bile flow and improve conditions such as liver congestion, bile duct inflammation, hepatitis, gallstones and jaundice.[140] 1 - 2, 250 - 500mg capsules three times daily.

4. An in vitro study on mice found that curcumin given over a period of 10 weeks significantly decreased incidence of gallstone formation relative to controls as well as a significant reduction in biliary cholesterol concentration.[141]

5. One study showed that N-acetyl cysteine (NAC) accelerated the dissolution of gallstone in vitro significantly.[142]

6. During my pregnancy with my third child, Eryn, I had gallbladder attacks in my second trimester and in the immediate postpartum time. I had experienced tremendous relief by using an herbal combination containing: Buplureum root, peony root, pinellia rhizome, cinnamon twig, dang gui root, rushen plant, zhishi fruit, scute root, atractylodes rhizome, panax ginseng root, ginger rhizome, and licorice root (marketed as LIV-C™ by NSP) and lecithin capsules. As soon as the pain and nausea began, I took 4 LIV-C and 2 - 3 lecithin capsules. Relief came within fifteen (15) minutes usually. I have to admit, too, that I had a strong attraction to fast food during that pregnancy as well. Could there be a correlation?

Note: Prevention is the key with gallstones. As I wrote this, I was eagerly awaiting the birth of our fourth blessing from the Lord. This pregnancy has been full of joy and vibrant health - just as we prayed it would be. I began preparing my body for pregnancy several months before conception (as soon as I felt my menstrual cycles about to resume and diligently took my supplements and followed the whole foods diet. The few short times of discomfort I experienced during that pregnancy came after slipping back into old (high fat or sugar, low-fiber) habits. Glory to God, I had no morning, afternoon or evening sickness with that pregnancy. A miracle He gave to me! Our sweet blessing was born and named Eliana, an answer from God.

Please see Strengthening the Liver for prevention information.

Gas (Flatulence)

We all know what this is: the bloated feeling we have with pain in our abdomen or side (sometimes even in our chests) until we are able to pass the gas without embarrassing ourselves in front of others. The normal, healthy person passes gas approximately 14 times per day. Pregnancy makes gas more likely because the digestive processes slow down intestinal motility. What we eat and how we prepare it can make a big difference in the amount of gas our bodies produce.

Lifestyle/Dietary Recommendations:

1. Watch out for dairy foods - the number 1 cause of gas in our country, says Dr. Michael Levitt of the University of Minnesota, an international authority on flatulence. Many people are not aware that they are somewhat lactose (milk sugar) intolerant. One sign of lactose intolerance is excessive gas after drinking or eating milk products. Yogurt does not produce gas and is acceptable for those with lactose intolerance because it basically comes predigested (those friendly bacteria eat up the milk sugar for you). Plain yogurt has more anti-lactose activity than flavored versions. Frozen yogurt does not have live bacteria so it is an offender.[143]

2. Beans are notorious for causing gas. You can de-gas your beans by about 50% by soaking them. The process is as follows: Rinse beans. Add them to boiling water and boil in a covered pot for 3 minutes. Let stand for two hours. Pour off old water and add new water at room temperature just to cover the beans. After two hours, pour this water off. Add more water and let soak overnight. Rinse again with room-temperature water. Add water to cover and cook until done, about 75 - 90 minutes.[144]

3. Add garlic and/or ginger to beans or other gaseous veggies. Both have been traditionally touted to relieve gas. Researchers at India's G.B. Pant University decided the tradition of adding spices to legumes and vegetables was based on "sound principles."[145]

4. Also of note is that when changing to a whole foods - more fiber-diet - many people experience an increase in gas. This usually will pass (no pun intended) in two to three weeks and is a great support for the "make changes slowly" way of moving toward a healthier lifestyle.

Nutritional Supplement Recommendations:

1. A small vial of peppermint oil carried along in the purse will make having a cup of peppermint tea while away from home much simpler. Simply place 2 to 3 drops of the oil in a cup of hot herb tea or water. Stir it well and drink.[146]

2. Papaya contains an enzyme, papain, that aids digestion thereby lowering the amount of undigested food in the intestinal tract to ferment and cause gas. Tablets

are available in the health food store. I like the combination of papaya fruit and peppermint tablets.

3. Activated charcoal has shown benefit in absorbing toxins and undigested food in the intestinal tract which decreases gas production.

One of the nicest things about being in labor is that "anything can go or pass" without need for embarrassment. This is a time of no worry about etiquette or propriety concerning bodily functions. One midwife says, "We get excited when moms start passing gas. It means their baby's head is pushing everything out of the way so that baby can come out to see mom!"

Genital Warts (Condylomata Acuminata) Human Papillomarvirus

This wart-producing virus is found in 2 to 10% of all women. It is primarily contracted through sexual encounters although some evidence exists of prenatal transmission either during birth or via the placenta causing infection in the baby. These wart-like growths may appear in one clump or in innumerable clumps of varying sizes around or inside the genitals. The growth seems to be stimulated by leukorrhea in pregnancy. If transmitted to baby during birth, baby can develop warts, hoarseness, difficult breathing and acute respiratory obstruction. Cesareans are not currently recommended as the best method of birth for those with genital warts. Allopathic treatment of podophyllum is contraindicated during pregnancy. Other alternatives are electrocautery, cryosurgery and CO_2 laser surgery.[147 148]

Lifestyle/Dietary Recommendations:
1. Practice good hygiene with a sitz bath after each bowel movement.
2. Change underwear frequently.
3. Be careful about relations with husband to protect him.

Nutritional Supplement Recommendations:
The specific herbal treatments for genital warts are not particularly suitable for pregnancy. The following recommendations are for warts in general.
1. Milk thistle has been recommended for internal use although further scientific investigation of efficacy is warranted.[149]
2. Immune system support is beneficial in fighting the virus causing the warts: garlic, echinacea and vitamin C.
3. Thuja occidentalis (yellow cedar, arbor vitae) contains a volatile oil, thujone, which is antiseptic and a special treatment for *topical* use in fungal and viral infections. Drops of the tincture may be applied to the external warts morning and night.[150 151] *Thuja should not be used internally during pregnancy because it is an emmenagogue (induces menstruation; abortifacient)* I've included this recommendation for those who are not pregnant.
4. A licensed naturopath should be consulted. When choosing a naturopath, one should choose one who has graduated from the National School of Naturopathy in Portland, Oregon or Bastyr College in Seattle, Washington or Southwest College of Naturopathic Medicine & Health Sciences. These are the only naturopathic medical schools that require on-site learning and internship in a clinical environment. If mom is unable to find someone from these colleges, she should be aware that choosing a "naturopath" who has not graduated from one of these universities means she is essentially contacting someone who has gotten an "N.D." from a

correspondence school. This is not necessarily bad; however, mom should know who she is paying for and how her practitioner was educated. Someone familiar with researching botanical medicine in the scientific literature or doing the research herself is often helpful as a starting point for a treatment plan. An excellent resource for research is *The Herb Research Foundation* located in Colorado. More information about this foundation is located Part 8, Resources.

5. Tori Hudson, N.D. has a treatment plan outlined in her manual, *Gynecology and Naturopathic Medicine*, that could be used prior to or after pregnancy. The manual is available from TK Publications, 19135 Butternut Drive, Aloha, OR 97007.

Group-b beta-hemolytic Streptococci Infections

One study identified colonization of these organisms in the vaginas of 1/4 of women studied in the third trimester. This number is higher than other studies that reported anywhere from 10% to a high of 30% colonization.[152] [153] Out of a study with 25% of women showing colonization, only one of 78 babies developed symptomatic group B strep infection, and he recovered after anti-microbial therapy.[154] The most common colonization rate in newborn infants ranges from 1 - 7%. Group-b streptococcus is the most common infecting microorganism of the newborn (30% of neonatal infections).[155]

Moms experience approximately 1.5 - 2.0% of puerperal infections (uterine) due to group B strep. This is mainly a complication of artificial rupture of membranes (AROM).[156] Morbidity among babies is 2 - 4 per 1000; mortality is 1 in 1000. There are two main syndromes:

1. Early-onset septicemia and pneumonia seen mainly in RDS (respiratory distress syndrome) cardiovascular collapse due to primarily premature infants born before 35 weeks, with male babies being more susceptible than girls.
2. Late onset seen after the 1st week of life. Baby symptoms can include lethargy, anorexia, jaundice. Meningitis is a common complication. Less frequently the infection is seen in the eyes, sinuses, joints, bones, skin, ears or lungs. This type may be due to nosocomial (caregiver transmits infection) infection rather than maternal infection.

Routine vaginal testing of mom is not recommended because of test unreliability, cost and the fact that although mom may have group B strep present, the percentage of those women becoming infected or infecting their babies is still low.[157] Out of 10 - 30% of pregnant women cultured positive, 50% of their babies were colonized, with only 1% of babies infected with the organism.[158]

Lifestyle/Dietary Recommendations:
1. All measures to strengthen immune function should be employed if mom has been cultured and shown positive for group B streptococcal infection.

Nutritional Supplement Recommendations:
1. Echinacea capsules, 500 - 1000mg three times daily or 2 ml of tincture/tinctract three times daily should be taken for one to two weeks, then mom should take an "echinacea break" for two to three days then repeat dosage for two more weeks.
2. Propolis has been advocated by some to boost immune function.[159]
3. Echinacea infusion may be used as a douche if under the direction of a professional maternal care provider. See douching instructions for pregnancy below.

Douching Instructions for Pregnancy

Douching during pregnancy is generally unnecessary and would not be considered a safe regular practice. The vagina is a self-cleansing organ. While some women do experience an increase in vaginal discharge (leukorrhea) during pregnancy, this is perfectly normal and should not be dabbled with.

There are times when douching may be beneficial; however, moms must take care to avoid forcing water into the uterus, possible causing infections, or forcing air into the vagina, possibly causing a deadly air embolus. **Douching during pregnancy should only be done under the direction of a qualified health professional**. A regular douche bag and hose may be used. Smaller bags make controlling the flow harder.

1. Fill douche bag with body temperature solution and attach a thoroughly cleaned vaginal tip (tip with fluted, wider end and holes in the sides).
2. Clear air from hose by opening the clamp and running liquid through until it comes from tip.
3. Hang bag 10 inches or less from the floor (bathtub faucet a good height).
4. Lie in the tub and gently insert the nozzle no more than 2" into the vagina (1 1/2" preferably).
5. Very gently release the hose clamp, and controlling the flow, allow the solution to run in and out of the vagina. Gentle kegels of 1 - 2 second duration may be employed, but moms should not attempt to retain water in the vagina during pregnancy. This could force water through the cervix.
6. When finished, clean equipment thoroughly with 1 - 2 drops of tea tree oil in warm water (water may be sudsy with antibacterial soap). Leave the bag uncapped and allow it to air dry.

If mom is already dilating, has placenta previa or ruptured membranes, **douching should NOT be attempted**. A sitz bath in a therapeutic solution is preferable if douching is not an option.

Hair Loss

Hair loss is very common in the first year after giving birth. My hair usually begins falling out "by the handful" when my babies are five or six months old. It usually lasts about six months for me. My vacuum cleaner and bathroom sinks clog up with all my hair. The laundry has my hair in it. Hair everywhere! It's a wonder I've any hair left!

The prevalent thought is this condition is caused by the changing hormone levels in a new mother's body. Normally, hair has a "resting" phase during which existing hairs die and are shed, and a "growing" phase when new hairs replace the shed ones. Pregnancy extends the growing phase and delays the resting phase, so several months after baby is born, mom sheds a greater amount of hair than during a normal resting phase.

The postpartum resting phase, that causes mom to lose more than twice the amount of hair she usually loses, peaks at six months postpartum and declines over the second six months of baby's first year. Difficult deliveries, particularly cesarean sections, and anesthesia used for childbirth seem to exacerbate the condition.

Lifestyle/Dietary Recommendations:

1. Avoid anesthesia during childbirth. It is not good for baby anyway unless a medical condition necessitates use.
2. Do not brush wet hair. Let hair dry before brushing, or comb gently with a wide-toothed comb.
3. De-stress lifestyle as much as possible. Stress increases hair loss.
4. Massage scalp daily. Increased circulation stimulates new hair growth.

Nutritional Supplement Recommendations:

1. In a double-blind, placebo-controlled study, long-term oral therapy with 18,000 IU of retinol combined with 70mg L-cystine and 700mg gelatin led to an improvement of diffuse hair loss relative to controls.[160] *This supplementation is not appropriate for pregnancy.*
2. A B-complex vitamin or a high-quality multivitamin may aid the body in adapting to increased stress levels.
3. Adding herbs that increase circulation may help: cayenne, ginkgo biloba, gotu kola. 2 to 6 capsules of one of these herbs daily.

Headache

An ache in the head, or headache, occurs when pain arises from the outer lining of the brain and scalp and its blood vessels and muscles. There are essentially two types of headaches: migraine, or vascular headache, characterized by throbbing, pounding, sharp pain in the head (can be behind one eye); tension headache characterized by a steady, constant, dull pain that starts at the back of the head or forehead and spreads over the entire head with a sense of pressure applied to skull.

Although early pregnancy can be a time of increased headaches due in some part to vascular changes in the body, I believe most headaches in pregnancy originate from hypoglycemia and liver congestion (loaded with extra hormones and toxins to de-toxify for removal from the body).

Lifestyle/Dietary Recommendations:

1. Allergy is the major cause of migraines.[161] The same allergens can cause tension headaches as well. Common allergens: milk, wheat, chocolate, food additives, MSG, artificial sweeteners like aspartame, tomatoes and fish.
2. Chocolate, cheese, beer, wine and aspartame may cause migraines due to "vasoactive amines" which cause blood vessels to expand. Many migraine sufferers are found to have low levels of platelet enzyme that normally breaks down dietary amines.
3. If mom is experiencing a number of headaches early in pregnancy, she should follow the Hypoglycemia recommendations as well as the suggestions for liver support (pg 85).

Nutritional Supplement Recommendations:

1. Magnesium deficiency is known to set the stage for migraines and tension headaches.[162] One function of magnesium is to maintain tone of blood vessels. Mom needs 350 - 500mg of magnesium aspartate or citrate daily.
2. Feverfew, while not to be used during pregnancy because of its emmenagogue properties (promotes menstruation; abortifacient), has been used for centuries for headaches. Modern research continues to confirm its historical use. A 1988 survey found 70% of 270 migraine sufferers who ate feverfew daily for prolonged periods claimed that the herb decreased the frequency and/or intensity of the attacks. This prompted clinical trials at the London Migraine Clinic, a double-blind study that used patients reporting help by feverfew. Those receiving placebo significantly increased the frequency and severity of their headaches, nausea and vomiting during the six months of study. Those taking feverfew showed no change. Two patients in the placebo group who had been in complete remission during self-treatment with feverfew said they developed recurrence of incapacitating migraines and had

to withdraw from the study. Self-treatment renewed remission in both patients.[163] A second double-blind study at the University of Nottingham showed feverfew to be effective in reducing the number of severity of migraine attacks.[164] Feverfew works by inhibiting the release of blood-vessel dilating substances from platelets, inhibiting production of inflammatory substances and re-establishing blood vessel tone.[165] Parthenolide is thought to be the active ingredient. To achieve the same results as those in the studies, each capsule should contain at least 0.2% of parthenolide per 25mg freeze-dried pulverized leaves twice daily or 82mg dried powdered leaves once daily. A higher dose (1 - 2 g) is needed during an acute attack. No side effects have been reported as long as the leaves are not chewed. This can result in small ulcerations in the mouth, swelling of the lips and tongue in 10% of users.

3. Nitrites may cause headaches according to neurologists William P. Henderson and Neil H. Raskin, of the University of California at San Francisco. If mom is prone to headaches, she needs to watch out for hot dogs, bacon, salami, ham and other meats cured with sodium nitrite or nitrate.[166] These foods are not the best for mom to choose since they can be contaminated with campylobacter bacteria, which can cause miscarriage or stillbirth.

4. Caffeine has been referred to as the nation's #1 headache instigator, says Dr. David W. Buchholz, director of the Neurological Consultation Clinic at Johns Hopkins University Hospital. Although some tests have shown small amounts of caffeine to be able to relieve headaches by temporarily constricting dilated and swollen blood vessels, the vessels swell up and dilate worse in a rebound action, worsening the headache. The other problem with caffeine is that it is addictive, and most people experience caffeine-withdrawal headaches as well as fatigue, mild depression, nausea and vomiting. Withdrawal symptoms usually start 12 - 24 hours after ceasing caffeine consumption and are usually over in a week.[167] To get off caffeine without feeling "Yuck," mix regular and decaf coffee over a week's period increasing the amount of decaf each day until it is all decaf (same for tea and soda pops). It is a good idea to wean off the decaf versions after overcoming the caffeine hurdle. The decaf versions have their own health risks.

5. Ginger acts much like aspirin in that it blocks prostaglandin synthesis which leads to a reduction in inflammation and pain according to Dr. Drishna C. Srivastava at Odense University in Denmark. It is safe to use for adults and children with no side effects reported. The recommended amount is 1 - 2, 500 - 600mg capsules taken with water up to four times daily as needed.[168] In China, birth practitioners caution against using too much ginger (20 - 28 grams = 20,000 - 28,000mg) in the early portion of pregnancy due to its stimulant properties.[169] I could find no scientific documentation of any abortive-aspects of this

herb in quantities recommended above, and scientific research on ginger does include studies of pregnant women, particularly those with hyperemesis gravidum (excessive vomiting during pregnancy).

6. Omega-3 fish oils may be a migraine headache preventive. This means moms cannot reach for it as a headache is coming on; rather, the supplement can be taken over the long-term in those who are prone to migraine attacks.[170]

Heartburn (Gastroesophageal reflux)

Heartburn is a burning sensation or pressure in the chest that extends upward to the back of the throat. Some people have even suspected a heart attack because of a bad case of heartburn. Heartburn occurs when the lower esophageal sphincter muscle relaxes and allow stomach acids, hydrochloric acid and pepsin, to spurt into the esophagus causing pain and a bad taste in the mouth.

Pregnancy hormones tend to relax muscles in the body so heartburn may be more likely to occur. There are measures to be taken that can lower the possibility of a heartburn attack.

Lifestyle/Dietary Recommendations:

1. There are several foods that can cause heartburn by relaxing the sphincter: chocolate, caffeine, fatty foods, alcohol, and possibly onions. Other foods increase stomach acidity making heartburn more painful: coffee, colas, beer and milk.[171] Avoid these foods and drinks if you are having a heartburn problem.
2. Eat slowly and calmly, chewing food well before swallowing. This allows the saliva to begin digesting the food prior to traveling to the stomach, a very important part of the digestive process.
3. Do not overeat. There is a consequence to gluttony, and it just may be heartburn.
4. Do not lie down immediately after a meal. If one does lie down, lie on the left side to prevent pressure on the sphincter muscle.
5. At the end of pregnancy when mom feels as though baby is in her throat, she may want to prop the head of her bed up on blocks so gravity can help keep tummy contents (acid) down. I personally find this to be helpful not only for heartburn, but for breathing easier at night as well.

Nutritional Supplement Recommendations:

1. Marshmallow root has a very high mucilage content that swells when combined with water to form a soft, soothing protective gel.[172] This can provide heartburn relief in 15 to 30 minutes. 2 capsules after meals.
2. Chamomile has been clearly shown in several studies to protect and heal the mucosa of the gastrointestinal tract and prevent ulcers from forming.[173] This is important for those suffering from chronic heartburn which can damage or ulcerate the esophageal lining. Although chamomile has been claimed, by those afraid of consumer herb use, to cause severe allergic reactions, this is only potentially possible in those who have an anaphylactic reaction to ragweed. In all the world's literature from 1887 to 1982, only 50 reactions were reported: 45 from Roman chamomile and 5 from the German variety, which is the variety most often used in the U.S. This herb would best be used, in this case, as a tea or infusion.

3. For those who anticipate a large or high-fat meal, it would be wise to take a dandelion preparation thirty minutes before the meal. This herb aids the flow of digestive juices and bile which provides for better digestion of fats and proteins.

4. I have also found Papaya tablets to be helpful in aiding digestion to avoid heartburn after indulging in a large or fatty meal.

5. Peppermint relaxes the stomach including the esophageal sphincter. Use in heartburn may increase problems with reflux.

Hemorrhoids/Varicose Veins

Hemorrhoids are actually varicose veins (enlarged blood vessels with weakened valves) of the rectum. Pregnancy may aggravate the problem of the pooling blood and enlargement of the blood vessels because of the blood volume expansion and hormonal relaxation of muscles. In late pregnancy, the weight of the uterus accentuates distension of the blood vessels. This blood vessel distension in the rectal area (hemorrhoids) can cause itching, redness, swelling and outright pain. Most hemorrhoids protrude out of the anus although some are located just inside the anal opening and may bleed during bowel movements with hard stool or vigorous straining.

Lifestyle/Dietary Recommendations:

1. A diet rich in whole grains has been shown to protect against many chronic degenerative (Western) diseases: cancer, especially colon cancer, heart disease, diabetes, varicose veins, inflammatory bowel disease (IBD), hemorrhoids and diverticulitis.[174]

2. A healthful diet full of fruits, vegetables, legumes and grains lends itself to regular, soft, bulky, easy to pass bowel movements. While many people keep reading material in the bathroom, one should only be spending a couple of minutes on defecation. Reading while on the toilet increases the amount of time of pressure on the rectal and anal area.

3. Have a footstool handy in the bathroom to use during bowel movements to reduce pressure on rectum and anus.

Nutritional Supplement Recommendations:

1. Topical treatment can provide temporary relief while mom is changing to healthier dietary habits. A witch hazel bark infusion can be used by soaking gauze in the infusion and applying to hemorrhoids.[175]

2. An ointment or infusion (for gauze compresses) made of Horse chestnut, mullein, white oak bark and yarrow is beneficial to help shrink hemorrhoidal tissue.[176] The cream Cellu-Var by Enzymatic Therapy may be used as well as the capsules per recommendation by Dr. Michael T. Murray, N.D. during a phone conversation.

3. The liquid TincTract™ **Circulatone by Mother's Choice**™ by Liquid Light is a formula containing Bilberry, Rose Hips, Cleavers and Ginkgo to enhance circulation and decrease varicosities.

4. Rutin supplements can help to shrink and tone blood vessels. 500mg daily (NOT for use in the first trimester).[177]

5. Butcher's broom has been termed a "phlebotherapeutic agent" - used to treat circulatory disorders especially varicose veins and hemorrhoids. Studies confirm this definition with patients improving when treated with Butcher's broom.[178] Butcher's

broom raises the blood pressure making it useful for those with low blood pressure. Broom gently raises the blood pressure by constricting the peripheral blood vessels resulting in an overall decreased blood volume. Although there are no safety restrictions on butcher's broom during pregnancy, there may be a safety concern due to decreased blood volume. The standard dosage is 2, 250-500mg capsules two to three times daily.

6. Bilberry has been shown in a study of pregnant women to reduce varices and various blood problems while exhibiting no side effects in mother or baby.[179] 2 - 450mg capsules three times daily.

7. Mom can apply calendula lotion by putting the lotion on a cotton swab and applying to sore tissue around or in the rectum after bowel movements.

Hepatitis

Hepatitis is an inflammation of the liver. There are several types of hepatitis. Each will be briefly discussed. All are of concern in that pregnancy creates a greater demand on the liver and a liver depleted from infection can compromise mother and/or baby's health.

Hepatitis A (infectious):

Type A hepatitis (HAV) is termed "infectious" hepatitis because it produces an acute infection that is relatively mild. This virus is transmitted by food and/or water contaminated by oral/fecal contact. It is an RNA virus with all the features of an enterovirus. It is very similar in pathogenesis to the polio virus except HAV infects the hepatocyte and polio targets the neuron.[180]

Different medical texts report an incubation period from 14 to 45 days (2 to 6 weeks).[181][182] The onset of symptoms is acute consisting of lethargy, loss of appetite with nausea and vomiting, headache, fever, and body aches. Jaundice follows by about one week and may persist for four to six weeks. Virus excretion in the feces may begin 2 - 3 weeks before the onset of symptoms and also last 4 - 6 weeks.

Long-term immunity normally follows recovery from the infection, although there is no cross-immunity between HAV and HBV. The effects on baby seem to be minimal. The infection is not thought to cross the placenta. The only risks to be defined were miscarriage (medically-termed spontaneous abortion) and premature births caused by the severity of mom's illness.[183]

Hepatitis B (serum):

Hepatitis B is a DNA virus. Exposure to Hepatitis B Virus (HBV) could result in one of the following outcomes:

1. An acute, self-limiting infection with or without symptoms of clinical hepatitis (as explained in HAV). This is the most common form of HBV infection. The period of infectivity may be longer than other viral infections, but infectivity is usually lost and antibody (anti-HBc & Hbs) appears in the blood.
2. An acute infection followed by development of an asymptomatic carrier state with the continuing presence of HBsAg.
3. An acute infection followed by chronic active hepatitis and persistent HBsAg and signs of continuing infection.[184]

The virus is transmitted by body fluids: blood, blood by-products, saliva, vaginal secretions and semen. Most medical texts include breastmilk as a means of transfer. Household items that come in contact with HBV-infected blood are also a risk: syringes, razors, toothbrushes, eating utensils, etc.

Vertical transmission (mother to infant) may occur during three periods:

1. Prenatal period through intrauterine or transplacental infection (5 to 6% of baby infections). This is an uncommon mode of transmission.
2. During the third trimester and birth, from contact with currently infected maternal blood and secretions (69 to 85%). This is the most common to infect baby if mother is in an acute condition or a carrier.
3. During the postnatal period (infancy) from breastmilk or bottle-feeding, overcrowded living conditions (49 - 53%).[185]

Cesareans are not indicated because both delivery methods put baby in contact with maternal fluid. Congenital defects are unlikely. Generally, baby will present with asymptomatic chronic Hepatitis B. Some will be jaundiced by three to four months of age. Immunoglobulin may be administered with hepatitis B vaccine as a preventive measure.[186]

Breastfeeding, while a risk factor, still shows a lower incidence of transmission to baby than bottle-feeding. A firm link between breastfeeding and neonatal infection has yet to be established.[187] Careful prayer and study should take place before decisions are made.

Hepatitis C virus (HCV)/Non-A, non-B Hepatitis (NANB):

Hepatitis C (HCV) is caused by another virus which accounts for 20% to 40% of all viral hepatitis in the U.S. Diagnosis is made by ruling out HAV and HBV. Blood tests are now available to detect the HCV IgG antibody; however, a 15-week delay between the onset of symptoms and a positive titer is common. HCV is most commonly transferred by blood transfusions or improperly sterilized syringes or needles but may also be transmitted by body fluids. Symptoms include: muscle aches, fever, headache, tiredness, loss of appetite, nausea, abdominal pain and joint pain, sometimes followed by dark urine and jaundice. Management and risk is similar to type B infection. Maternal transmission to baby is possible.[188]

D Hepatitis (Delta):

The type D hepatitis requires type B to reproduce. Type D may transform mild, chronic HBV into severe, chronic active hepatitis leading to cirrhosis of the liver. It has been transmitted perinatally at least once,[189] but percentages and risks are unknown at present.

Hepatitis E virus (HEV)

This virus was previously classified in the Non-A/Non-B virus group. Hepatitis E (HEV) is transmitted by oral ingestion of fecal-contaminated water or food. HEV has been found in India, Africa, Asia, Mexico and several Middle Eastern countries. Fatality rates for pregnant women range from 15% to 20%. Blood tests are available which can detect both IgM and IgG antibodies for HEV.[190]

Lifestyle/Dietary Recommendations (For all forms of hepatitis):

1. The need for a high-quality food diet prior to and during the illness has made the greatest difference in terms of maternal and perinatal mortality. A diet high in carbohydrates, protein, vitamins and minerals as well as adequate liquids is of prime importance.[191] If mom is vomiting severely, an IV should be discussed with her health care provider.
2. Rest is imperative in an infection of this nature. This is the time for bed, not carpooling.
3. Mom needs to limit her contact with others during the infection so as not to infect those in her household, friends, relatives and strangers who do not need to get sick either.
4. Reduce fat intake - absolutely no alcohol.
5. Water with a wedge of lemon squeezed in is nourishing to the liver and helps to alkalize the rest of the body.
6. Some may find that taking one tablespoon of extra virgin olive oil daily is helpful.
7. During the illness and healing phase, foods should be steamed instead of eating them raw. Plenty of green leafy vegetables should be eaten.
8. Hospital birth for carrier-moms or moms with current infection is a necessity.
9. Mom should handle baby carefully postpartum (gloves if caring for open wounds, wash hands frequently, and watch out for wet kisses).

Nutritional Supplement Recommendations:

1. Liver-supportive herbs, such as milk thistle and dandelion, are definitely helpful to protect and build liver function.[192] [193] Three capsules of each three times daily.
2. Licorice root has been validated in experimental work to be useful in the treatment of hepatitis, cirrhosis and related liver disorders.[194] Three to six capsules daily.
3. Immune-enhancing herbs would be beneficial to support the body in fighting the infection. Echinacea has documented immunostimulant activity.[195] [196] [197] Astragalus, a Chinese herb, has definite positive action on the immune system and glands (liver included). In some Chinese journals, astragalus has been reported to inhibit hepatitis (even chronic HBV).[198] [199]
4. Daily doses of 300 and 600mg of calcium pantothenate and 90mg and 180mg of pantethine taken for 3-4 weeks has positive immunomodulatory action and effects on blood serum levels of immunoglobulins and phagocytic activity of peripheral blood neutrophils in hepatitis patients.[200]

5. Supplementation with coenzyme-B12 or cyanocobalamin at a dosage of 100mcg IV daily may product a normalizing effect on blood enzyme levels during hepatitis.[201] [202]

6. One study showed that Ginkgo biloba arrested the development of liver fibrosis of chronic hepatitis.[203]

Herpes Simplex Viruses

Herpes Simplex Viruses both Type I (HSV-1) and Type II (HSV-II) are recurrent viral infections that may remain dormant for short or long periods after initial, primary infection and recur anytime, usually during times of physical or emotional stress.

HSV-I

Type I is the cause of the common fever blister in, on or around the mouth. It may also be found on the fingers of the hand in individuals who touch their fever blisters often.[204] If lesions (fever blisters) are present, oral contact with others should be avoided. Type I may be transmitted to the genitals (10% of genital herpes is Type I). Handwashing should be employed often with warm, soapy water.

HSV-II

Type II herpes is almost always transmitted sexually. Skin to skin contact is necessary to contract herpes.[205] The incubation period from exposure is usually 6 to 10 days, and initial symptoms are intense vulvar itching, burning, tingling and tenderness. There are one or many small or large thin-walled, fluid-filled vesicles that may appear over the vulva, vestibule, perianal area, or inner surfaces of the thigh, inside the vagina and/or on the cervix. Urination may be painful because of lesions. Vesicles rupture forming painful ulcers. At this stage, most moms feel ill and have a low-grade temperature.

Lesions usually regress, with the pain disappearing in 2 to 4 weeks. Lesions recur in 50% of persons infected with the herpes simplex virus. Recurrences are usually less severe and of shorter duration.[206] Prior to recurring outbreaks, some experience a prodromal phase of tingling, neuralgia, sensation of pressure or increased vaginal discharge.[207]

HSV-II may transplacentally infect baby and cause congenital defects, although this is rare. Congenital defects most often occur with a primary infection of mom prenatally. There is an increased risk of miscarriage and prematurity for babies with mothers who are infected during pregnancy.

Babies born to mothers infected at the time of birth have a 40 to 60% chance of infection. Cesareans are indicated if mom has a current outbreak during labor.[208]

Lifestyle/Dietary Recommendations:

1. Avoid foods high in arginine: almonds, Brazil nuts, cashews, hazelnuts, peanuts, pecans, walnuts, chocolate, gelatin. Restrict amounts of: coconut, barley, corn, oats, wheat, pasta, brussel sprouts.[209]
2. Do eat foods high in lysine: milk (see discussion on milk in Part 2), soybeans, beef, poultry, sour cream, yogurt, fish, eggs, buckwheat.[210]
3. Icy cloths or ice packs may provide pain relief for lesions.

4. Keep lesions clean and dry - cotton underwear is a must.
5. Wash hands often and do not touch or pick at lesions.

Nutritional Supplement Recommendations:
1. L-Lysine is an amino acid that is highly recommended to combat herpes outbreaks. 1,200mg to 3,000mg of l-lysine daily.[211]
2. *Lactobacillus acidophilus* may help relieve symptoms of outbreaks as well as prevent future recurrences. Three capsules daily or 1/4 to 1/2 teaspoon three times daily of powder. Only purchase refrigerated probiotic supplements.[212]
3. Herbs exhibiting anti-viral activity in current research against herpes are: Uva ursi,[213] 2 capsules three times daily (use caution during pregnancy due to uterine stimulating properties); Bilberry,[214] 2 capsules three times daily; Buckthorn,[215] 1 capsule three times daily (use caution during pregnancy due to bowel stimulating properties); Echinacea,[216] 500mg every 2 - 3 hours during outbreak; Red raspberry,[217] 2 capsules three times daily; Blue-green algae,[218] 1,000mg to 3,000mg daily; Licorice,[219] 2 to 4 capsules daily (use caution during pregnancy due to phytosterols in plant). Obviously mom will not want to use all of these herbs. She would be well-advised to use the safest choices for pregnancy.
4. For herbal topical antiviral herbs, clove oil and tea tree oil have both been found to inhibit the herpes virus.[220]
5. Peppermint has been shown to inhibit and kill the herpes simplex virus, among many other microorganisms.[221]
6. Herpilyn, by Enzymatic Therapy, may be applied topically to lesions for speedier healing.
7. Bee Propolis has been shown in studies to reduce the viral titer of herpes simplex virus and reduce viral synthesis as well as cut recovery time in half for patients with postherpetic trophic keratitis and/or postherpetic nebula.[222 223]

Echinacea root and burdock root, in equal amounts, have been reported to prevent outbreaks and eradicate the herpes virus from the body system if taken for six months (10 days on, 10 days off - 500mg to 1,000 mg of each two to three times daily). I have no clinically-documented experience with "eliminating" the herpes virus, but this combination of herbs, at the very least, has proved beneficial in clinical practice in limiting an outbreak and preventing recurrence.

Hyperthyroidism

The high estrogen levels of pregnancy cause an increase in thyroxine binding globulin (TBG). This may cause the thyroid to enlarge causing a slight goiter. Symptoms of hyperthyroidism are similar in many ways to normal pregnancy changes: emotional fluctuations, intolerance to heat, irritability, increased perspiration, variable appetite, and variable weight gain. Hyperthyroidism causes these symptoms to be pronounced and causes: enlarged thyroid, bulging eyes, an elevated heart rate, and a slightly higher blood pressure and an elevated basal body temperature.[224]

There is a risk of miscarriage, particularly in the first trimester, if the problem is not treated. The other risk of untreated hyperthyroidism is the possible development of thyrotoxicosis (a "thyroid storm" or crisis). This condition can be fatal if left untreated.[225]

Lifestyle/Dietary Recommendations:

1. The increased rate of metabolism means extra calories are needed to ensure mom and baby's nutritional well-being.

Nutritional Supplement Recommendations:

1. Astragalus is an herb that has been used extensively in Chinese medicine. In recent years, it has been introduced in Western herbal medicine as an important immunostimulant and glandular herb. One particular study published in the *Journal of Chinese Medicine* in 1986 showed the effectiveness of astragalus in treating hyperthyroidism.[226] 2 capsules three times daily.
2. In doing research for plant medicines associated with hyperthyroidism, I found very few substantiated remedies that would be safe for pregnancy. The safest two mentioned (besides astragalus) were balm (Melissa officinalis) and thyme. In animal studies, they did inhibit thyroid-stimulating hormone (TSH).[227] Others mentioned were bugleweed (Lycopus virginicus), gypsywort (Lycopus europaeus) and motherwort (Leonurus cardiaca); however, all three of these have antigonadotropic hormonal action.[228] Since gonadotropin is the pregnancy hormone, it would be ill-advised to take an herb with anti-pregnancy hormone effects on the body.
3. A physician should be consulted, preferably one with extensive knowledge of preventive, natural and dietary medicine.

Hypoglycemia

Hypoglycemia is often called "low blood sugar." It is caused by faulty carbohydrate metabolism. The pancreas causes too much insulin to be released in response to the ingestion of simple sugars or refined carbohydrates (white foods: flour, sugar, pasta, bread). These simple sugars enter the bloodstream quickly (sometimes within seconds of eating these foods) and overwhelm the body system with glucose. The pancreas responds by releasing too much insulin which causes a dive in blood sugar levels. The adrenal glands then release epinephrine (adrenaline) which causes a headache, sweating, weakness, hunger, heart palpitations, and inward trembling. The liver then releases stored glycogen (sugar) to regulate blood sugar and insulin levels.[229][230]

Highly processed foods are so lacking in essential nutrients that nutrients are leached from the body system to make up for what is missing. As the entire body becomes nutrient depleted, cravings for sugar and/or fruit are common. This is an attempt to keep up glucose levels. A cycle of up-down blood sugar fluctuations ensues. This physiologic process designed to protect us in emergencies, if abused by regular ingestion of refined carbohydrates, can lead to a "wearing-out" of the pancreas, adrenals and liver.

Common symptoms of hypoglycemia: nausea and vomiting in early pregnancy, lack of appetite, morning sickness (the overnight fast results in blood-sugar bottoming-out around 4 a.m.), headaches, fatigue, fainting, dizzy spells, ketones in urine (reveals that the liver is depleted of glycogen, stored glucose) decreased baby movement, night-waking (when blood sugar goes "low," waking up is very common).[231]

Lifestyle/Dietary Recommendations:

1. Basically, the same recommendations dietary-wise as for diabetes — high complex carbohydrate, high-fiber diet.
2. Eat often, every one to two hours, in small amounts.
3. At bedtime, have a high-protein snack: peanut butter on whole-wheat bread, cheese, yogurt (plain - add fruit or unsweetened preserves), etc.
4. If mom wakes up hungry in the night, she should have a snack ready by the bed or go to the kitchen, or keep an ice chest (cooler) by the bed for foods that have to be refrigerated like chicken or eggs.
5. If mom does throw-up after getting up in the morning, she should try to get down some food as quickly as possible afterwards. I found in my pregnancies with morning sickness that starchy foods such as boiled potatoes, pasta or rice worked well as a first morning meal until my tummy felt calm enough for something with more protein.
6. Have a high-protein snack when a craving for something sweet occurs.

7. All sugars should be eliminated, even naturally-occurring ones such as high-sugar fruits and honey unless combined with or followed by a protein such as yogurt or whole-wheat bread, etc.

Nutritional Supplement Recommendations:

1. Chromium is a mineral that has received a great deal of attention regarding blood sugar regulation. Make certain mom's prenatal formula contains an adequate amount in an absorbable form - chromium picolinate 100mcg three times daily before meals.[232]

2. Use liver-supportive herbs such as dandelion or milk thistle since the liver regulates how much glucose stays in the system through its storage and release of glycogen. One milk thistle tablet or capsule containing at least 70% silymarin three times daily.

3. One week prior to labor, a mom who is hypoglycemic or has that tendency should begin complex-carbohydrate loading until the birth. This reduces the likelihood of hypoglycemia during labor which can occur in long labors or because of nausea and vomiting.[233]

Hypothyroidism

Hypothyroidism occurs when the thyroid gland is not producing adequate thyroid hormones. This can increase the risk of miscarriage because of the need for increased production of thyroid hormones by six weeks gestation.[234] Hypothyroidism is most often caused by inadequate iodine intake. The thyroid combines iodine with the amino acid tyrosine to create thyroid hormones. This is why iodized salt was introduced into our society. Those people not eating fish and seafood or sea vegetables usually do not get enough iodine in their diet.

Hypothyroidism is usually mild in pregnant moms because infertility is the major side effect of severe cases. Checking basal body temperature is one way of ascertaining if the thyroid is functioning normally. To check basal body temperature (BBT), place a thermometer in the armpit for 10 minutes after waking but before doing anything in the morning and while still reclining in bed. Temperature may also be taken vaginally. This eliminates variances in oral temperature due to respiratory infections.

Normal, axillary (armpit) temperature in a non-pregnant woman ranges from 97.4 to 98.2 F (36.3 to 36.8 C). Consistently lower readings may indicate low thyroid function; higher readings could mean an overactive thyroid. At ovulation, BBT is raised by approximately half a degree (called the "thermal shift") making the normal, pregnant range 97.9 to 98.7 F (36.65 to 37.05 C). A slight drop between weeks 9 and 12 gestation may be due to the influence of HCG (human chorionic gonodotropin).[235]

The most common symptoms of hypothyroidism are: weakness, dry or coarse hair and skin, lethargy, slow speech, edema of the eyelids, feeling cold, minimal perspiration, thick tongue, cool and pallid skin, impaired memory, constipation, weight gain, difficult breathing, headaches, fatigue, susceptibility to infections, poor appetite and heavy periods.[236]

Lifestyle/Dietary Recommendations:
1. Include more iodine-containing foods in the diet: seafish, sea vegetables such as kelp, dulse, spirulina, etc.
2. Decrease the intake of vegetables known as goitrogens (foods that block iodine utilization): turnips, cabbage, mustard, cassava root, soybeans, peanuts, pine nuts and millet. If mom is eating these foods, she should cook them to inactivate the goitrogens.[237]
3. Use iodized sea salt for seasoning to supply extra iodine.

Nutritional Supplement Recommendations:
1. Naturopaths use organic thyroid glandular supplements derived from cattle. Recommended amount: 1 tablet daily while monitoring BBT to check effectiveness.[238]

2. As with hyperthyroidism, Siberian Ginseng improves thyroid responsiveness to changing demands in the body. It has an adaptogenic effect meaning it normalizes glandular function whether high or low.[239]

3. Other herbs that stimulate thyroid function such as ephedra combined with white willow bark or caffeine-containing herbs are not appropriate for pregnancy in the dosages necessary or the methods necessary for positive results. Outside of pregnancy, moms can consult the excellent book by Michael T. Murray, N.D., *Natural Alternatives to Over-the-Counter and Prescription Drugs* published by William Morrow & Co., NY, NY, 1994.

Irritable Bowel Syndrome

Irritable bowel syndrome (IBS), sometimes referred to as spastic colon, is very common in the U.S. with as many as 15 to 30% of Americans suffering from this uncomfortable condition. Many of the more current studies point to diet as the major cause of IBS. Food intolerance or allergy is evident in approximately two-thirds of patients with IBS.[240][241]

Symptoms of IBS include: abdominal pain and distension (bloating); constipation alternating with cramps followed by more frequent bowel movements or diarrhea; pain usually relieved after bowel movements; excessive production of mucous in the colon; flatulence (gas); nausea; loss of appetite; and, commonly, feelings of stress or depression prior to crampy bowel movements. Pregnancy can increase problems with IBS because of the hormonal relaxation of the intestines. Prevention is the key in this disorder as in so many others. A high-fiber, processed-food-free diet is essential.

Foods that may cause IBS from food intolerance or allergy:

1. Milk - One study revealed 74% of IBS patients had some degree of milk intolerance.[242]
2. Dietetic sugars, particularly sorbitol. One study of healthy adults found almost half of subjects were sorbitol-intolerant. Sorbitol is found in some natural products and supplements as well as dietetic candies. Foods rich in sorbitol are: peaches, apple juice, pears, plums, prunes, sugarless gums, dietetic jams and chocolate.[243] Fructose may cause some individuals a problem.
3. Coffee, tea.
4. Wheat and corn cereals.
5. Potatoes.
6. Onions.
7. Citrus fruits.

Dr. John O. Hunter, gastroenterologist at Addenbrookes Hospital in Cambridge, Massachusetts believes that irritable bowel syndrome induced by food reactions is not caused by the typical allergenic reaction involving the immune system. He believes the problem is an abnormal imbalance of bacteria in the intestines, triggered by eating certain foods or taking antibiotics. Dr. Hunter found excessive numbers of aerobic (require air) bacteria in fecal samples of IBS patients after they ate an offending food. These aerobes wreck normal friendly bacteria activity which triggers colon disturbances leading to constipation, diarrhea, pain and bloating.[244]

Lifestyle/Dietary Recommendations:

1. Eliminate foods to which mom may be allergic or intolerant for 2 to 3 weeks then add one back at a time to see if a reaction occurs.

2. Eliminate sugar and dietetic sugars as well as natural sugar additives such as fructose. Sugar adversely affects normal bowel function.[245]

3. Add water-soluble fiber such as that found in vegetables, fruit, oat bran, brown rice, guar gum, psyllium hulls or husks and legumes (beans, peas).

Nutritional Supplement Recommendations:

1. Ginger aids in the elimination of gas and relaxes and soothes the intestinal tract which may offer some relief of IBS-sufferers.[246] Fresh ginger (1/4" slice) added to fresh fruit or vegetable juice may be used or ginger capsules (2 to 3 capsules as needed).

2. Psyllium hulls may be added to daily supplement routine until normal bowel bacteria are back in balance. 4 to 6 capsules daily.

3. A special peppermint oil product (Peppermint Plus - an enteric-coated oil capsule) inhibits intestinal spasms and relieves gas.[247] The enteric-coat does not allow the oil to be released in the tummy which could cause heartburn. 1 - 2 capsules between meals three times daily.

4. A product containing "Active Immunoglobulin Concentrate" derived from raw milk whey (Inner Strength by EN) has shown a remarkable ability to not only aid repopulation of normal bacteria but to attack the membrane coating of pathogenic (bad) bacteria, viruses and yeast. This attack renders the pathogens unable to infect the body and are then eliminated.[248] Inner Strength is enhanced when taken with probiotics such as *l. acidophilus* or *b. bifidus*.

Indigestion

Indigestion is characterized by a feeling of gaseousness or fullness in the abdomen caused by either increased secretion of hydrochloric acid (HCL) or decreased secretion of HCL as well as other digestive juices and enzymes.

Common symptoms of low gastric acidity:
Bloating, belching, burning and flatulence immediately after meals
Sense of "fullness" after eating
Indigestion, diarrhea or constipation
Multiple food allergies
Nausea after taking supplements
Itching around rectum

Common signs of low gastric acidity:
Weak, peeling or cracked fingernails
Dilated blood vessels in the cheeks and nose
Acne
Iron deficiency
Chronic intestinal parasites or abnormal flora
Undigested food in stool
Chronic candida infections
Upper gastrointestinal gassiness[249]

Several studies have shown that the ability to secrete gastric acid decreases with age.[250] Some moms may find that pregnancy is a time of decreased amounts of gastric acidity which leaves them feeling symptoms of indigestion.

Lifestyle/Dietary Recommendations:
1. To find out if the problem is too much hydrochloric acid (HCL) or too little HCL, the following at home test may be performed: Take 1 tablespoon of apple cider vinegar or lemon juice when experiencing indigestion. If this eliminates the symptoms, too little HCL may be the problem. If it makes the symptoms worse, an overproduction of HCL is the problem. If the vinegar has helped, it can be taken with meals or an HCL supplement could be taken instead. Since HCL supplements make the condition of hiatal hernia, gastritis and duodenal ulcers worse, do the above test before self-treating with the HCL supplements.[251]
2. Foods or substances that stimulate the flow of HCL production are: hot peppers, onions, salsa, peppermint, papaya, pineapple, alcohol, milk, coffee (caffeinated and de-caf), tea with caffeine, 7-up, Coca-Cola, etc.

3. Avoid foods th

4. If

2 cup cooked rice ties up excess stomach
Ava H. Der Mandersoian, Ph.D., profes-
chemistry at Philadelphia College of
may neutralize or absorb stomach acid:
u, whole grain bread. The only caution
"don't eat too much." Excess food will

e quite helpful around the Parker
eshen the breath."
body to produce its own HCL for
most helpful are: cayenne pepper
chewable tablets, 1 to 2 taken 30

aya (papain) and fresh pineap-
have been shown to aid diges-

of fats, proteins and starches;
althy choice.
estion are fennel and clove tea.[254]

Insomnia

Insomnia is a term used to essentially say "I cannot sleep!" Insomnia may occur in pregnancy due to several factors: hypoglycemia, pressure on the bladder caused by the growing uterus, pressure everywhere caused by growing uterus OR it may simply be due to factors we all deal with: excess stimulation, exercising before bed, hot baths before bed and/or stress.

Lifestyle/Dietary Recommendations:

1. Eliminate natural stimulants - caffeine, alcohol.
2. Nocturnal hypoglycemia is an important cause of sleep-maintenance insomnia. Nocturnal hypoglycemia causes a release of hormones like adrenaline, glucagon, cortisol and growth hormone which regulates glucose levels. These compounds stimulate the brain signaling "time to eat." Eat a good snack 30-45 minutes before bed - oatmeal, other whole grain cereals, breads, muffins. No sugars.
3. Relax. Do birth relaxation techniques before bed.
4. Exercise in the morning or early evening for 20 minutes.
5. Do not overeat at the dinner meal.
6. Adopt regular bedtime habits - go to bed at the same time and rise at the same time. "Early to bed, early to rise" is a good admonition.

Nutritional Supplement Recommendations:

1. Valerian root in scientific studies has been shown to have the ability to improve sleep quality and relieve insomnia.[255] One large double-blind study revealed the aqueous extract of valerian root improved insomnia and left no "hangover" the next morning. It has been suggested to be as effective in reducing sleep latency (time required to get to sleep) as small doses of benzodiazepines. Valerian also reduced morning sleepiness. Thirty to forty-five minutes before bedtime: 1 - 2g of dried root (or as tea) or 4 - 6mg (1 - 1.5t) of tincture or 1 - 2 mg (0.5 - 1t) of fluid extract or 150 - 300mg capsules of valerian extract containing 0.8% valeric acid.
2. Passionflower and Chamomile are other natural herbal sedatives that may be taken as teas or in capsule form before bedtime.[256]
3. An herbal calcium supplement such as ChamoCalm by Mother's Choice™ makes a good instant, "no-steep" tea before bed.

Kidney Stones

Kidney stones is another of those maladies associated with our "Western" diet.[257] Calcium-containing stones are made up of calcium oxalate, calcium oxalate mixed with calcium phosphate, or (rarely) calcium phosphate alone. Dietary patterns that have been shown to be associated with calcium-containing stones (as in kidney stones) are: low fiber, highly refined carbohydrates; high alcohol; large amounts of animal protein; high fat, high calcium foods; high salt; and high vitamin D enriched food.[258 259]

Kidney stones are very common in the U.S. Almost 6% of our U.S. population develop a kidney stone each year. Men are two to three times more likely to experience kidney stones than women. The discouraging note is that if someone has stones once, the chances of recurrence are high (40% in next 5 years; 80% in next 25 years).[260] An encouraging word would be that this problem may be entirely preventable with lifestyle and dietary modifications.

Lifestyle/Dietary Recommendations:

1. An increase of fluid intake is vital. More liquid in — more liquid out. A daily output of 1 1/2 to 2 quarts is recommended. These liquids do not include coffee, tea, colas, sweetened juices or punches. They should be pure water (home purification is the most reliable means of ensuring pure water. See Part 2), fresh fruit and vegetable juices. Lemon juice and cranberry juice are particularly effective.[261]

2. Lower animal protein intake and increase fresh fruits and vegetables. Going completely vegan (no animal products whatsoever) does not seem necessary. Meat eaters who do not focus their meals on meat, rather they make fresh fruits and vegetables the mainstay, have a lower incidence of stones.[262] Animal protein increases the amount of calcium in the urine which when combined with uric acid (also increased with high meat consumption) can lead to stone formation.

3. Eat whole wheat, brown rice or corn. These fiber-rich foods reduce urinary calcium which results in lowered risk of kidney stone formation.[263]

4. Leave the milk in the cow. Milk (in the supermarket) is fortified with vitamin D which increases calcium absorption and calcium concentration in the urine. Milk fortified with vitamin D also lowers magnesium levels in the body.[264] This makes vitamin D-fortified milk a risk factor for stone-formers.

5. Include leafy greens in the diet - kale, leafy lettuce, parsley. The high amount of vitamin K may help lower the incidence of kidney stones. Vitamin K is necessary for the synthesis of a natural compound in urine that inhibits crystalline growth of calcium oxalate.[265]

Nutritional Supplement Recommendations:

1. Magnesium supplements combined with Vitamin B6 (pyridoxine) have been shown to be effective in preventing kidney stone recurrence. 400mg magnesium daily with 50mg of B6.[266] [267] Foods rich in magnesium and vitamin B6 include: barley, bran, corn, buckwheat, rye, soy, oats, brown rice, avocado, banana, lima beans and potato.

2. Calcium supplements should be from a chelated form rather than bone meal, oyster shell or calcium carbonate. Calcium chelates such as calcium citrate are more easily absorbable by the body. Supplementation should not exceed levels recommended in Part 2, in chapter titled "Nutrient Needs of Pregnancy."

3. If mom has a history of kidney stones, it would be wise to limit vitamin C intake (daily over long-term) to 2,000mg. High levels of vitamin C over extended periods can contribute in creating stones.[268]

4. Herbs found to be helpful in dissolving and/or eliminating stones are: Cornsil,[269] Cranberry,[270] Flax,[271] Gravel root, Hydrangea, Marshmallow and Horsetail[272] [273]

Low Blood Pressure

Low blood pressure readings are not a problem unless the reading is very low and associated with symptoms indicating a health problem. In fact, those persons with low blood pressure have been shown to live longer than people with normal blood pressure.[274] Low blood pressure readings are generally found in young people or elderly people who are in good health, vegetarians and women who exercise regularly. In pregnancy, a slight drop in blood pressure around 28 weeks is a healthy sign that mom's blood volume is expanding according to plan.

For those moms who have low blood pressure combined with other symptoms such as nausea, dizziness upon rising, fainting, visual disturbances and/or breathlessness with exertion, an underlying problem may be present. Anemia and hypoglycemia may be contributing factors in causing mom to feel unwell and have low blood pressure.[275] The main thrust of any (if any) treatment is nutritional counseling and aiding the circulatory function.

Lifestyle/Dietary Recommendations:

1. Exercise. A nice daily walk is to be encouraged for all pregnant moms regardless of blood pressure readings.
2. Slowly rise to a standing position instead of jumping up. A quick rise temporarily will decrease the blood flow to the brain.
3. Be diligent to follow the whole foods diet as outlined in Part 2. Eat often to prevent hypoglycemic reactions.

Nutritional Supplement Recommendations:

1. Herbs to avoid because of their hypotensive effects demonstrated in clinical studies are: Agrimony, Ashwagandha, Black cohosh, and Goldenseal.[276]
2. Siberian ginseng has also been shown to have an ability to raise blood pressure in those with hypotension.[277] 4 capsules daily.
3. Ginkgo may help both blood pressure problems by increasing circulatory function. 2 - 4 capsules each day.
4. Korean (Panax) ginseng helps with low blood pressure by its adaptogenic factor. This basically means that it lowers blood pressure in hypertensive individuals and raises it in hypotensive people.[278 279 280 281] 4 - 6 capsules daily. Panax ginseng is not recommended for use during pregnancy.

Metabolic Toxemia of Late Pregnancy (MTLP)

Allopaths view Metabolic Toxemia of Late Pregnancy (MTLP) as a group of symptoms to treat. Nutritionists, midwives and Dr. Tom Brewer, both an OB/GYN and a general practitioner who has studied women, view toxemia as a metabolic disorder brought on by poor nutrition. As we discussed in the beginning of Part 3, Glandular System - Liver, the liver which is responsible for over 500 metabolic functions has a greater demand placed on it during pregnancy. Hormones increase to the equivalent of 100 birth control pills that the liver has to break down and send out for excretion; the liver selects amino acids to combine for protein which will attract the right amount of fluid in the bloodstream; and digestion slows to enhance nutrient absorption which allows toxic byproducts to develop that the liver then has to process for excretion.[282]

With all this extra work, is it surprising that the liver will need more nutritional support? MTLP is a preventable condition of pregnancy. The key is good nutrition. Herbal liver support is a must for women who, prior to pregnancy, had liver problems and/or who show signs that the liver is not handling the heavier burden easily in early pregnancy.

If the liver is well-nourished, mom and baby will be well-nourished by adequate blood volume expansion which peaks at 28 weeks. Signs of a contracting blood volume are:

1) IUGR - placenta functions poorly, produces poorly-nourished baby;
2) Rising hemoglobin at 28 weeks (there is generally a drop of one to two points from the early pregnancy value due to expanded blood volume diluting the hemoglobin concentration);
3) Tired mother who may complain of nausea and headaches;
4) Marked edema (if mom pushes her edematous [swollen with fluid] skin, a pit will form instead of the skin "bouncing back," so to speak);
5) High blood pressure - this may not occur until condition is severe (on the verge of convulsions or after the onset of convulsions). The heart tries to supply adequate blood flow to the placenta but does not have enough blood volume;
6) Epigastric pain - pain around the liver from liver damage;
7) Maternal convulsions because of neurological irritation to the brain;
8) Hyperreflexes due to extreme stress on the nervous system;
9) Proteinuria - a late sign of kidney damage. The kidneys respond to falling blood volume by producing renin which constricts blood vessels placing greater demand on the heart. Thicker blood and reabsorption of fluids cause the kidneys to be damaged;
10) Oliguria occurs as urine production decreases as the body tries to preserve the minimal blood volume. When this occurs, kidney shutdown is imminent.[283]

Lifestyle/Dietary Recommendations:

1. Prevention with adequate caloric intake of fresh, preferably organic, whole foods (as God created them, not processed until they are empty of nutrients) is the key.

The daily food plans outlined in Part 2, if followed, will ensure adequate protein intake in a highly nutritious form.

2. At the first sign of true toxemia (MTLP), dietary intervention should begin immediately with mom having a high protein food every waking hour, while not ignoring other basic whole food requirements.

3. If mom is under stress or started out below ideal weight or is carrying more than one baby, she should add 20 - 30 extra grams of protein daily.

4. Pregnant moms should *salt to taste* during pregnancy. DO NOT restrict salt intake. Salt is necessary for retaining fluid for expanding blood volume.

5. Weight gain should be encouraged through nutritious foods (the average weight gain is 25 lbs; women who are underweight need to gain 35 lbs to 40 lbs). While the average weight gain is only 25 pounds, most midwives, whose clients typically have bigger and healthier babies, recommend a gain of one pound per week of pregnancy (40 lbs total).

6. Liquid intake should be at least 2 quarts per day of purified water, natural juices and herb teas.

7. Mom needs to snack to prevent hypoglycemia from causing nausea and to provide adequate caloric and protein intake.

8. If mom is used to junk food (processed, fatty foods), she should slowly switch to a natural food diet. She could immediately switch to more whole grains, brown rice, whole wheat bread, fruits and vegetables, but a too radical change (junk food to vegan - no animal products whatsoever) could cause a release of built-up toxins into her system, which is not healthy for baby.

Nutritional Supplement Recommendations:
1. Milk thistle should be (and is) first on the list for liver and digestive support. It has been demonstrated to protect and support liver function.[284][285][286][287] A minimum of three tablets daily (standardized to contain 70 - 80% silymarin) for moms needing liver support (history of liver disease, toxemia, morning sickness, hypoglycemia, headaches during pregnancy). If the early signs (#s 1 - 3 of above symptoms) develop, up to four tablets per day of milk thistle may be taken.

2. Dandelion is recognized for its liver stimulant properties. It is rich in organic sodium and iron making dandelion beneficial for pregnancy.

3. A quality prenatal is essential. I prefer one of the following three brands: NF Prenatal Formula (particularly if mom has a history of anemia), Opti-Natal or the Professional Prenatal Formula.

4. Yellow dock is stimulating to the liver. Some moms may find it is stimulating to the intestines too. 2 to 4 capsules daily.

Morning sickness (Nausea)

It has taken me many pregnancies to figure this one out. Morning sickness is not exactly an accurate term. Many women experiencing it would call it "all-day sickness." Basically it is nausea, and sometimes vomiting, that may occur during the first trimester of pregnancy. I have tried many remedies during my pregnancies — some have worked well, some worked a little, others worked not at all. I had hyperemesis gravidum (vomiting repeatedly; unable to hold anything down) with my eldest child which was medically treated with Dramamine (unsuccessful), Tigan (unsuccessful) then Thorazine (this was somewhat helpful in that it kept me knocked out most of the day so that I only threw up when I was awake). With my fourth child, I had *no morning sickness whatsoever!* Praise the Lord!!

I have come to believe through my own experience and the experience of others that the root of the problem for many women is inadequate liver support during a period of greater demands on this vital organ. If moms begin preparing their bodies for pregnancy prior to conception, they will have a better chance of avoiding morning sickness (as well as other health risk factors).

Lifestyle/Dietary Recommendations:

1. Two to three months prior to pregnancy, if possible, or as soon as pregnancy is confirmed, the Whole Foods Diet should be adopted and followed regularly. Mom should aim to eat every 2 hours while awake, have a high-protein snack before bed and keep a high-protein snack by the bed for the middle-of-the-night blood sugar drop.
2. Some moms find that eating before getting out of bed in the morning helps; others prefer to quickly rustle up something after rising. Mom can try both to see what works for her.
3. Deep-breathing when the feeling of nausea comes can be very helpful. I certainly found this to be beneficial as our family vehicle drove around hairpin turns on the side of the North Carolina mountains during my pregnancy with Ellie (heights and sheer drop-offs make me queasy!!).
4. Drinking water with a wedge of lemon squeezed in it is refreshing and liver-cleansing.
5. Herb teas to try: peppermint, chamomile, and red raspberry.
6. If caffeine consumption is a regular part of the diet, eliminating caffeine may lower the incidence of morning sickness.

Nutritional Supplement Recommendations:

1. A basic quality prenatal formula such as NF Prenatal, Opti-Natal or the Professional Prenatal Formula is essential to avoiding morning sickness by providing

much-needed nutrients. A few women feel sick after taking their prenatal. These moms should try taking them with meals — not on an empty stomach.

2. I have found milk thistle (standardized to contain at least 70 - 80% silymarin) to be invaluable in preventing morning sickness. I began taking 2 tablets each day two months prior to this pregnancy and increased to 3 tablets daily when our pregnancy was confirmed. Milk thistle is liver supportive and protective. I feel this is why it worked so well to prevent the nausea and vomiting I have had with every other pregnancy. This would be especially helpful for those moms who vomit bile during pregnancy.

3. The herb ginger has received a great deal of praise and validation from the scientific community due to its superior ability to curb nausea and vomiting associated with pregnancy, seasickness (motion sickness), stomach virus and post-operative nausea. Ginger was shown to be better than Dramamine in a study by Daniel B. Mowrey, Ph.D.[288] Morning sickness treated with ginger had a 75% success rate in the clinical trials Mowrey performed. Mowrey states in his book, *Herbal Tonic Therapies*, that the best form of ginger for effective application in the gastrointestinal tract is the encapsulated powder. The main rule of thumb, according to Mowrey, to using ginger root is: "Use it till you taste it." This means one has taken enough when after taking the capsules, one can taste the ginger or feel a warm sensation in the esophagus after swallowing the capsules. This is ginger root's own built-in dosage regulator. A general dosage for morning sickness is: 3 to 5 capsules before getting out of bed. After taking the capsules, mom should stay in bed until the nausea is relieved, then she should take 3 to 5 capsules at the slightest hint of nausea.

For motion sickness: Severe - take 4, 400mg, capsules twenty minutes before journey; Mild to moderate - 2 capsules 15 minutes before journey, then 2 to 4 capsules when the slightest bit of nausea occurs.

For stomach flu: Take at first hint of nausea, or better yet, as soon as being exposed to someone with a virus, Use the above ginger rule of thumb.[289]

Mouth Sores/Inflamed Gums

Mouth sores or ulcers (canker sores) and inflamed gums can be a problem during pregnancy. They both are painful conditions that fortunately respond well to natural treatment. While these two discomforts are separate entities, I have grouped them together here because the treatment is the same for both.

Canker or mouth sores are generally small, round sores that are white in the center with a red, raised border. Certain foods seem to aggravate them and may even bring them on (food allergy). Dentists now recommend more frequent cleaning visits during pregnancy as gingivitis has been associated with low birth weight in babies.

Inflamed gums can be a discomfort in pregnancy due to hormonal changes which affect the acidity/alkalinity of the mouth making gums more susceptible to bacteria and plaque.

Lifestyle/Dietary Recommendations:
1. Eliminate foods that are allergens.
2. Brush teeth, tongue, gums, inside of cheeks and palate twice daily to remove build-up.
3. Floss at least once daily.

Nutritional Supplement Recommendations:
1. Allow a 25 - 50mg zinc lozenge to dissolve on the sore or inflamed area up to twice daily until inflammation is gone.[290]
2. Dissolve one teaspoon of acidophilus in water and gargle/swish twice daily. This is okay, even good, to swallow.
3. Vitamin C with bioflavonoids: 1000mg three times daily for 3 days then 1000mg daily on a regular basis. The positive effect of vitamin C on dental health has been scientifically confirmed.[291]
4. Deglycyrrhizinated licorice (DGL) in a gargle or as a lozenge three times daily.
5. John Bastyr, pioneering naturopath, developed an excellent formula: Mix tincture of echinacea with myrrh gum powder to make a paste and apply locally to the inflamed area.
6. Propolis tincture is recommended by herbalist Christopher Hobbs. Put a few drops on the gums or the sore and let sit. A few studies have confirmed antibacterial effects of bee propolis on wounds. NOTE** Propolis may cause allergic reactions.
7. A product I have found helpful is called "Oxyfresh Gel" manufactured by Oxyfresh USA, Inc., P.O. Box 3723, Spokane, WA 99220. It contains OXYGENE (which is stabilized chlorine dioxide as well as purified deionized waterr, carrageenan, chamomile extract, aloe vera, methylparaben and propylparaben. I rub this gel on my gums or sore spots as needed.

8. Another product I recently have benefited from for better oral care is FoliCare™ by Advanced Medical Nutrition, Inc., 2247 National Avenue, Hayward, CA 94545. It is an oral care rinse to be used twice daily that contains folic acid which is recommended by Drs. Murray and Pizzorno, authors of the *Textbook of Naturopathic Medicine*.[2] A dose of 4mg per day for 30 days of folic acid increased resistance of gingiva to local irritants and reduced gum inflammation in a double-blind, placebo-controlled study of human subjects.[292]

Nocturnal myodonus

Nocturnal myodonus is an intimidating name for the problem of muscle twitching at night. It is a nerve and muscle disorder characterized by repeated contractions of one or more muscle groups (the legs are a popular spot) during sleep. The twitching lasts less than ten seconds. Most people are not aware they are experiencing this unless their spouse alerts them (like I do with my husband) with a polite elbow jab to "be still."

Nutritional Supplement Recommendations:

1. Vitamin E at 400 IU daily (a quality prenatal will probably supply this amount) has been shown to benefit "muscle twitchers."[293]

Nosebleeds

Mild nosebleeds occur frequently during pregnancy. This condition is due to increased blood volume bringing vascular changes. Nosebleeds may be due to a lack of vitamin C and bioflavonoids which help decrease capillary fragility. Another cause of "nose-spotting," so to speak, upon waking in the morning is dry air in the home.

Lifestyle/Dietary Recommendations:
1. Eat plenty of dark, leafy green vegetables and citrus fruits.
2. Consider a humidifier or vaporizer for overly-dry indoor air. If mom chooses to use one of these, she should be diligent to keep it clean and free of molds and mildew which can create other problems for the family.

Nutritional Supplement Recommendations:
1. Extra vitamin C and bioflavonoids should be considered until the condition is resolved.
2. If the nose is dry and itchy, mom may apply a *thin* layer of vitamin E oil, comfrey ointment, aloe gel or unpetroleum jelly to moisten nasal membranes.

Palpitations

Heart palpitations are generally painless although very uncomfortable. Palpitations are characterized by a pounding heartbeat that is faster than normal and feels as though the heart is filling the chest cavity. When I have experienced these, I feel as though the blood vessels in my neck and head are bulging, and I have a sense of breathlessness.

Frequent palpitations may be a sign of anemia. The blood deprived of adequate oxygen causes the heart muscle to work faster and harder to supply vital organs with oxygen. Hemoglobin should be checked and anemia treated if this is the root problem. Palpitations may be occurring as a response to stress, caffeine consumption or overexertion of physical activity.

Palpitations need to be dealt with since the reason for occurrence is the body's attempt to pump more oxygen to the cells which includes the baby's cells.

Lifestyle/Dietary Recommendations:
1. Follow the whole foods diet with an emphasis on dark, leafy green vegetables.
2. Slow down and relax to relieve stress.
3. If palpitations occur during strenuous physical activity, discontinue that activity.

Nutritional Supplement Recommendations:
1. I have found the most effective supplement for palpitations is a combination of ginkgo and hawthorn in a powdered capsule - 2, 450mg, capsules as soon as the palpitations start. If chronic or frequent, 2 capsules each day, 1 in the morning and 1 thirty minutes before bedtime. This has always stopped my palpitations within 2 - 3 minutes of taking the capsules.

Parasites (Protozoa disease)

Most people do not consider parasites to be a risk for them unless they have been, or are going out of, the country. The unfortunate fact is that parasitic infections are all too common in United States.

Our community or well water supply is often contaminated with the little fellows — some of them resistant to municipal water treatment methods such as chlorine. People who handle our food or the food itself may be infected. The most common means of transfer person-to-person is in day care centers. My own personal thought on another means of picking up one of these nasty infections is from the ever popular kiddie play equipment at restaurants geared to children. Little tots are not known for their meticulous hygiene habits, and where there are lots of little ones, there is to be expected intermingling of germs and parasites.

The three most common parasites causing symptoms are: *Entamoeba histolytica*, *Giardia lamblia*, and *Blastocystis hominis*. Symptoms for these infections include: diarrhea, gas, bloating, weight loss, loss of appetite, fatigue, nausea, abdominal cramping and/or fever. A physician should be consulted if some or all of these symptoms are present and remain for more than the standard 24 to 48 hours for a gastrointestinal infection. A stool sample test can be performed to identify the infectious agent. Although it may be necessary to follow allopathic treatment for severe cases, natural measures can benefit recovery and help fight the protozoa disease. Some of these parasites, if untreated, can remain in the system causing re-infection when the body is susceptible. While the person may be asymptomatic, they can still transfer the parasite to others; therefore, treatment is a must.

Lifestyle/Dietary Recommendations:

1. Prevent occurrence by drinking only distilled or reverse osmosis water preferably treated at your home (see resource section for water treatment system suppliers).
2. On trips, use only bottled distilled or reverse osmosis water. Do not sip from sparkling streams while camping. Do not eat fresh fruits and vegetables (which may have been rinsed in contaminated water) while out of the country — eat only cooked foods, or peel fruit yourself.
3. Eat bananas that have not fully ripened (slightly green) and basmati rice with plain yogurt containing live cultures.
4. Eat a high-fiber diet if well tolerated.
5. Avoid high-risk settings such as day care centers and indoor playgrounds.
6. Pumpkin seeds are effective in expelling worms or helminths and internal parasites. They may be eaten raw or slightly roasted.[294]
7. Clove tea is also helpful in the recovery from protozoa disease.

Nutritional Supplement Recommendations:

1. The product Inner Strength (EN), containing Active Immunoglobulin Concentrate derived from raw milk whey, may be taken 1/4 to 1/2 teaspoon three to four times daily. If combined with the super strain of *acidophilus* or *bifidus* found in certain brands of *acidophilus* and *bifidus* (EN and UAS Labs), the re-population of beneficial bowel bacteria will be enhanced.

2. Garlic should be eaten freely and taken in supplement form. Garlic was proven superior to antibiotics in a recent test by Egyptian doctors at Ain Shams University in Cairo. Small doses of fresh garlic combined with garlic capsules virtually wiped out symptoms of *Giardia lamblia* in one day. All were protozoan-free after three days.[295] Garlic tablets or capsules (equivalent to 4 - 5 fresh cloves) - 3 to 6 daily or, as the researchers did, whip up thirty peeled fresh garlic cloves with a little water in a blender at short bursts until it is homogenized; chill the mixture. The dosage given to the children was one-third cup of the garlic solution twice a day.

3. Bee Propolis in a concentrated strength from 10%-30% can be an effective treatment for those suffering with giardiasis.[296]

4. Pau D'Arco demonstrated anti-parasitic function in several studies. The most notable study was a carefully controlled animal study at the Naval Medical Research Institute in Bethesda, Maryland that showed lapachol (Pau D'Arco constituent) to be protective against the deadly parasite, *Schistosoma mansoni*.[297][298] 3 to 6 daily. Pau D'Arco is not recommended for use in pregnancy.

5. Elecampane contains the chemical alantolactone that helps expel intestinal parasites especially pinworms and *Giardia lamblia*.[299] Recommended dosage: 2 to 3 capsules three times daily.

Pregnancy Induced Hypertension (PIH)

PIH is often viewed as an indicator of metabolic toxemia of pregnancy. Though hypertension is one of the symptoms associated with Metabolic Toxemia, alone it does not merit the aggressive toxemia treatment. In fact, normal, healthy women had their blood pressure monitored throughout the day in recent (1989) research at the University of Cambridge, England. Dr. Kevin Dalton, in conducting this study, found that systolic pressure fluctuated up to 40 points and diastolic readings fluctuated as much as 20 points. The average fluctuation was between 20 to 30mm.Hg. within a ten-minute period.[300]

It is important to view these normal fluctuations as just that - normal. If a mom is having a consistently high blood pressure or a significantly rising blood pressure, measures should be taken to help bring it back to normal. If mom is experiencing other symptoms such as feeling poorly, marked edema, protein in the urine, rising hemoglobin and poor growth of the baby, toxemia should be considered since it is a dangerous condition for mom and baby.

Values that are considered high blood pressure in adults are: Borderline - 120-160/90-94; Mild - 140-160/95-104; Moderate - 140-180/105-114; Severe - 160+/115+. A common reading for an adult is 120(Systolic)/80(Diastolic). In non-pregnant adults (because any drug can be a problem in pregnancy), prescription drugs do not seem to be the answer for those in the borderline to moderate range. In fact, these drugs often produce unncessary side effects that increase the risk for heart disease. Two definitive trials, the Australian and Medical Research Council trials, as well as five other large trials, including the famous Multiple Risk Factor Intervention Trial (MRFIT) have shown that the drugs offer *no benefit in protecting against heart disease in borderline to moderate hypertension.*[301] These studies actually compared drug treatment with NO treatment (placebo). The natural alternatives, if employed, would obviously then lend substantial benefit.

The *American Journal of Cardiology* published an article in which the following quote was found, "Few patients with uncomplicated marginal hypertension require drug treatment... there is little evidence these patients (with marginal hypertension) will achieve enough benefit to justify the costs and adverse effects of antihypertension drug treatment."[302]

How costly in dollars is this treatment? Yearly sales of blood pressure medications are estimated to be greater than 10 billion dollars. Eighty percent of patients are in the mild to moderate range which could result in an 8 billion dollar loss to drug companies each year as well as dipping into the pockets of doctors. A *Journal of the American Medical Association* article stated that "treatment of hypertension has become the leading reason for visits to physicians as well as for drug prescriptions."[303]

Lifestyle/Dietary Recommendations:
1. Eliminate high-risk lifestyle factors: coffee consumption, alcohol intake, lack of exercise, stress and smoking.
2. Dietary high-risk factors should be eliminated: obesity, too much sodium and not enough potassium; low fiber, high-sugar diet; high saturated fat and low essential fatty acids intake; and diet low in calcium, magnesium and vitamin C.
3. Increase potassium intake. Sodium restriction is not advised but increasing potassium intake is advised. Researchers recommend a potassium to sodium ratio of 5:1 for maintaining good health. Current American diet has a 1:2 ratio. The benefit of added potassium really needs to come from the diet — not from drugs or supplements. Pregnant women should salt to taste.
4. Increase plant food consumption. Vegetarians generally have lower blood pressure levels and lower incidence of high blood pressure and cardiovascular disease.
5. Sucrose, table sugar, elevates blood pressure probably due to the increased adrenaline production resulting in increased blood vessel constriction and increased sodium retention. Complex-carbohydrate high-fiber foods, on the other hand, lower blood pressure.
6. Omega-3 fatty acids not only lower cholesterol, they decrease blood pressure. Double-blind studies demonstrate that fish oil (EPA or eicosapentaenoic acid) supplements or linolenic acid from flaxseed oil are effective for lowering blood pressure.[304] One tablespoon of flaxseed oil per day - cold-processed oil used as salad dressing or in supplemental form.
7. Special foods shown in studies to be particularly helpful in lowering blood pressure: celery - 4 ribs per day; garlic - 3 or more cloves per day and onions; nuts and seeds or their oils for their EFA (essential fatty acid) content; cold-water fish; green, leafy vegetables (rich source of calcium/magnesium); whole grains and legumes for fiber; and foods rich in vitamin C like broccoli, green peppers, and citrus fruits.
8. Blood pressure rises with five or more cups of coffee per day. This amount of coffee may be detrimental to baby as well.
9. Alcohol should not exceed one ounce of alcohol daily (2 oz. of liquor, 4 oz. of wine, 12 oz. of beer) for those with high blood pressure. *Pregnant women should not consume alcohol in any amount.*
10. Relax and pray.
11. Exercise.

Nutritional Supplement Recommendations:
1. Calcium should be taken at 1000mg - 1500mg daily and magnesium at 500mg - 1000mg daily. The highly absorbable forms are citrate, orotates, aspartates, or Krebs-cycle chelate intermediates.

2. Ginkgo and Hawthorn combination taken 2 in the morning and 2 before bedtime. This combination of herbs generally takes two weeks to see a change in lowering blood pressure.[305]
3. Coenzyme Q10 may be taken at 20mg three times daily.

Plantar Warts

Plantar warts are common on the sole of the foot. They typically are extremely tender, flattened by pressure. Unlike corns or calluses, they tend to pinpoint bleed when the wart surface is pared away. Standard allopathic treatment includes applying 40% salicylic acid tape for several days after which the physician debrides (scrapes away) the wart, finally destroying the wart through freezing or the use of caustic agents such as 30% to 70% trichloroacetic acid.[306] Nutritional and botanical supplementation centers on immune system and liver support as well as topical application of anti-viral herbs.

Lifestyle/Dietary Recommendations:

1. Eliminate alcohol and sugar (even "natural" sugars from fruit juices, fructose, maple syrup, etc.) since they depress the immune system.
2. Keep socks on around the house to protect other family members from the wart-producing virus.
3. Support the liver with dark, leafy greens and fermented foods such as yogurt, apple cider vinegar, miso, sauerkraut.

Nutritional Supplement Recommendations:

1. Apply the fresh juice of Cheledonium (Greater Celandine) to wart, cover and leave for several days. Cheledonium exhibits anti-viral activity which explains why it has been used so successfully for warts since they are induced by a virus.[307]
2. Thuja (Tree of Life) oil may be topically applied to the wart(s) two to three times daily. The addition of garlic oil to Thuja oil may enhance the chemical activity of both.[308] Thuja should not be used during pregnancy.
3. The use of Milk Thistle (containing at least 70% silymarin) aids liver function. Assisting the liver is necessary part of botanical protocol for any growth on or in the body. 1 tablet or capsule three times daily.[309]
4. Immunostimulating herbs such as astragalus and echinacea may be taken internally. Echinacea should not be taken for more than three months because a tolerance to the immune-stimulating effects may build. 2,000mg daily of each. Licorice may be beneficial due to the anti-viral activity of the herb (De-glyzirrinated licorice is the best choice for this type of use). 1 to 3 capsules or tablets daily.
5. Vitamin A acid (2% in petrolatum, one time daily, topically) produced good results in 50% of patients with plantar warts after four weeks of treatment. Complete cure occurred in two of the patients.[310]

Poison Ivy, Oak, Sumac

The problem of skin reaction to poison ivy or oak or sumac is not related to pregnancy. The reason it is included is that it is uncomfortable, and I thought moms would want to know what to do for it.

The sap from the plant contains urushiol, one of the most toxic skin agents known to humanity. Urushiol is not only potent but long-lasting. Gloves that crumbled a poison ivy leaf 6 to 12 months ago may still be coated with active oil. The rash is not contagious. Oil, however, may be transferred by hands, fingers and clothing.

Lifestyle/Dietary Recommendations:

1. Wash with mild soap and running water immediately upon contact with the plant.

Nutritional Supplement Recommendations:

1. Apply Jewelweed (Impatiens biflora). Pick the leaves and juicy stems. Crush them in the hand; put the plant and juice directly on the rash. Jewelweed may be placed in boiling water for five minutes; let steep and strain. Freeze tea into ice cubes and apply to poison ivy rash. Jewelweed relieves the itch and reduces inflammation. Although scientific evidence is scant, at least one study indicated jewelweed was as effective as pharmaceutical cortisone creams in treating poison ivy rash.
2. Grindelia (gumweed/gum plant) has pain-relieving and anti-inflammatory qualities. Christopher Hobbs recommends "Put a few drops of the tincture on the lesions and spread it with your fingers. The drops actually form a bandage-like, resinous, shiny coating over the top of the rash. It can be applied before going to bed, and it helps prevent you from scratching and spreading the rash." Hobbs also recommends taking Echinacea orally to boost the immune system for severe cases of contact dermatitis.
3. Tea tree oil may be applied to lesions.
4. For the camper, the Tecnu Poison Oak-N-Ivy Cleanser made by Tec Labs of Albany, Oregon helps cleanse urushiol from the skin after contact if water is not available.

Restless Legs

This discomfort makes me crazy! It is the feeling of restlessness in the legs that makes me want to kick or beat my legs against the bed after lying down for a night's sleep. Restless legs feels like all the energy of the entire body is focused in the legs. This is unfortunate since the rest of the body wants to go to sleep.

Lifestyle/Dietary Recommendations:
1. Foods rich in folic acid: Daily - 1 cup of orange juice (.07mg), 1/3 cup whole grain cereal (0.1mg), 1/2 cup cooked spinach (.13mg) and 1/2 cup cooked dry beans (.12mg).

Nutritional Supplement Recommendations:
1. Make certain that mom's prenatal contains at least 400mcg of folic acid, preferably 800 - 1,000mcg.
2. L-Dopamine has been found to be effective in the treatment of restless legs syndrome at a dosage of 100-200mg daily.[311] Please check with health care provider before using during pregnancy.

Salmonella/Campylobacter/Listeria

Salmonella, Campylobacter and Listeria are bacteria commonly known for causing food poisoning - gastrointestinal infection actually. These infections have become more prevalent in recent years due to antibiotic usage in our food (meat, most commonly chicken and eggs) supply. Drs. Michael A. Schmidt, Lendon H. Smith and Keith W. Sehnert in their book, *Beyond Antibiotics*, state that "Roughly, 40% of all antibiotics produced are used in animal husbandry. In most cases, antibiotics are used in animals raised for slaughter and eventual sale to consumers."[312] Even though these animals or their by-products are sometimes tested for antibiotic residue, if antibiotic-resistant bacteria have already been created, it is too late for the consumer who purchases bacteria-infected pork, beef, chicken, eggs, shellfish, sushi and dairy products.

There are almost 500,000 reported cases of *salmonella* or *campylobacter* infections each year. The actual number of infections (reported and unreported) may be as many as 20 to 80 million people in the United States.[313] The symptoms which include nausea, abdominal cramps, diarrhea, fever, headache and sometimes vomiting, mimic the "stomach flu" or a gastrointestinal virus. The incubation period is from 6 to 72 hours after eating infected food.

Campylobacter infections are on the rise, numbering two times more than salmonella last year in the U.S. Pregnant women, the elderly and very young babies are at most risk. Pregnant women who contract campylobacter during pregnancy are at very high risk for miscarriage or stillbirth. Common sources of campylobacter contamination: deli meats, uncooked hot dogs, leftovers, raw milk or pasteurized milk that has not been heated to 145 degrees Fahrenheit for 35 minutes, eggs and raw or undercooked poultry.

Lifestyle/Dietary Recommendations:

1. To prevent the occurrence, purchase organically-grown meat if possible. This does not totally eliminate the possibility of infection but greatly reduces one's risk.
2. Cook meat, especially chicken and turkey, thoroughly until there are no pink juices running.
3. Keep food preparation area clean. Do not allow raw meat or its juices to touch other food.
4. Wash hands or utensils in hot, soapy water after handling raw meat. Mom might even want to wear disposable gloves for poultry.
5. Wooden cutting boards may harbor bacteria - plastic ones are supposed to be better.
6. Thaw meat in the refrigerator, not on the kitchen counter or in the microwave.
7. Keep the refrigerator below 40 degrees F and the freezer at or below 0 degrees F.

8. Do not eat raw eggs. Prepare as follows:
   - Scramble 1 minutes at 250 F (121 C).
   - Poach for 5 minutes in boiling water.
   - Fry uncovered sunny-side up for 4 minutes at 250 F.
   - Fry over-easy 3 minutes one side, 2 minutes other side at 250 F.
   - Boil in shell for at least 7 minutes.[314]

Nutritional Supplement Recommendations:

1. Take 1 teaspoon of acidophilus (one of the super-strains) powder every hour until symptoms subside.
2. Take 1/2 teaspoon of Inner Strength (Probioplex - EN) with acidophilus. Mix in lukewarm water and drink.
3. Seek medical care if no improvement is seen in 24 to 48 hours.
4. If numbness, tingling or paralysis follows a meal, seek emergency care immediately. A very serious food poisoning, such as botulism, may have occurred.

Shingles

Shingles are caused by varicella-zoster or herpes zoster — the same virus that causes chicken pox. Shingles occurs when the virus which has been lying dormant in the body is activated by fatigue, stress, chicken pox exposure, anticancer drugs, immune system deficiency, Hodgkin's disease or other cancers. The virus travels to the nerve endings near the skin's surface. The result is burning, itching or pain that develops into blisters and a ring of rash on the abdomen or chest area. Shingles sometimes affects the neck, lower back, forehead or eyes. Althought the lesions usually crust over and heal after 1 to 2 weeks, persistent pain may develop due to nerve damage by the virus (postherpetic neuralgia).

The incidence of baby infection in the womb is low with shingles although it is possible. Moms with shingles should definitely avoid contact with pregnant women who have NOT had chicken pox because of the higher incidence of congenital baby infection from the varicella or chicken pox virus.

Allopathic treatment for shingles is risky for pregnancy - Acyclovir (Zovirax) and steroids.

Lifestyle/Dietary Recommendations:

1. Eat foods high in lysine and low in arginine: chocolate, peanuts, leeks, cereal grains (see Herpes Simplex).
2. Apply cool or cold wet dressings to the affected area. Some even put the wet cloth into the freezer to make it colder. Avoid heat.
3. Vitamin E capsules can be pricked with a pin and the oil applied directly onto lesions.

Nutritional Supplement Recommendations:

1. Vitamin E - 600 IU daily.
2. Vitamin C - 2 to 3 grams daily until lesions clear.
3. Lysine - 500 - 1,000mg three times daily during outbreak.
4. Vitamin B12 injections has helped with postviral neuralgia.
5. Intramuscular injections of adenosine monophosphate (AMP) should be discussed with physician for safe use during pregnancy. One study showed 88% of patients treated with AMP became free from pain and remained pain-free from 3 to 18 months after treatment.[315]
6. Follow Herpes Simplex herbal regimen.

Sinusitis

Sinusitis is an infection located in the sinus cavities of the head. Symptoms include swelling, congestion with thick, yellowish-green discharge, pain, headache that is worse upon bending over and all-around feeling unwell. Sinusitis occurs when mucous becomes thick and blocks the single exit out of the sinus cavities. Once blocked, bacteria find a home in which to thrive. The condition can become chronic if preventive measures are not employed.

Lifestyle/Dietary Recommendations:

1. Keep mucous thin by drinking 1 glass (8 oz.) of water every hour during a respiratory infection or allergy. Lemon added to the water supplies extra vitamin C without adding extra sugar.
2. Eat hot, spicy food - Mexican salsa, red peppers, chicken soup loaded with onions and garlic.[316]
3. Keep air moist with humidifier. Be certain to clean humidifier so mold and mildew do not grow.
4. Apply a hot cloth to the face for a few minutes to encourage circulation and mucous flow.
5. Pinch the sides of the upper nose with fingers to relieve pain and stimulate the flow of mucous.
6. Avoid allergens.

Nutritional Supplement Recommendations:

1. Vitamin C with bioflavonoids is always a good supplement to take during any infection. Moms in the first trimester should limit vitamin C intake to 3,000mg daily. Moms in the 2nd or 3rd trimester can take up to 1,000mg every 2 hours.
2. Bromelain has clinically-documented efficacy in treating sinusitis[317] by reducing inflammation, promoting drainage and decreasing swelling. 250 - 500mg three times daily taken 30 minutes before meals.
3. Echinacea is always a good choice for immune stimulation, and it has shown antibacterial effectiveness in studies.[318][319] When I feel pressure in my sinuses, I take 500 - 1,000mg every 2 hours.
4. A product called E.H.B. (NF) was very helpful for our family one Christmas when we developed sinusitis. Although it has goldenseal in it, the amount was not enough to cause me to have a hypoglycemic reaction and was not enough to stimulate contractions in my pregnancy. The caution against using goldenseal during pregnancy still applies.

5. Garlic has potent antibacterial properties. The equivalent of 3 to 4 cloves may be taken daily, or if family can stand it, eat 3 to 4 cloves daily. For those resistant infections, mom may need to take 3 to 4 cloves every 3 to 4 hours during the acute stage of the illness.

6. Tei Fu oil rubbed on the temples and forehead stimulates circulation and drainage. Just be careful not to get in the eyes.

Skin Infection, Mild

Mild skin infections from wounds or lesions are those not causing a systemic (whole body) response. There is no fever or general feeling of illness with a mild skin infection. This condition can be prevented with good hygiene and immuno-stimulant herbs.

Lifestyle/Dietary Recommendations:
1. Add to diet plenty of foods rich in vitamin C and bioflavonoids to aid healing: peppers, cantaloupe, guava, citrus fruit and their fresh juices, papaya and kiwi.
2. Wash affected area with soap and water several times daily to keep wound clean.
3. Eat onions and garlic which stimulate immune response.

Nutritional Supplement Recommendations:
1. Take 1,000 - 2,000mg Echinacea daily to stimulate immune function.
2. Apply 3 drops Echinacea tincture or tinctract and 1 drop of tea tree oil to inflamed area three times daily. Soothing Salve Drops by Mother's Choice™ may be used instead of trying to combine the drops to apply to the wound oneself.
3. Apply aloe vera gel 2 to 3 times daily to aid healing and provide protection for wound.

Sore Throat

A sore throat - does it really need a definition or will "OUCH" do? The throat becomes sore because of inflammation or irritation due to allergies, dry air, viruses or bacteria. It is sometimes difficult to distinguish one cause from another. The most common cause of a sore throat is a virus causing the "common cold" which is responsible for 80% of all sore throats.[320] A cold usually causes a scratchy or sore throat that is gone in a day or two followed by sneezing, coughing and increased mucous production.

Another cause of sore or scratchy throat is allergies or dry, indoor air. This type of sore throat usually is only felt in the morning upon waking and gets better as the day progresses. Eating and drinking usually relieve this type of sore throat.

The third cause of sore throat is a bacterial infection such as the *streptococcus* bacteria. The symptoms that accompany this sore throat are: fever of 102 or higher, fatigue, headache, stomach ache and/or nausea. The throat appears red with white patches on it. If a strep infection is suspected, a throat culture, not just a quick strep test, should be performed to determine if it is indeed bacterial. If antibiotics are used, the timing of initial treatment is crucial. Studies have shown that antibiotics taken within the first 48 hours of a strep infection actually *increase* the risk of a recurrent infection by two to eight times.[321] If antibiotics are used, concurrent nutritional support should definitely be used. Whatever the cause of the sore throat, the nutritional supplementation is the same.

Lifestyle/Dietary Recommendations:
1. Licorice root tea or a teaspoon of licorice tinctract in a cup of water has an anesthetizing effect. It helps to soothe the throat and suppress coughs.[322]
2. Jim Duke, Ph.D., U.S. Department of Agriculture's expert on medicinal plants, recommends: "pineapple juice with a pinch or so of ginger, nutmeg, rosemary and spearmint and a bit of licorice as a sweetener." Thyme and cardamom may also be added.[323]
3. Hot liquids such as chicken soup are always of benefit for respiratory illness and sore throats.
4. If sore throat is due to dry indoor air, use *a clean* humidifier. If due to allergens in home, consider an air purifier.
5. Change toothbrush every 1 to 2 months.
6. Investigate for milk allergy if recurrent tonsillitis is a problem.
7. Eat blackberries. Their astringent tannins may help.

Nutritional Supplement Recommendations:
1. LymphaRub by Mother's Choice™ contains essential oils that work extremely well for sore throats. The product may be rubbed on the throat 3 to 6 times daily. Family members other than mom may decide to put one to three drops in a cup

of water and sip slowly one to three times daily. Essential oils should not be taken internally during pregnancy.

2. Zinc lozenges containing at least 23mg of zinc may be taken every 2-4 hours. This amount of zinc should not be taken for more than one week.

3. A warm fenugreek tea or sage tea gargle may help relieve sore throats due, respectively, to their high mucilage and astringent tannins content.[324] [325]

4. Even the FDA calls slippery elm "an excellent demulcent" (soothing agent).[326] It is available in lozenges, teas or liquid combinations.

5. Echinacea may be taken at first sign of a sore throat to aid the immune response. 500 - 1,000mg every 2 to 4 hours.

Strengthen Bladder Function

I have included this here to help those moms who may have poor bladder muscle tone. This condition most often occurs at the end of pregnancy when baby's head may make it difficult to completely empty the bladder when urinating.

Lifestyle/Dietary Recommendations:
1. Exercise the pubococcygeal (PC) muscle by doing 100 -200 Kegel exercises daily.
2. Do not Kegel while on the toilet. This can lead to urine retention.
3. Relax pelvic floor muscles entirely when urinating and just let it flow.

Nutritional Supplement Recommendations:
1. Nettle and dandelion tea is very helpful in improving bladder and kidney function. 3 - 4 cups daily.

Strengthen Immune Function

As discussed in Body System Changes During Pregnancy, the immune system is mildly depressed during pregnancy. This does not mean we are susceptible to everything that come along. For some moms who start their pregnancies ill or become ill early in pregnancy, it is important to strengthen the immune function nutritionally.

Lifestyle/Dietary Recommendations:

1. If mom has been ill or feels unwell, rest is essential to healing and restoration of normal immune response. If mom keeps going and going, so will her immune response.
2. Follow the whole foods daily plan for pregnancy for maximum nutrition.
3. Include plenty of garlic and onions in meal preparation.

Nutritional Supplement Recommendations:

1. Astragalus (Astragalus membranaceus) is one of the best herbs for general stimulation of the immune response for chronic decreased immunity. Astragalus is a very safe herb for internal use even in large doses.[327] [328] 2 to 6 capsules daily for 1 to 2 months.
2. Echinacea is a potent immune stimulator. If used for general immune stimulation, it may be taken 1,000mg -2,000mg daily for 10 days. Stop for 3 to 5 days. Repeat dosage for another 10 days.
3. Vitamin C - 1,000mg - 3,000mg daily.

Toothache

A toothache anytime is anything but pleasant, but a toothache during pregnancy can be misery because of the limited avenues of relief. While the means of relief are limited, this is not to say we must be in misery. There are several natural remedies that may be safely used during pregnancy. I personally have used some of these during one of my pregnancies.

A visit to the dentist is appropriate to identify the cause of the toothache. It may be that a build-up of plaque and bacteria have caused inflammation around a particular tooth. A thorough cleaning at the beginning of pregnancy with a six-month follow-up can help prevent many problems. X-rays are definitely a danger to the developing baby and should be avoided.

Lifestyle/Dietary Recommendations:

1. Regular brushing (at least twice daily) and flossing (at least once daily) is essential for dental care. Our family does not use fluoride toothpaste because of our concern about the toxicity of fluoride. The book, *Fluoride: The Aging Factor* by John Yiamianis, 6439 Taggert Road, Delaware, OH 43015, is an excellent resource on fluoride as well as *The Fluoride Report: The Truth in H_2O Foundation*, PO Box 219, Buckeyestown, MD 21717-0219 or 301-874-2948. We use herbal toothpaste instead.

2. A diet of whole, natural foods promotes a healthy mom and baby. Dried fruits should be limited in the amounts eaten due to their high natural sugar content and stickiness. If mom does eat them, she should brush her teeth immediately afterwards.

3. A warm cloth over the facial area in pain may be helpful and soothing.

Nutritional Supplement Recommendations:

1. Dip a cotton swab into a mixture of: Essential oil of Clove - 15-20 drops, Olive Oil Extra Virgin - 1 teaspoon, Brandy - 1 teaspoon. Rub the saturated cotton swab on tooth and surrounding gum every 2 hours. Do not overuse. Clove extract has shown the ability to suppress plaque formation, specifically active against streptococcus mutans, a major cause of dental caries (cavity) formation.[329]

2. Echinacea, Myrrh, and Yarrow help stimulate the immune system and fight inflammation. Christopher Hobbs in his book, *Echinacea: The Immune Herb!*, recommends applying drops of tincture right on the tooth every 15 minutes until pain is relieved.

3. Sedative herbs such as valerian, skullcap and chamomile may be used for short periods to relieve toothache pain. 1 teaspoon of herbal tinctract combination, Peace Treaty from Mother's Choice™, every 2 to 3 hours.

4. For those having dental surgery (not during pregnancy), bromelain has been shown to reduce swelling by 7.5% one day after surgery at a dosage of 240mg daily. The study was done on patients with impacted or dislocated lower wisdom teeth.[330]

5. Vitamin B6 and zinc supplementation may lead to a reduction in dental caries (cavities), even in those who consume a diet that leads to caries.[331]

Toxoplasmosis

Toxoplasmosis is a protozoal infection caused by the intracellular parasite *Toxoplasma gondii*.[332] Trophozoites in the acute stage pass to the tissue to form cysts which remain viable, and oocysts are passed in cat feces.[333] This disease is transmitted to humans via raw or poorly cooked meat, as well as cat or bird feces. One third of the population has antibodies to toxoplasmosis. Symptoms may manifest as: fatigue and malaise; muscle pain; and swollen lymph nodes. However, most cases are sub-clinical or asymptomatic.

This infection crosses the placenta resulting, if contracted by baby, in first trimester miscarriages or malformation of the baby. If contracted later in pregnancy, problems such as prematurity, central nervous system defects, anencephalus, hydrocephalus and destructive changes in the eyes or brain may be seen.

Virology testing is available to check antibody status although it is not performed routinely. Kitty may be tested by the vet. Many adult cats will have previously contracted the disease, thus will no longer be at risk.

Lifestyle/Dietary Recommendations:

1. Avoid cleaning cat litter boxes or working in dirt where cat feces may be present.
2. Cook all meats thoroughly before consuming. Microwaving and stir-frying do not destroy toxoplasmosis.
3. Wash hands thoroughly after touching raw meat or wear gloves when handling raw meat and wash gloves with soap and hot water.
4. Do not buy kitten or bird during pregnancy.

Nutritional Supplement Recommendations:

1. Echinacea - 500 - 1,000mg every 2 hours if infection is suspected.
2. Garlic - 2 to 3 cloves daily or their supplemental equivalent.
3. Bayberry - 1/2 teaspoon of tincture or tinctract twice daily or 500mg of powdered herb twice daily. Exceeding these dosages may result in an upset of the sodium/potassium ratio of the body.

Urinary Tract Infection

The most common urinary tract infection is called cystitis which is an infection of the bladder. We women are much more likely to have UTIs than men. This may be for a variety of reasons, some of them being:

1) Our urethra is closer to the anus than men;
2) Sexual relations (intercourse) can deposit bacteria near the urethra;
3) Improper wiping after pottying;
4) Using feminine hygiene sprays, douches and bubble baths - these irritate the normal cleansing process of our bodies;
5) Wearing synthetic-material panties when plain (or pretty), breathable cotton is best;
6) Not drinking enough to supply the urinary tract with a constant supply of urine to flush it out.

Since pregnancy hormones relax just about all of the body's structures and functions, it is important to practice good hygiene and preventive measures for urinary health.

Lifestyle/Dietary Recommendations:

1. Wipe from front to back after bowel movements.
2. Urinate after sexual relations, and practice good hygiene (washing up) afterwards.
3. Avoid feminine hygiene sprays, douches (not to be used during pregnancy except under direction of caregiver), and bubble baths.
4. Wear loose clothing and cotton underwear.
5. Drink 2 quarts pure water daily. Add lemon for increased urine acidity. Urinate often. Do not hold urine while finishing a task — urinate then come back to finish the task.
6. If urinary symptoms persist with a negative urinalysis - suspect yeast (See Vaginal Yeast Infection).
7. If dad is having symptoms too, suggest he follow supplement guidelines.

Nutritional Supplement Recommendations:

1. Cranberry juice concentrate capsules - 1 three times daily with 8 ounces of purified water.[334][335]
2. Buffered vitamin C or Ester-C — 500 - 1,000mg every 4 hours until infection has cleared. Maintenance - 1,000 - 1,500mg daily.
3. Uva ursi, grindelia, pipsissewa, and couchgrass are all herbs that research has shown to be beneficial to the urinary system especially in the treatment of cystitis.[336] Uva ursi should not be used in large amounts during pregnancy due to its uterine stimulant properties.

Vaginal Infections

The most common vaginal infections are: yeast *(Candida albicans)*, *Trichomonas vaginalis*, and *Bacteriosis vaginosis* (often caused by Gardnerella). As always prevention is the best course of action. I will list the lifestyle and dietary recommendations first, then I will list each infection separately along with the specific supplement recommendations.

Lifestyle/Dietary Recommendations:
1. Wear cotton underpants.
2. Eliminate or decrease sugar and refined carbohydrate consumption.
3. Use perfume/dye-FREE toilet paper and laundry detergent.
4. Use no feminine hygiene products such as sprays, powders, etc. Daily bathing is sufficient.
5. Clean hands and body before and after intimate relations with husband (this implies relations only with husband - chastity is necessary for the avoidance of some vaginal infections which are sexually-transmitted).
6. Eat one cup of plain yogurt with live cultures daily.
7. Eat plenty of garlic and make sure the mainstay of the diet is complex carbohydrates and fiber from vegetables, fruits and legumes.

Yeast or *Candida Albicans:*

Symptoms include genital itching, dryness and inflammation, discharge is heavy, thick, white cottage-cheese-like clumps smelling "yeasty." Antibiotic therapy is a common cause.

Nutritional Supplement Recommendations:
1. Microwave underpants.[337]
2. Place pure acidophilus capsules high in the vagina at bedtime. Be careful not to push capsule(s) into the opening of the cervix.
3. An acidophilus powder or cranberry concentrate powder (1 tablespoon to 1 quart of water) as a douche may be helpful. Douching during pregnancy is a definite risk to mom and baby. Douching should only be done during pregnancy under the care and instruction of a professional health care provider. Douching instructions listed under Group B beta-hemolytic Streptococcal Infection.
4. Mom may peel clove of garlic (without damaging clove or it will be very irritating (burning) to vaginal tissue) and insert into vagina for overnight stay. *Anytime mom inserts anything into her vagina, she should be careful not to push it (capsule or clove) into cervix.

5. Take 1/2 teaspoon acidophilus powder (EN, UAS Lab, Progressive Labs) with 1/2 teaspoon Inner Strength™ (EN). Combine with warm water and drink 4 to 6 times daily during infection to resupply body with "friendly" bacteria.

6. Swab tea tree oil mixture around vagina using gauze soaked in: 1 cup water with 3 drops of tea tree oil or use a tea tree oil suppository once daily for 7 to 10 days.[338] Some women may experience a burning sensation vaginally with intravaginal use of tea tree. Proceed with caution. Do not use un-diluted tea tree oil. This will burn and cause tissue swelling. Experience speaking. Ouch!

7. Echinacea may be taken orally. Initial dose: 1,000mg or 2 mg tincture/tinctract; then 500-1,000mg every 2 to 3 hours for 2 days; then three time daily for 3 days; finally twice daily for 5 more days.

8. Pau D'Arco - 500 - 1,000mg twice daily for 2 to 3 weeks. Caution in pregnancy.

9. Grapefruit seed extract - 130 mg twice daily with plenty of water. This option as well as #8 are short-term therapies - 2 - 3 weeks maximum.[339]

10. A product by Nutrition Now called Yeast Defense was very helpful for me during a pregnancy in which I had to take antibiotics for a terrible sinus infection. I used 2 capsules of Yeast Defense plus one tablet of Garlic every 3 hours plus 1 tablet of pure Grapefruit Seed Extract 3-4 times daily. Continued therapy for at least 10-14 days.

Trichomonas vaginalis:

Symptoms include: itching and inflammation of vulva and vagina and a prurient greenish-yellow discharge that is slimy or foamy. Anal sexual contact is a major cause of "Trich" because Trich normally resides in the rectum. Trich may only be passed through sexual contact. Men may harbor the organism in their penis without symptoms. It is imperative that both mom and dad be treated. Since trich cannot live in an acidic environment, the goal is to acidify the vagina.

Nutritional Supplement Recommendations:

1. For dad: 1 to 2 teaspoons Goldenseal/Myrrh tincture or tinctract three times daily for 10 days plus use a Pau D'Arco sitz bath to wash dad's penis: Make a strong infusion of Pau D'Arco (Taheebo or Lapacho). Soak penis 15 minutes twice daily. Instructions for making infusion: Steep 1/2 ounce of Pau D'Arco in 2 cups of water for 20 minutes.

2. Mom can take 2 tablespoons of apple cider vinegar or lemon juice in water twice daily plus 5,000mg vitamin C.

3. A douche of: 2 tablespoons white vinegar and 1 tablespoon activated charcoal powder to 1 quart of water may be used daily for 1 week, then every other day for the following week and then twice weekly for 2 more weeks.

4. Garlic cloves (as described for yeast) may be used every 3 hours for 3 days, then once a day for overnight for 4 more days. The third week, garlic suppositories or capsules may be used every other day then twice in the fourth week.[340]

5. In one study Pau D'Arco (lapacho) extract was applied in the vagina using gauze soaked in the extract. A fresh-soaked gauze was renewed every 24 hours. The treatment was highly effective.[341]

6. A lactobacillus vaccine called Solcotrichovac was used in a study of 444 women which yielded a 92.5% cure rate after one vaccination of the inactivated microorganisms.[342]

7. Bee propolis extract has been shown to have lethal effects on Trich in vitro.[343]

Bacteriosis vaginosis (Gardnerella)

Symptoms may include: itchy, inflamed vagina with a white or yellowish, thin, highly odorous (fish odor) discharge that may be blood streaked; frequent, painful urination, cramps or lower back pain may also be present. Dad needs treatment too.

Nutritional Supplement Recommendations:

1. Echinacea - 1,000mg four times daily or 1/2 teaspoon Echinacea tincture or tinctract.

2. An echinacea infusion (1 ounce to 2 cups boiling water, steep 10 hours) may be used for douching - 3 tablespoons infusion to 1 quart water. Douche daily for 7 days. May also douche with Bayberry bark. Douching during pregnancy is a risk for mom and baby. Douching during pregnancy should only be done under the care and direction of a professional health care provider.

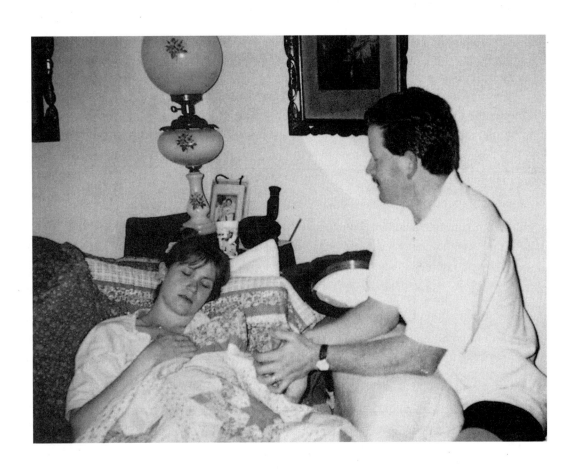

PART FOUR

Laboring to Love

"Your eyes saw my substance, being yet unformed, And in Your book they all were written, The days fashioned for me. When as yet there were none of them." Psalm 139:16

THE APPOINTED TIME HAS COME

Labor. The word brings to mind a jumble of emotions: excitement, trepidation, joy, frustration. The one emotion that stands out for me as I think about my labors is love, the love I feel for this child making his or her way out into my arms. I have walked several different roads as I have journeyed through motherhood. Some have been easy, others difficult, yet all of them have taught, sharpened, grown me into a woman and mother who respects the design of the Father in pregnancy and birth.

Emotions as diverse as, "I'm tired of being pregnant." "I do not want this pregnancy to be over," "I just do not want to wait any longer to see my baby," can all be expressed during the last weeks of pregnancy. These are just a few of the sentiments mothers express in the last month of pregnancy. Even for those of us quite comfortable in waiting on the Lord have a hard time waiting for and surrendering to God's appointed time for the birth of our child. Our fear of the unknown, and what we know of other('s) pregnancies, sometimes cause us to lose touch with the comfort of the Lord and the peace of surrendering to His will.

Surrender, or the yielding to and giving up to, of ourselves is the necessary ingredient of labor, of love itself. Perfect love is not selfish nor boastful, two qualities we mothers sometimes exhibit when we approach laboring to bring forth our child. One mother may opt for a drug-filled labor in order to "avoid the pain." Another may triumphantly declare her fortitude in making it through her baby's delivery "completely natural." I do not mean to imply that either pharmaceuticals are never appropriate for labor or that non-medicated delivery is wrong. The problem lies not with method, although certainly natural childbirth is generally superior to medicated deliveries in terms of health of mom and baby. Loving our baby and God means that we, as mom and dad, must examine our motivation for the decisions we make prior to and during labor.

I have personally found it so very easy to get caught up in the "goings on" in my life near the completion of my pregnancies so that I forget what and who this is all about. As I draw closer to the birth, I think of all the ways the unknown date of the birth will affect my family's life. "Will I be able to go to the family Thanksgiving celebration this year, or will the baby already be born?" "Should I schedule any book seminars or wait until the baby is here?" "But Lord, I want an October baby!" How our designs confuse and rob us of our peace!

God knows the time of our baby's birth, the moment, the hour, the day, the month, the year. We know what we feel we must accomplish in this ninth month and postpartum time; God knows what we need to accomplish in this ninth month and postpartum time. His design clearly shows what we must do: Rest, for we tire more easily; Prepare our home and family for the baby's coming, for we have that "nesting" instinct; Wait, for the Lord has appointed the time of birth; Nurture at our breasts, for the Lord compares His comfort of Zion to a nursing mother.

Our calling as mothers is one of sacrifice. We must sacrifice our fleshly desire to avoid the work, labor, of birth, through chemical means. If we routinely chose to escape the work of life through chemical means in any other instance, we would be labeled "drug abusers," yet when another life is vulnerable to the effects of drugs routinely used during birth, we seem to find this acceptable. As stated earlier in this book, pharmaceuticals do have their place in healing; however, the use of medications should be reserved for those times of necessity rather than being the first thing we ask for when the first contraction comes.

Labor *is* work. Sometimes labor is *very* hard work. Sometimes labor goes as smoothly and calmly as in our dreams. We must prepare for this work, physically, mentally and spiritually. The Hebrew women were "lively." We women of today are very rarely as "lively" as those women; therefore, I think we must avoid the supposition that we can continue all the activities that we may be engaged in prior to pregnancy, especially if those activities were not all that healthful to begin. Pregnancy, for some of us, will be a time of quiet activity, no lugging around 50-pound bags of wheat for this lady anymore during pregnancy.

For those women who are planning a Vaginal Birth After Cesarean (VBAC), the best advice I could possibly give would be to begin to consider yourself "just another birthing woman." The statistics are in your favor. Choose carefully a supportive caregiver and surround yourself with those who will encourage you when you are doubtful and exhort you to birth preparation, physical, mental and spiritual.

Mental, or emotional, preparation coincides with spiritual preparation. We cannot be emotionally at peace if our focus is not on trusting our Divine Creator in His wisdom and plan for this child, this pregnancy, this birth. We delight in our husband's washing us with the Word of God, allowing the Scriptures to bring us peace, comfort and BOLDNESS in the approaching birth. Joy is found in trusting the Lord, *sacrificial trusting* that surrenders our own plans, even our own hopes, to the Will of God.

As the time of birth draws near, may our spirits be cleansed and renewed in our trust in the grace of the Lord, may our hearts be gladdened with the assurance of His mercy, may our bodies open in the fullness of time under His pillar of strength, may our hearts be turned to our babies in the perfection of His love.

Natural Labor Induction in the Post-Dates Woman

There are times when the hormonal activity of a pregnant mom may need to be "encouraged" with herbs. This hormonal assistance may need to be started prior to due date in the woman who experiences no noticeable Braxton-Hicks contractions by the 34th week of pregnancy or is feeling no cervical twinges or "pressure" sensations by the 37th week. These herbs may be of benefit to the woman who has had previous babies with postmaturity syndrome, the woman planning her first vaginal birth or a mother past the 37th week with prolonged ruptured membranes. These herbs should NOT be utilized for the reason, "I'm tired of being pregnant. I want it to come out now!" Since the Lord appointed a time for baby to be born when He formed the baby, any intervention in this area should be done only after prayer and confirmation from the Lord that this intervention should be implemented.

Preparing the uterus:

One of the following herb formulas may be taken from the 34th week until birth:

BirthPrep™ (Mother's Choice™)- A formula dating back to early naturopathy that prepares the uterus for birth as well as aiding the softening of the cervix. To be used two to three times daily for the last five weeks of pregnancy.

PN-6 (NW) - Time-honored formula for the last five to six weeks of pregnancy used by many women to tone the uterus in preparation for labor. Recommended dosage is to begin taking one capsule per day the first week, adding one more capsule daily each week until at the end of the six weeks, mom will be taking six capsules daily.

5-W (NSP)- A widely used-formula containing the herbs Black Cohosh (Cimicifuga racemosa), Squaw Vine (Mitchella repens), Dong Quai or Angelica (Angelica sinensis), Butcher's Broom (Ruscus aculeatus), and Red Raspberry (Rubus spp.). Recommended by many midwives to tone the uterine muscle in preparation for birth and provide the body with hormonal precursors so it can produce what is needed. I usually recommend moms start out with two capsules per day and be up to 6 capsules per day by the end of one week and stay at 6 daily until term. If taking six daily causes too many Braxton-Hicks contractions at night, reduce dosage by one capsule until rest is possible.

Equinox Botanicals Uterine Tonic - This tincture (alcohol-based) of herbs is recommended by some midwives. The tincture will be absorbed better than the capsules in most women at the end of pregnancy; however, the alcohol in the tincture may be hard on mom's system. Take as directed on bottle.

In addition, some women may find these nutritional supplements beneficial for hormonal support:

Evening Primrose Oil or Black Currant Oil - These oils contain prostaglandin precursors, and prostaglandins are known to ripen the cervix. The daily dosage is 500 mg three times daily beginning at the 36th week. Some midwives and physicians have opened the capsules and rubbed the oil directly on the cervix beginning at term or at the start of the attempt to initiate labor.

Pituitary glandular extract - While I am not personally familiar with the usage of this remedy, it has been reported by some maternal care providers to help prime the pituitary gland to produce adequate oxytocin. This is usually started at 36 to 37 weeks. Three tablets are taken daily.

To initiate labor:

StartUP™ (**Mother's Choice**™) - This herbal combination utilizes herbs that stimulate uterine contractions to assist the body's natural laboring process. 1/2 to 1 teaspoon may be used every two hours until labor is well-established and consistently progressing.

Master Gland - This combination of vitamins, minerals and herbs is used to nourish the glandular system so that it might function normally. Since the glands produce our hormones, it makes sense that this would help initiate labor. My own personal experience in recommending this to midwives and having them use it with clients is that it has not failed to work in the post-dates woman who is ready for labor but not going into labor. The herbs it contains are: Licorice, Lemon bioflavonoids, Asparagus, Alfalfa, Parsley, Kelp, Black Walnut, Thyme, Parthenium, Schizandra, Siberian Ginseng, Dong Quai, Dandelion, Uva Ursi, Marshmallow. Recommended amount: 2 tablets every 30 minutes until labor is underway and throughout the labor. If headache occurs, discontinue for that day and start again the next day. I have seen no problems with using this dosage for two to three days. It seems to make the labors go faster, too.

Labor tincture - This is available from Equinox Botanicals and may be given 10 drops every thirty minutes for three hours. You might like to alternate with the Master Gland if the Master Gland alone is not achieving desired results.

Goldenseal or Goldenrod may be used for those women unable to take herbs with estrogenic properties. 2 capsules every 2 hours may be taken to stimulate contractions.

Blue Cohosh, Black Cohosh and Ginger tincture - For those who need just a little help getting started, this can be quite effective. Recommended amount: 10 drops of each of these tinctures every 2 to 3 hours increasing the dosage to every half hour when contractions start. This should not be used for more than one day without taking a break to allow the liver time to process the Blue Cohosh. If nausea, vomiting or headache occurs, discontinue and start again the next day.

Moms should be in a well-nourished condition before attempting to initiate labor. Birthing is hard work. The week prior to labor should be a week with plenty of carbohydrate intake to provide the necessary glycogen (fuel) for labor work.

Hemorrhage

A hemorrhage is an abnormal, excessive loss of blood. Obstetrically speaking, an excessive amount is more than 500 milliliters (2 cups or 500 cc's).[344] Hemorrhage may occur as a sudden gush, a steady flow or a prolonged trickle, without normal clotting. A postpartum hemorrhage may be caused by:

1. Atonic uterus (won't contract) from retained placenta, overdistended uterus, oxytocin induction or augmentation, rapid labor or delivery, prolonged 1st and 2nd stage of labor, grand multiparity (has had more than four babies) or a history of uterine atony with previous deliveries.
2. Cervical lacerations (cervix is torn during delivery).
3. Extensive vaginal and perineal lacerations.
4. Abruptio placentae - placenta prematurely separates from uterine wall.
5. Very rarely, uterine laceration or rupture.
6. Surgical intervention at birth.[345]

All natural measures for hemorrhage are to be used *while seeking medical assistance.* Mom should be listened to as she is the one who will know if she feels like the bleeding is too much for her body. One woman may handle a loss of 2 cups of blood well while another may be more susceptible to problems. Mom's care of baby is affected by the amount of blood lost combined with her ability to handle the blood loss. Caregivers should make certain mom and baby get the best possible start even if this means a slight change in the birth plan to accomodate pitocin, methergine or IV fluids. A little help and discomfort in the beginning can make a world of difference in how mom faces those first weeks postpartum.

Lifestyle/Dietary Recommendations:
1. If there has been any "extra" bleeding at the birth and mom is not handling it well, mom should avoid the usually pleasant herbal bath for her and baby. The heat of the water could encourage bleeding to renew.
2. Mom should immediately lie down if she is in an upright position with her head lower than her bottom.
3. The uterus should be grasped tightly and massaged to encourage the muscle to contract.
4. Have baby nurse to give mom nipple stimulation which will release oxytocin which causes the uterus to contract.
5. If the bleeding has not diminished within five minutes and mom is at home, transport immediately unless your caregiver is present with medical intervention available.

Nutritional Supplement Recommendations:

1. An herbal combination used to aid in halting heavy bleeding is HemHalt™(available from Mother's Choice) which contains: Shepherd's Purse, Blue Cohosh, Bayberry, Yarrow and Capsicum. The herbs stimulate uterus to contract and halt bleeding.[346][347] 1/2 - 1 teaspoon under tongue; hold for three minutes then swallow. Repeat in five minutes if necessary.

2. Immediately mom should begin to drink liquid chlorophyll until bleeding stops or medical intervention is available.

3. A tincture of cayenne may be used, but the above herbal combination (HemHalt Formula) should follow the cayenne. While cayenne initially may halt the bleeding, it is a stimulant herb that may cause bleeding to renew shortly.

Internal Bleeding Recovery (Hemorrhage)

Internal bleeding or hemorrhage depletes the body of vital nutrients and causes pronounced fatigue. Sometimes nausea and loss of appetite may occur after a hemorrhage. The lifestyle and nutritional steps mom takes after internal bleeding or hemorrhage can make a great difference in how soon she is able to resume her activities and care for her body.

Lifestyle/Dietary Recommendations:

1. Fluids need to be taken in slowly but steadily - sipping one cup of water every hour for the first day after bleeding to replace body fluids.
2. Foods rich in vitamin K (necessary for blood clotting) should be eaten: alfalfa, dark, green leafy vegetables, soybeans and *lactobacillus*-containing yogurt.
3. To avoid a scar if there is a wound or tear that caused bleeding, mom can apply comfrey ointment or a plantain poultice which have been shown in studies to prevent scars from forming and soften those that do form. Vitamin E also helps to soften scar tissue already formed.
4. Soothing Salve drops may be directly applied to tears for healing.

Nutritional Supplement Recommendations:

1. The HemHalt™ (Mother's Choice) may be continued two to three times daily until mom's bleeding is stopped.
2. Chlorophyll supplements (algae-based green foods: spirulina, chlorella, blue-green algae and grasses of wheat, barley and alfalfa) may be used to replace lost nutrients.
3. Vitamin C, 2g to 5g of vitamin C with bioflavonoids plus 25mg to 50mg zinc.
4. Bioflavonoids, especially rutin, may be taken with the vitamin C.
5. Vitamin B12, folic acid and iron in a B complex formula.

Labor Exhaustion

Maternal exhaustion during labor occurs because of a variety of or a combination of factors including hunger, lack of sleep, prolonged labor and/or a difficult labor. If labor is progressing slowly, mom must continue to rest as much as possible. Staying upright to facilitate contractions is only effective if mom is not getting too tired. Her body will expend all its energy on outside activity rather than the hard work of opening and drawing up the cervix.

Lifestyle/Dietary Recommendations:

1. Mom should take naps or at least lie down and be completely at rest often during a long labor.
2. Mom may continue eating light foods during labor. She should definitely continue drinking vegetable and fruit juices and water throughout labor to maintain adequate hydration.
3. Since mom will probably have a bottle of liquid chlorophyll at her home if she is planning a home birth, she can mix the chlorophyll with water and sip a half-cup each hour during labor.
4. A soothing bath with lavender drops added (7-10 drops per full tub of water) can provide relaxation for mom to allow her to gather her reserve strength to continue laboring.
5. Ginseng has been studied to ascertain whether it truly improves endurance and increases energy, and the results were positive. While ginseng is not an herb to be used indiscriminately during pregnancy, its use during a long labor with a tired mom may be warranted. Mom may take up to 3 grams daily during labor.

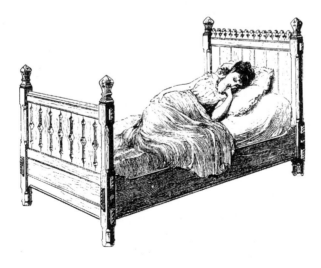

Perineal Tears

Perineal tears can almost always be avoided by mom and dad doing perineal massage (massage of the perineum - area between vagina and anus) for the six weeks prior to estimated due date, good perineal massage and support during the delivery of baby by mom's caregiver or husband, and gentle, exhale pushing (not pushing baby out with one strong push). When perineal tears do occur, the extent of the laceration or tear is measured by: 1st degree — tear extends through the skin and the superficial structures above the muscles; 2nd degree — tear extends through the muscles of the perineal body but does not involve the sphincter ani; 3rd degree — tear also severs the sphincter; and 4th degree — the anterior rectal wall is also torn.

Different care providers have varied opinions about the need to stitch, or even whether an episiotomy should be performed. Episiotomies heal more slowly and not as well as a natural tear and can certainly be avoided through the careful management of the second stage of labor (See book resource section). First degree tears generally do not need stitching, as well as some second degree tears. If mom will keep her legs together so healing can occur, painful stitches can be avoided. Perineal injuries not involving the levator ani (Pubococcygeus [PC] muscle) produce no permanent disability even when they are not repaired or stitched.[348] Third and 4th degree tears do require stitching.

Lifestyle/Dietary Recommendations: For prevention...
1. Begin perineal massage six weeks prior to estimated date of delivery. See box on next page.
2. A healthful diet helps insure tissue integrity and strength.
3. Do not blast baby out. Let the uterus do the work unless there is an urgent need to get baby out quickly (example - fetal distress).
4. Have someone with experience perform perineal massage and support baby's head during delivery. Personally, I have found that moms who are very aware of their body's signals do not need a lot of perineal support during the delivery of the baby's head. It is simply a matter of realizing what that burning sensation means (tissues are stretching)— no forceful pushing, breathe baby out!

Nutritional Supplement Recommendations: If a tear has occurred...
1. Apply St. John's wort oil or Lavender oil (Lavandula officinalis) was shown to be effective in relieving perineal discomfort following childbirth. The new moms used the oil in their baths for ten days after the birth of baby.[349]
2. A combination of 1/4 cup comfrey, 1/4 cup uva ursi, 1/4 cup chamomile, 1/4 cup shepherd's purse may be used as a healing perineal wash. Combine and add to water. Bring to boil, lower heat and simmer for 20 minutes. Use this tea as a rinse for the perineal area or use to make compress with sterile gauze or cloth.

Perineal Massage

Perineal massage is an activity that can accomplish several objectives: create a more elastic perineum to ease baby's passage (and mom's comfort during that passage); help mom become comfortable with her body's function; and get dad involved in the birth preparation. Some moms may prefer not to do perineal massage. Perineal massage is a personal choice. Moms who do elect to practice perineal massage seem to increase the likelihood of avoiding a tear or episiotomy.

Perineal massage should be started about six weeks before the due date and should be done daily. A lubricant such as olive oil, almond oil or vitamin E oil reduces friction during massage as well as increases suppleness of mom's tissue. Supple, elastic tissue does not equate with stretched out, loose tissue. A ballerina who can do "the splits" does not have loose, flabby tissue and muscle tone; rather she has worked at stretching her muscles and toning her tissue. If I were to try to do the splits today, there is a 99% likelihood that I would tear my ligaments in my groin. If I practiced for six weeks, stretching each day, by the end of that time, I would probably be able to gently lower myself into the "splits" position. So it is with birthing a baby. "Practicing" the baby's birth by doing perineal massage lessens mom's likelihood of tearing her muscles and tissue during the birth. Perineal massage does not create a flaccid vaginal wall; rather it increases mom's awareness of muscle control and the tone of those muscles.

Instructions:

It is best to have mom's husband help her with the massage, although it is possible for mom to do perineal massage alone. A mirror is helpful for mom if she is going to do the massage herself. Fingernails should be short and a fresh pair of inexpensive, disposable latex gloves are sometimes easier on mom's vaginal area than rough hands (wash hands before beginning). Positions for perineal massage are: semi-sitting, squatting against a wall or standing with one foot raised and resting on tub, toilet or chair. Pour the chosen lubricant over the fingers and thumbs rather than dipping hand into oil (risk of contamination). With oiled fingers, rub oil onto the perineum to insure adequate lubrication. Add more oil if necessary.

If mom is doing the massage alone, the thumbs will probably be easier to use. Dad can use his index fingers. Place the thumb or index fingers inside the vagina (up to the second knuckle); move them upward along the sides of the vagina in a rhythmic U or sling-type movement. This movement will stretch the vaginal tissue, the muscles surrounding the vagina, and the skin of the perineum. Mom can also massage by rubbing the skin of the perineum between the thumb and forefinger (thumb on the inside, finger on the outside or vice versa). The vaginal and perineal sensations will be of tightness at first, but as the weeks progress, daily massage will relax and stretch the tissue.

As dad is doing the massage, mom should concentrate on relaxing her muscles as she feels pressure. As dad becomes more comfortable massaging, he should increase the pressure just enough to make the perineum begin to sting from the stretching (just as it does when baby's head is born). Mom and dad should continue the massage for at least five minutes and should consult with their caregiver if they have any questions about the massage.

Premature Labor

Premature labor is the term used to describe labor which begins between the 20th and 36th week of pregnancy. A small baby does not necessarily mean baby was premature. Approximately 7% of all pregnancies end in low-birth weight babies. This includes small-for-dates (gestational age) or growth retarded babies.[350] Prematurity is based on the gestational age of baby, not on his birth weight. An attempt to halt premature labor is best for baby unless: 1) the pregnancy is of at least 37 weeks gestation; 2) the membranes are ruptured; 3) the cervix is 4 - 5cm dilated; 4) the baby has congenital defects necessitating delivery; 5) mom has severe toxemia, abruptio placentae or another serious condition making delivery necessary.[351]

Lifestyle/Dietary Recommendations:

1. The conditions necessitating premature delivery for mom's safety (toxemia, abruptio placentae) can and should be minimized through whole food nutrition.
2. Membranes are more likely to rupture if an infection (urinary, vaginal [ureaplasma, mycoplasma]) is present, so prompt treatment of these variations is imperative.
3. Bed rest is the order of the day to reduce gravitational pressure on the cervix.
4. Some midwives recommend a glass of wine and a warm tub bath (if membranes are still intact) to see if that will stop contractions.

Nutritional Supplement Recommendations:

1. CarryOn™ by Mother's Choice™: As with miscarriage, Black haw and cramp bark are research-supported uterine relaxants. These may be taken in combination with false unicorn (normalizes hormone function) and wild yam (antispasmodic to abdominal region). 1 teaspoon every 2 to 3 hours, reducing dosage as cramping and bleeding eases.
2. Melatonin administration inhibited uterine contractions after a drug induces contractions was given to mice. We do not know if this effect occurs in people.[352]
3. L-arginine supplementation significantly reduced the number of contractions in women suffering from preterm onset of uterine contractions.[353]

Relaxing During Labor

Relaxation during labor is one of the main factors influencing the perception of and outcome of the birth. A relaxed mother generally (not always) opens, or dilates, quicker than a tense and fearful mother. Submitting oneself to the process of birth is "the work" of labor. I personally find it "work" to relax anytime. I much prefer to be actively doing *something*. There is no "secret" to relaxation. Relaxation is a process of allowing the tension held in the body's muscles to leave.

Lifestyle/Dietary Recommendations:

1. Eat lightly and drink regularly during labor to avoid hunger which makes it harder to relax.
2. Practice relaxing on a daily basis during pregnancy so the act will be natural and happen readily during labor.
3. A soothing lavender bath can be very helpful for promoting relaxation.

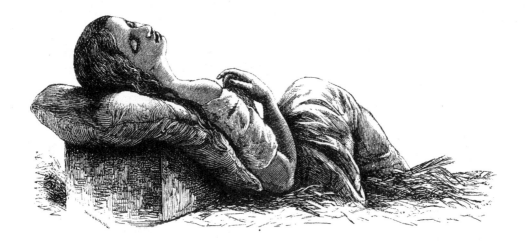

Rigid Cervix

The cervix is the opening of the uterus which stretches to allow the baby to pass through for birth. The softening and thinning-out process of the cervix prior to or during labor is called effacement. The stretching or opening of the cervix is referred to as dilatation or dilation of the cervix. The cervix must dilate to 10 centimeters (called complete dilation) to allow baby to be born. If mom's cervix is not softening and thinning out, feels rigid or inelastic or if mom has had a tear in her cervix before due to a lack of elasticity, the following measures may be helpful.

Lifestyle/Dietary Recommendations:

1. A very warm tub bath (only if the membranes have not ruptured) with a few drops of lavender oil may help mom relax to allow her body to work efficiently.
2. A change of position or moving to another room may give mom a fresh outlook.
3. My personal physician recently told me after Ellie's birth (and my extension of a previous tear in my cervix) that next time I should try massaging my cervix during early labor just as one would do perineal massage on the perineum during the pushing stage of labor. Since evening primrose oil encourages softening and opening, I planned to squeeze the oil from several capsules of the oil and massage my cervix during early labor the next time. With the assistance of my physician, we gently stripped back my membranes from my cervix and massaged the inner portion of my cervix prior to labor. When labor began in earnest, I sank into a warm tub of water and stayed there until around 8 cm. As usual, I experienced a "stall" at 9 cm for about four hours. During that time, we did not do much massage on the cervix until just a "lip" was left which my midwife gently pushed back as I pushed through a contraction. This process was gentle and no further laceration of the cervix occurred even though my Zeb weighed a whopping 9 lbs., 4 oz., a full pound and 2 ounces bigger than my previous biggest baby.
4. Pray for a gentle opening of the "gate" through which baby will arrive.

Uterine Infection

A uterine infection in the immediate post-partum period is called a pueperal infection. The two major risk factors for postpartum infection are cesarean section and lower socioeconomic status. Other risk factors such as prolonged labor, prolonged rupture of membranes, frequent vaginal exams during labor or invasive monitoring techniques do not produce consistent infections each time they occur (meaning every mother with prolonged labor does not get an infection; only some do).[354]

Symptoms of a uterine infection include: mom's temperature rises to 100.4 degrees F (37.8 C) in two of the first 10 days after the first 24 hours, foul-smelling lochia, uterine tenderness, chills, achiness and overall malaise. The uterus may be larger than it should be (not reducing in size relative to time of delivery). Mom should contact her caregiver immediately if she begins to manifest any of these symptoms so a culture may be done to determine what organism is responsible. If mom decides to use herbs, she should see some improvement following supplementation in 6 - 12 hours. If she worsens before that or is not healing in the 6 - 12 hours, antibiotic treatment should begin immediately. Any time antibiotics are used, it is a good idea to continue immune-stimulant supplements as well as probiotics ("friendly" bacteria that help keep down the overgrowth of the "unfriendly" bacteria).

Lifestyle/Dietary Recommendations:

1. Practice good hygiene after the birth. Use the perineal wash of mom's choice each time she urinates or has a bowel movement. Change maternity pads at least every 3 hours.
2. Be sure to drink plenty of fluids and continue with the pregnancy diet to ensure nutrition for mom and new baby.
3. Intimate relations with husband should not be resumed until all bleeding (lochia) has stopped.

Nutritional Supplement Recommendations:

1. Echinacea - 500 - 1,000mg every 2 hours throughout waking hours.
2. Astragalus - 500 - 1,000mg every 2 hours.
3. Vitamin C - 1,000mg every 2 hours.
4. Goldenseal may be used - 500mg three to four times daily. Use no more than one week and be certain to supplement with acidophilus and Inner Strength.™.

PART FIVE

Postpartum Care for Mom and Baby

"Then you shall feed: On her sides shall you be carried,
And be dandled on her knees. As one whom his mother comforts,
So I will comfort you...." Isaiah 66:12,13

Taking Care of Mom After Her Blessing Has Arrived

The immediate postpartum period is designed by God to be a time for family and baby to bond together and mom and baby to get settled into a loving breastfeeding relationship. Our female bodies were designed to need at least a couple of weeks of rest in order to heal from the birth, and it takes a full six weeks for the uterus and cervix to "shrink" (involute) back to their non-pregnant size. Most maternal care givers recommend that mom stay in bed with baby for the entire first week of baby's life. The bathroom should be the longest journey mom takes in that first week. I have found that remaining in my nightgowns all week prevents me from the temptation to do more than I should. Mom can get dressed that second week and begin getting out of bed to eat with the rest of the family and sit up during the day. Heavy lifting (i.e., heavy is anything bigger than baby!) should be avoided until at least six weeks postpartum and then gradually resumed. This allows mom to rebuild muscular integrity to support the uterus, bladder and rectal wall.

Some women feel so well after their baby is born that they immediately jump back into their daily routine of caring for other children, cleaning house, cooking meals, homeschooling, working in the family business, etc. While most of us would view this bounce back to everyday life a blessing (and feeling well *is* a tremendous blessing), when we step outside God's physical plan for our bodies, we reap the physical consequences of heavier vaginal bleeding, increased risk of breast infection, higher risk of losing structural support of uterus, bladder and rectum because of heavy lifting, and the loss of a precious time with baby that will never be regained.

Dad needs time to get acquainted with his new child as well. If dad is able to take vacation time from his job, it is a blessing to him and the rest of the family if he plans to take it upon arrival of baby. We have found that this allows my husband an opportunity to get to know our baby, help care for me as I rest in bed and gives the older children special time with dad that helps make up for limited time with mommy. One of mine and Keith's most special reasons for choosing homebirth is being able to roll over after the birth in my bed, snuggle next to my husband with our new baby in between us and sleep for a day.

Uterine Massage and Bleeding

Once the placenta has been delivered, fundal massage (massaging from the top of the uterus down toward the cervix) should be done every ten minutes for the first couple of hours after the birth. This helps expel any clots that may be forming on the site where the placenta was located. These clots need to be removed by massage because some can form that are large enough to block the cervix. The initial bleeding associated with placental delivery should slow down so that mom should not feel any flow of blood while lying down (there will be a small flow as that associated with a menstrual cycle, but mom should not feel blood flowing out of the vagina).

It is common for some blood to collect while mom is lying down that will flow as she rises from the bed for a bathroom trip. The amount expelled at bathroom visits should be no more than occurs during the menstrual cycle. Any flow of blood that mom feels should be followed by fundal massage to ensure the uterus is firm and clamped down. Periodic checks on the uterus should be performed for the first twenty-four hours. It is a good idea for mom to massage the uterus in a downward motion during bathroom trips to expel clots that may have formed. A frequently nursing baby will aid in keeping the uterus firm and contracting. As baby suckles at mom's breast, the pituitary releases the hormone oxytocin that stimulates contraction of the uterus.

Mom's caregiver should be called back to the home or to the hospital room immediately if the flow of blood is soaking a menstrual pad (or its equivalent) in a thirty-minute time period. See instructions for Hemorrhage to ascertain what measures are to be taken while waiting for the caregiver to arrive.

Bleeding immediately after birth is usually bright red with a flow similar to a menstrual period. This blood is made up of blood from the placental site, the endometrium (lining) of the uterus, and amniotic fluid. Sometimes mom may see "stringy" bits of the amniotic sac that were torn away when the bag of waters broke. This is normal. After the first few days, bleeding will turn to a pinkish-brown discharge eventually fading to clear yellow. Any renewed bright red bleeding occurring after discharge has turned pinkish-brown signals that mom is doing too much. Mom may find this to be a nuisance because she wants to get back to her "normal" life; however, renewed bleeding is a sign of excess stress on her body. She should heed this signal and rest. Her "normal" life will still be there several weeks later. Baby's first few weeks will not be.

The odor of postpartum bleeding and discharge is similar to menstrual flow. If a bad odor or continued bright red bleeding occurs, a uterine infection or retained placental products may be present. Mom should contact her care provider immediately while beginning the guidelines listed under Uterine Infection (please read this section to find out how to avoid a uterine infection).

Perineal Care

Hopefully, perineal massage and a gentle delivery has allowed mom to avoid an epiosiotomy or tear. If delivery was very fast and a tear has occurred, the following measures may be observed:

Perineal Rinse - Each time mom uses the toilet, she should rinse off or spray the perineal area using a peri-bottle with a solution of Betadine, Phisoderm, or for those desiring a more natural alternative, a Tea Tree Rinse (1 - 2 drops of Tea Tree Oil added to warm water in peri-bottle). For moms with stitches or large tears, another perineal rinse is the Comfrey Rinse:

> 1 ounce of comfrey leaves, cut and sifted
> 1 ounce of Echinacea plant, cut and sifted
> 1 pinch of goldenseal

Bring the above herbs to a slow boil in one quart of water. Turn off heat and let steep one hour. Store in refrigerator and use as perineal rinse with each bathroom visit. This rinse may be used as an herbal compress by soaking sterile gauze and applying to the lacerated or stitched area.

Lavender Bath - A recent study concluded that the perineal area of mothers who bathed in a bath to which drops of lavender oil had been added healed much quicker than mothers who did not bathe in the lavender. I added 5 to 7 drops of lavender oil to 8 inches of very warm bath water with my last babies. This was a relaxing and healing to my sore vaginal area (I did not tear, but my tissue was tender).

Light therapy - If mom has torn or been stitched, sitting with bottom up in the sunlight (in a window not facing the neighbors, of course) for 15 to 30 minutes several times daily increases circulation to the area as well as acting as an astringent and drying the area. If mom has no windows she can use, a 40 to 60 watt light bulb may be held one foot from her bottom for 10 to 15 minutes for similar results.

Keep Knees Together - Tailor sitting is beneficial before baby arrives, but definitely not helpful if you have lacerations or stitches. It is of utmost importance to stay in a reclining or semi-reclining position with knees together until healing of perineal tissue is underway. This allows the tissue to knit back together as it was before and prevents stitches from coming undone; re-stitching may not be possible.

Kegel, Kegel, Kegel - Starting the day after baby is born, mom should begin Kegel exercises to strengthen her PC muscle. This muscle supports and "holds up" mom's internal structures, so it must be strong. Exercising the PC muscle also helps hold together any tissue that has torn until healing can occur. Mom should work up to 200 Kegels per day every day for the rest of her life!! This exercise is essential to good muscle tone in the vagina. A strong PC muscle will hold the bladder and rectal wall in their places and not allow them to protrude (as in a cystocele or rectocele) into the vagina. Kegels to strengthen the PC muscle will hold the uterus in its designated position rather than allowing the uterus to fall down or even out of the vagina due to poor muscle tone.

Bathroom Habits and Hygiene

Mom will need to be meticulous in hygiene practices while urinating and having bowel movements to prevent pathogens from traveling up the urethra or into the vagina up into the uterus. Mom should not wipe after pottying for the first three days; instead, she should use her peri-bottle to rinse off her bottom and pat herself dry. After these first few days, she can begin again to wipe from front to back after urinating or having a bowel movement.

Empty the bladder completely and often. In the first few days after birth, mom's body will be eliminating all of the fluid she stored up in preparation for the birth. She will likely experience profuse perspiration and need many potty trips.

Change feminine pads at least every two to three hours even if bleeding is minimal. Mom should wear cotton underpants since natural fibers allow moisture to evaporate, thereby reducing infection risk.

Symptoms necessitating mom contact care provider:

- Temperature that stays above 99 F. Some moms experience a slightly elevated temperature right after birth due to dehydration or on the second or third day when the milk comes in.
- Pulse rate over 100 per minute. If rest does not decrease pulse rate and it is associated with an elevated temperature, an infection may be present.
- Uterine or abdominal pain not associated with after-birth pains.
- Foul-smelling discharge. The smell of mom's lochia may be strong to her in the first few days, but a strong smell is not necessarily a bad smell. On the other hand, a putrid odor signals infection.
- Flu-like symptoms. If these body aches, chills and a possible fever are combined with a hard, red lump on the breast that is painful, mom may have a breast infection (also called mastitis). Rest, moist heat and frequent nursing are the best treatments for this condition.

BABY CARE IN THE IMMEDIATE POSTPARTUM PERIOD

Baby is now here, soft and wrinkled and warm. Baby should be immediately brought up to mom's chest, skin-to-skin, with towels over her to keep her warm. Mom's breast should be offered to baby in the first few minutes after the birth as this helps the uterus to clamp down and slow mom's bleeding. If baby is not interested in nursing just yet, be patient. Little ones sometimes need about ten minutes to get used to their new surroundings before they want to nurse.

Sometime in the first hour or two after the birth, baby should be looked over thoroughly. The birth attendant will be checking for the following:

Color - Newborns generally look very pink, almost purple immediately after birth due to blood flow during the birthing process. The birth attendant will want to make sure baby is "pink-ing" up nicely if baby was a little blue or grey at delivery. Sometimes, it may take a day or two for baby's hands and feet to get rid of a blue-ish tinge when baby is cold. Within the next couple of days, this very pink color will fade into a lighter skin tone. All babies have this light skin tone regardless of race. Melanin, which gives skin its color, will become active after birth and give baby her natural skin tone within several days or weeks. Babies of color (not of Caucasian parents) usually have a blue area, Mongolian spots, that resembles a little butterfly over the base of the spine and across the lower back. This is the beginning of true skin color. Baby may look slightly yellowish on the third day (see Jaundice). Some babies, especially those a little bit early have a white, creamy covering called vernix caseosa that has helped keep baby's skin moist. This vernix does not need to be washed off; rather, mom can massage it into baby's skin during their after-birth herbal bath.

Birthmarks - Any birthmarks will be noted on the newborn exam sheet. Common birthmarks include:
1. "Stork bites" or "Angel kisses" which are red areas usually located at the base of the head, on the forehead, bridge of nose or eyelids. These are caused by dilation of the capillary vessels and minute arteries. They usually fade by the time baby is one year old. Some references report that if they do not fade by three years of age, they may be permanent. My Emily had an "Angel's kiss" on her forehead. It was in a nice V shape. While it had faded by age 5, I can still see it (no one else can) especially when she cries;
2. Strawberry mark which appears in the first six weeks as a bright red spot. These marks can increase in size until baby is one year old but will usually fade by the

teen years. I have one of these on the inner part of my lower thigh in the shape of a diamond. I told my husband it is a sign he got a "priceless jewel" for a wife;

3. Port wine stains which are red-to-purple spots that can occur anywhere. They are usually very dark and prominent. They are not a common birth mark. Betty Peckman in her book *Christian Midwifery* tells of a cure that sounds very odd; however, she says it does work: Mom should lick the stain after each of baby's baths until the stain fades or disappears. She tells of personally seeing this cure take place, so it sounds as though it is worth a try (even though it sounds weird).

Head - The attendant will check baby's anterior and posterior fontanels (soft spots). The anterior fontanel located above the forehead on the top of the head will close at 12 to 18 months. The posterior fontanel located on the back of the head will close in 6 to 8 weeks. Sometimes, the posterior fontanel will be closed in "overdue" babies. The cranial bones may appear to be overlapped across the suture lines (the bone lines betweeen the fontanels and across the occiput in a Y shape) right after the birth since baby's head molds to fit through the birth canal. This overlapping will subside in a day or two. If baby's head is very pointed from molding after the birth, it may take several days to round out, but be assured it will. My husband thought our first daughter's head looked like a razorback hog's head when she appeared on the perineum because the skin on her head was a wrinkled ridge. This "ironed" out within an hour or two. Baby's head may appear to rest right on top of her shoulders. The neck is usually very short and hidden in folds of skin. Baby's hair will be wet from the amniotic fluid. If the amniotic fluid was stained with meconium, baby's hair may be colored as well. This will wash out in the herbal bath. Because the hair is wet, it may look a darker color than baby will actually have later.

Eyes - Baby's eyes normally will be open as she takes in her surroundings and finally sees mom and dad. Attendants will check for any drainage or swelling around the eyes. Most care-providers are required by law to administer eye care (or eye prophylaxis) to baby in the form of antibiotic ointment in hopes of protecting baby from any undiscovered sexually-transmitted disease mom may have. Parents may refuse this by signing or writing a statement to withhold eye care from baby in some states.

Genitals - Baby's genitals are usually enlarged at birth. If baby was born breech, the genital area may be bruised. This is especially so with little boys. Little girls may even have a blood-tinged discharge in the first week after birth, also related to breech birth. This is normal. The enlargement and discharge is a result of mom's hormones circulating in baby's system. The breasts of little girls may be enlarged as well and will sometimes even leak a few drops of "milk."

Circulation - The birth attendant will check for any squeaks, whistles or whooshing sounds during the heartbeat to rule out developmental problems. Baby should appear pink and have no "extra" sounds during the heartbeat. Blue extremities combined with the above sounds signal a problem, and baby should be evaluated by her doctor immediately, especially if the problem worsens as baby cries or moves her arms or legs.

Breathing - Baby's breathing pattern will be irregular during her first 24 hours. There may be shallow breathing with deep breathing mixed in and even short periods of apnea (no breathing for a very short time, then "catch-up" quick, short breaths which end in a deep breath). Baby should be next to mom in bed so mom will know if baby has long or frequent periods of apnea that need to be checked out. Newborns generally breathe 30 to 60 breaths per minute. If the amniotic fluid was stained with meconium, the attendant should make certain there are no "rubs" (rubbing sounds as baby takes in a breath) when listening to the lungs. Many times when baby is "gurgle-y," breastfeeding and being in the warm herbal bath with mom will clear out any fluid from the lungs.

Urination - The number of wet diapers should be noted by parents or caregiver. Baby should urinate during her first day and be having at least 6 to 8 wet diapers after mom's milk comes in. Urine should be clear or pale yellow.

Bowel Movements - Baby's first bowel movements (for two to three days) will be meconium. Meconium is composed of bile, waste blood cells, waste or dead cells from her time in utero and digested amniotic fluid. It looks like tar and is the consistency of tar. Mom should apply unpetroleum jelly to baby's bottom before she has a bowel movement to prevent the meconium from sticking to her delicate skin. Meconium is hard to wash off. Mom may also want to hold off on dressing baby in her prettiest outfit until the meconium stools have given way to nice, yellow breast-fed baby stools.

Attendants should thoroughly check baby's mouth, nose, ears, neck, abdomen, extremities, spine, anus and neurological signs for anything that may need medical attention. Mom's birth attendants will help mom get started with breastfeeding baby and make sure baby is nursing well. More about the breastfeeding relationship can be found in Part 6.

Baby will most likely spend much of her time sleeping. Most newborns sleep from 16 to 20 hours a day. It is common for baby to breastfeed then take a long nap after the birth. Mom and dad should take advantage of this and rest after the labor of birth. Baby should be placed on her side to sleep. This position is natural for babies who are sleeping Babies sleeping on their tummies have a higher risk of SIDS (sudden infant death syndrome) as well as increasing the risk of baby getting stuck face down unable to turn head to breathe. Babies sleeping on their back may breathe fluid in if they spit up in this position. Attendants will likely stay with mom and dad for two to three hours after the birth, but this should not stop these new parents from getting much needed rest with baby. In cases where baby was slow to get started breathing and nursing or if mom had any complications such as a hemorrhage, the attendants should stay for at least six hours to ensure all is well before leaving.

The American Red Cross recommends that if baby spits up, turns pale or bluish and begins to gasp or swallow repeatedly or cease breathing, mom or dad should immediately turn baby on her side at a 45 degree angle with her head lower than her feet. The back should be patted firmly and mouth and nose suctioned out thoroughly, if needed. Panic is counterproductive to taking care of baby quickly. An infant CPR course is an excellent idea for parents-to-be to give them the knowledge necessary to take care of baby in an emergency.

Danger Signs

Serious physiological problems in baby are rare occurrences; however, it is prudent for parents to be aware of warning signals. If any of the following is observed in the baby, the pediatrician should be called:

- Extreme paleness (white) or blue-coloring of the skin and mucous membranes. This may begin in the extremities.
- Blueness around the mouth or of the nail beds after baby is 24 hours old.
- Shrill, high-pitched, shrieking crying not associated with hunger, wet or "poop-y" diaper, diaper pin stick or need for comfort.
- Eyes rolling up or down. (Baby's eyes will normally roll around a bit, look cross-eyed until she is several months old and has good muscle control.)
- Convulsions.
- Grunting or other difficulty breathing, chest retractions - pulling of the skin in between the ribs and at the base of the rib cage.
- Refusal to nurse for longer than 6 hours in the first few days.
- Repeated projectile vomiting. This is different than spitting up. Projectile means it projects forcefully out from baby.

Blocked Tear Duct

A blocked tear duct in baby will cause baby's eyes to appear runny or dry and matted. This condition can occur as a "side effect" of newborn eye prophylaxis when the caregiver uses silver nitrate. Silver nitrate has been replaced by the antibiotic erythromycin as the less-irritating choice for newborn eye care.

The parent's goal is to unclog the blockage. This is accomplished by gently massaging the inside corner of the eye, the tear duct, as well as using the herbal eyewashes recommended under the heading Eye Care. If mom and dad do not see improvement within a day or two, medical assistance should be sought immediately. If baby has a gonorrheal infection in the eye, permanent blindness can result without antibiotic treatment.

Colic

The term colic is used to describe baby's crying due to abdominal cramps and gas. Mom will recognize colic by observing: baby cries and mom has ruled out a wet or poopy diaper, hunger, need for closeness, or being too cold or too hot; baby pulls legs in jerky movements up to stomach; baby passes gas; baby has nursed recently. Colic may occur more often in children with allergies. This makes it especially important for mom to avoid foods that she is allergic to during her pregnancy as she can pass on these particular allergies to baby if she insists on eating those foods during the prenatal period.

Lifestyle/Dietary Recommendations:

1. Be certain to burp baby after he nurses. Some babies need to be burped in the middle of nursing; others do not burp much at all. If baby is having a problem with gas, taking time to burp baby may be helpful.
2. Cut back on gas-forming foods in mom's diet: dairy products, cauliflower, cabbage, broccoli, beans that haven't been soaked well, carbonated juices or sodas, caffeine, chocolate, spicy foods, onions and garlic. I hesitate to mention garlic on this list because recent studies have shown that babies actually nursed better when mothers added garlic to their diet. Mom can eliminate these foods for a few days and reintroduce them one at a time to see if baby has a reaction.
3. Eliminate all foods to which mom is allergic; baby may be allergic to them, too.
4. Gently moving baby's legs towards the abdomen in a bicycling motion may help the gas to pass. Mom should never force baby's leg upwards if it does not move there easily.
5. Holding baby like a football, head down (make sure baby's head is supported with face to the side so baby can breathe), may help some babies calm down and ease tummy cramps.

Nutritional Supplement Recommendations:

1. Catnip and fennel tea (with NO HONEY added - honey may cause botulism in babies whose digestive systems are not equipped to handle the botulism spores) or a TincTract™ (glycerine-based liquid herb processed in three stages) of catnip and fennel has been very helpful for many families dealing with colicky babies. Baby only needs a very small amount - 1 to 2 drops. This may cause baby to relax enough to fall asleep. Mom need not be alarmed, instead, she should take a nap also.
2. The tummy-friendly **TumEase**™ by Mother's Choice™ contains peppermint, catnip, fennel, marshmallow, Oregon grape, licorice and ginger. These herbs have documented digestive functions in alleviating intestinal cramping and aiding the passage of gas. 1 to 2 drops is usually sufficient.

3. Mom may want to drink chamomile tea while nursing. It is far better to begin with mom taking the digestive supplements mentioned above or drinking the chamomile tea as she nurses to see if this helps before progressing to giving them to baby.

Cradle Cap

Cradle cap is caused by overproductive sweat and oil glands on the scalp. It is the common name for seborrheic dermatitis. Mom may notice that baby has areas of build-up that look dry or oily, flaky and crusty. Some babies even develop cradle cap behind the ears. Cradle cap is not dangerous for baby and does not necessarily need treatment as long as mom bathes baby regularly and washes the scalp. Mom need not be afraid of washing over baby's fontanel (soft spot) as long as she does not apply downward pressure to the fontanel (pushing in very hard).

Lifestyle/Dietary Recommendations:
1. Wash baby's head at least every other day to remove flaky build-up.
2. If simple washing does not take care of the problem, mom may massage olive oil onto baby's scalp before bed and comb build-up out during the morning bath.
3. Mom should make certain she is following the whole food diet with an emphasis on foods rich in essential fatty acids: deep-sea fish, nuts and seeds.

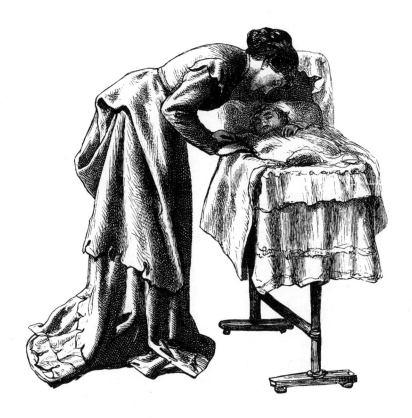

Diaper Rash

Diaper rash is a condition most of us have seen or treated at some time on somebody's bottom. Diaper rash may be mild with a pink to red rash on bottom or severe with baby's bottom being fiery red and oozing from open lesions. Rashes may occur from the waste products in urine and feces, yeast, allergy to something mom is eating, or sensitivity to plastic products (disposable diapers or plastic diaper covers). It is best to begin treatment as soon as a rash is discovered.

Health care providers now believe it to be unnecessary to powder baby's bottom at each diaper change. In fact, using baby powders inappropriately (shaking onto baby's bottom instead of into mom's hand away from baby) may cause the powder to be inhaled by mom and baby. This powder inhalation results in lung irritation. Using cornstarch in lieu of commercial powders is not a good alternative either. Cornstarch can cause a yeast diaper rash to spread rapidly (putting a tiny bit of cornstarch onto rash if mom suspects yeast is a good at-home test; if it is yeast, the cornstarch will cause a major spread of the rash).

Lifestyle/Dietary Recommendations:

1. Change diapers frequently.
2. Avoid foods to which baby's bottom reacts.
3. Launder baby's clothes with natural or mild soap instead of heavy-duty detergents. Rinse clothes and diapers twice.
4. Avoid disposable diapers if baby is consistently red from using them.
5. Avoid plastic diaper covers. There are many good cotton or wool covers available.

Nutritional Supplement Recommendations:

1. If mom wants to put something on baby's bottom for protection, there are several natural alternatives to lotions or petroleum jelly: cold-pressed oils, unpetroleum jelly and natural baby creams.
2. I have found the Chamomile Concentrate by ChamoCare to be quite effective in healing bottom rashes. Applied directly to the skin with a Q-tip may sting baby's skin if the bottom is inflamed. Two to three drops in baby's bath water is much more pleasant for baby and just as healing.
3. Aloe vera gel is great for a mild rash. Just open a leaf and spread gel onto bottom. Commercial gel preparations usually have citric acid in them that stings baby's already irritated bottom.
4. Soothing Salve Drops by Mother's Choice™ may be applied directly to the bottom.
5. Plantain leaves are healing to the skin and may be put fresh in the diaper or soaked in hot water (and cooled before placing on baby's skin) and placed in the diaper for a healing poultice.

6. There are some commercial preparations that have been used successfully containing goldenseal, comfrey, calendula, plantain and other healing herbs. These may be applied with each diaper change.

7. If the rash is caused by an overgrowth of yeast, mom should supplement her diet with garlic and echinacea to stimulate immune response. She should also add some probiotic supplements as well (*lactobacillus acidophilus, bifidobacterium bifidus,* etc.).

8. For yeast rashes, mom can apply ointments containing goldenseal, rinse baby's bottom in apple-cider vinegar and/or apply plain, unflavored yogurt with live culture to baby's bottom.

Eye Care

Most hospitals, physicians and yes, even midwives, administer prophylactic eye care to newborn infants. The reason behind this is to hopefully prevent an infection in baby's eyes from mom's presumed sexually-transmitted disease (gonorrhea, chlamydia, etc.). Eye prophylaxis is a treatment health professionals are required by law to perform in most states; however, if mom and dad feel strongly about refusing eye care (mom is absolutely positive she tests negative for STDs or for religious reasons), they should investigate the possibility of signing a waiver to decline this procedure. For those parents who may choose to decline eye prophylaxis, I have included the natural measures parents may take if they want to at least do something to pacify their caregiver or reassure themselves. I would like to add that in the presence of one of these STDs, baby is at risk for permanent blindness. Parents should also be aware that if mom does have an STD, one application at birth only is not going to cure the problem.

Nutritional Supplement Recommendations:

1. An eye wash of goldenseal and eyebright is a standard for any eye infections. Simmer one-half ounce of eyebright and one-half ounce of goldenseal root (the powder is very fine and will not filter well) for eight hours. Strain out with cheesecloth or an unbleached coffee filter (do not use a washcloth as the goldenseal will stain it yellow). This strong tea may be frozen for use within a month or refrigerated for use within three days.
2. Many mothers simply express colostrum, baby's first food, from the breast into the eyes to treat or prevent eye infections. Simple water helps with simple eye irritation.

Fussy Baby

Most fussy babies get labeled with the term "colic." Baby may indeed have colic if crying is associated with jerky leg movements toward abdomen and gas that occurs within 30 minutes after nursing. If this is the case, see Colic. Whatever the case, babies always have a reason for crying. These reasons include hunger, being too hot or too cold, gas, uncomfortable clothes or they just may need to be held and cuddled, and, as they grow older, boredom and because it elicits a response in mom or dad. The newborn period is not the time to teach baby to be independent. These precious creations from God are totally needy at birth. They depend on us as parents to provide their food, keep them dry, warm, and comfortable. They are completely dependent on us for love and affection. Cuddling or holding babies often during this period of their growth will not spoil them or mean that they are ruling us; rather, it will mean that we, as parents, are being responsible for the gift that God has blessed us with by providing our arms as safety and comfort as our Creator does for us.

Baby has been embraced within mom's womb for nine months. The womb is dark, warm and snug. It may take a little time for baby to adapt to light, as well as the new feeling of perhaps insecurity due to the new environment. There is no reason baby should not be embraced within mom's arms now instead of her womb. Mom can and should take time while she herself is recuperating from the birth to draw her baby to her breast, snuggling baby next to her body. Dad can help by rocking baby, jigging baby on his shoulder, walking with baby or bathing baby in nice warm water while mom takes a nice soothing bath herself. Mom might even elect to include baby in her bath. Mom and dad may also choose to take turns "wearing" baby by using an over-the-shoulder baby holder that has been shown in studies and everyday practice by moms to decrease fussiness. I've never been able to use these myself as they make my babies fussy due to their mother's short stature squishing them in the sling.

A fussy baby can cause mom and dad to feel more frustration than appreciation of this gift of God at times. Mom and dad can be assured that their newborn is not crying or being fussy to manipulate them; rather, this particular baby has a great need to be held closely for longer periods than some other babies they may have observed. Since both mom and dad will be expending a great amount of energy taking care of baby, house and business, their diets need to continue to conform to the whole foods pregnancy diet and prenatal supplements. I feel compelled to add that this sacrifice of lifestyle will only last a short time period. Baby will soon be older and more able to wait for gratification. Fussiness in newborns generally arises from some need or physical problem.

Jaundice

Jaundice occurs when the liver's detoxifying process (breaking down blood cells, hormones, other body chemicals) is deficient. In physiologic jaundice, which usually occurs around the third day postpartum, this is believed to be caused by liver immaturity or intestinal immaturity. The excess red blood cells which have accumulated in baby before and during birth are no longer needed. Jaundice appears when the red blood cells are incompletely broken down by the liver and released into the bloodstream, or they may be incompletely eliminated in the intestinal tract which causes reabsorption in the bloodstream. When bilirubin, a by-product of this red blood cell breakdown, is released or reabsorbed into the bloodstream, it causes the skin and whites of the eyes to look yellow. Normal bilirubin levels are 5% to 9%. A rise up to 14% is not uncommon. Physiologic jaundice which causes this mild rise in bilirubin levels occurs in as many as 50% to 70% of newborn infants. Symptoms are: yellow skin color, yellow whites of eyes, and elevated bilirubin levels. A baby with "normal" physiologic jaundice is active and breastfeeds well.

A rise of bilirubin above 16% is cause for concern. This could be due to incompatible blood types of mom/dad/baby, drug use by mom, or a damaged or malformed liver. This type of jaundice, pathological jaundice, occurs in the first week of life, often in the first day, and causes baby to be lethargic and dehydrated because of refusal to nurse in addition to being yellow, almost orange, all the way to the palms of the hands and soles of the feet.. Medical care should be sought immediately as brain damage can occur with bilirubin levels above 20% for more than a 24-hour period.

A very rare form of jaundice is Jaundice of Late-Onset, sometimes labeled as "breast-milk jaundice." It occurs when high levels of a particular hormone (present in only 100 - 200 women) is difficult for baby's liver to process or breakdown. This type of jaundice has a late onset (10 - 14 days after the birth) and baby has symptoms similar to physiologic jaundice. There is no evidence that weaning is of benefit to baby.

Lifestyle/Dietary Recommendations:

1. As always, prevention is the best avenue to pursue. Mom's prenatal diet should consist of whole foods: grains, leafy greens, legumes, raw fruits and veggies and meat in small quantities if desired. Dark, leafy greens are cleansing to the liver and help mom grow a baby whose liver is capable of processing the extra red blood cells.

2. Drugs during the pregnancy and labor should be avoided unless the benefit outweighs the risk. Pitocin, a drug used to initiate or augment labor, is known to increase bilirubin levels. Any drug mom receives requires more work for the baby's liver since the liver breaks this toxin down for elimination from baby's body.

3. Baby should be nursed frequently during the first week. This helps to bring mom's milk in quicker, provides hydration which aids in cleansing bilirubin, and stimulates the liver to process and direct elimination of excess red blood cells. Schedules, whatever mom and dad may plan to implement later, are not appropriate for baby's first six weeks.
4. Expose baby to indirect natural lighting (sunlight) several times daily. Mom can do this by placing her rocking chair (or whatever is available) near the window to nurse two to three times daily.

Nutritional Supplement Recommendations:
1. Mom may want to supplement her diet in the last few weeks of pregnancy and her first week postpartum with milk thistle. Milk thistle contains silymarin which has been shown to protect and enhance the function of the liver. What mom eats or drinks while pregnant or breastfeeding, baby will benefit from also. Three tablets or capsules daily containing at least 70% silymarin.
2. Dandelion is another herb well-known for its mild liver-stimulating properties. 2, 450mg capsules daily.

Thrush

Thrush is caused by the organism *Candida albicans*, better known as "yeast." Symptoms of thrush include: red gums or inside cheeks of mouth; small patches of cottage-cheese-like curds on baby's tongue, gums or the inside of the cheeks; fussiness while trying to nurse. The recommendations which follow are for both mom and baby. The nipple of mom's breast and baby's mouth both need to be treated to eliminate the yeast entirely. Persistence and perseverance are necessary as it takes several days to stop the yeast over-growth and replace beneficial organisms.

Lifestyle/Dietary Recommendations:

1. Biblical hygiene standards are a must: wash hands after eliminating, changing baby's diaper, touching baby's mouth or mom's nipples; and throw items used to treat thrush (example - cotton swabs) in the garbage.
2. Mom should increase garlic in food. Baby's like breastmilk after mom eats garlic; yeast organisms do not.

Nutritional Supplement Recommendations:

1. White oak bark tea may be used as a wash for baby's mouth and mom's nipples. Decoct 1/2 to 1 ounce of the bark in 1 1/2 pints of boiling water; simmer 10 to 15 minutes. Cool and apply with cotton swab to inside of baby's mouth and mom's nipples after each feeding.
2. Other herbs that may be prepared as the above tea and used in a similar manner are: bilberry, cedar berry, elecampane, and fennel.
3. The herb Mathake (Tropical Almond), *Terminalia catappa*, produces a pleasant-tasting tea that has powerful anti-fungal activity, particularly on *Candida albicans*.[355] The tea of this herb may be prepared the same as the above teas and applied in the same fashion. It may be used up to three months at a time.
4. Oral supplements for mom should include: Echinacea (1000-2000mg daily), Garlic (equivalent to two to three cloves daily), Pau d'Arco (1000mg daily), Grapefruit Seed Extract (1/4 to 1/2 teaspoon daily) and Caprylic acid (2 to 3 tablets or capsules daily).

PART SIX

The Breastfeeding Relationship

"...thou art He that took me out of the womb: thou didst make me hope when I was upon my mother's breasts." Psalm 22:9

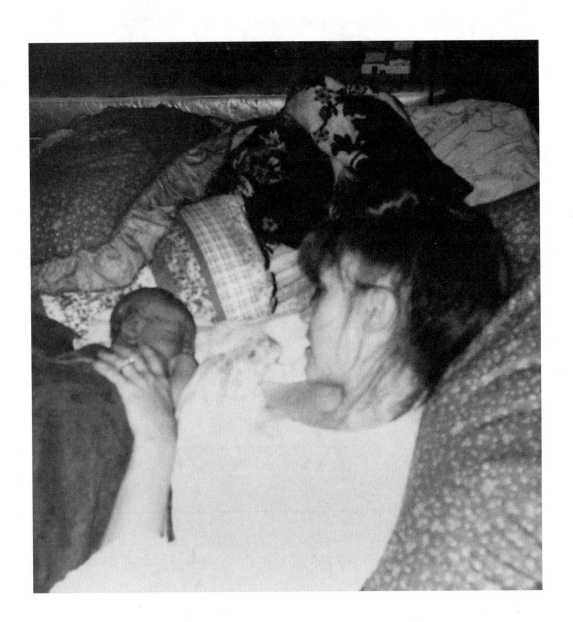

Breastfeeding the New Baby

This chapter of the book will address the beginning of the breastfeeding relationship between dad, mom and baby. The following chapters will discuss the growing child's breastfeeding needs and the weaning process. I enter into this area with a firm understanding of the physiological needs of the newborn/infant stage (birth to six - nine months), yet it is with some concern that I address the additional issues of emotional needs, spiritual needs of the newborn for I know that there is a great divisive wall separating Believer from Believer on the issue of Scheduling versus Responsive Breastfeeding. It is not my intention to accuse mothers who schedule of being poor mothers or poor followers of the Lord nor is it my intention to accuse mothers who wholly give themselves to breastfeeding and pacifying their children with their breasts that they are poor spiritual leaders of their babies. My hope and prayer is that each father and mother will prayerfully consider all the information available on the subject of breastfeeding and go to the Word of the Almighty God to receive their instruction on how to nourish and nurture their tiny blessings from Him who created them. It is not obedience to God to follow man's or man's ministries' advice. It is obedience to follow God's word and to listen (while praying for our spirit's protection by the Holy Spirit) to the counsel of godly men and women. There is no man or woman who is totally right in what they do, say or write, including this author. The Parker way of breastfeeding is what works for the Parkers. The Smiths may find a better way for their family.

The basic physiologic need is for sustenance, and God has conveniently provided sustenance right on mom's body that is absolutely perfect for baby. Breastfeeding has many benefits for the family: baby's healthier, happier, smarter; mom's healthier, happier, skinnier; dad's just glad mom looks great and baby's healthy. Many book sources discuss the benefits to baby of breastfeeding. This book will address the benefits to mom:

- Breastfeeding causes the uterus to contract and return to normal size more quickly after birth.
- The fat stores that pregnancy planted on the backs of mom's arms, thighs, buttocks and belly will be used to provide fuel for baby's meals rather than just sitting there.
- Nursing the baby will allow much-needed rest time for mom as she recovers from the labor of birth. Many maternal care providers say that the female body requires a year to completely recover from a birth.
- The time of amenorrhea associated with sole breastfeeding, no other food supplements, provides mom with natural child spacing.

Many women love the idea of the first three benefits, yet balk at the fourth, natural child spacing, because it implies we are trying to control what is God's province, birth. I have a concern about this type of thinking. I've seen women wean their babies so that God could bless them with another child because they weren't having as many children as the Jones family. Now that seems to be the flesh controlling what is God's area.

If God designed the breasts to nourish our babies and provided amenorrhea to coincide with this nourishment, why do we feel the need to say He was wrong in this and wean our babies to have more? This leads to babies not receiving the maximum benefits of breastfeeding, which for health benefits needs to last at least 18 months. Mom won't be nursing every 2-3 hours at 18 months or 12 months of baby's age, but her period of amenorrhea may last that long. This is God's design for the female body. We need not balk. He's still in control, even if we're not pregnant every year or two like some of our friends who have a shorter period of amenorrhea. That is God's design for our friends. Our body may require a longer recovery time after birth than our friend. or we can just realize that God has a different purpose for our friend's life than ours. Yielding to God's lordship is more than how many babies we can have in our fertile years. Yielding implies giving in to His design and control over our life.

Methods of Breastfeeding:

Scheduled Breastfeeding

Scheduled breastfeeding refers to parents who adhere strictly to a schedule of feeding their newborns usually every three to four hours except during the night where they expect them to sleep all night. This method is physiologically based on the needs of a bottle-fed infant, not the breastfed infant. It is promoted by several ministries whose founders/leaders, knowing the child is born with a sin nature, believe the child must *immediately* after birth be brought into submission to the parents by way of enforcing a schedule that meets the parents' desires, not the "demands" of the child. The followers of these ministries believe this is the biblical model of structure and obedience designed by our Creator, often believing it is the only biblical model. The advantages of this method are: parents do not have to alter their life much to meet the needs of the new baby, parents can sleep all night fairly soon after the birth, mom can leave baby for longer periods of time, and dad gets his dinner on time. The disadvantages are: mom's breasts may not reach full potential of providing adequate breastmilk for baby due to lack of demand that leads to lack of supply, baby stays hungry for a couple of hours (breastmilk is digested in 1 and 1/2 hours) howling until she eventually learns a meal will not be provided until mom is ready, or baby may become very ill or die from lack of nourishment medically termed "failure to thrive."

The major advantage promoted by these ministries is training out a child's sin nature. I would submit that the sin nature is not something to be "trained out." It can be brought under the authority and submission of parents until such time of regeneration by the Holy Spirit enabling them to follow Jesus, who frees us from the bondage of that sinful nature. This is not to say that we should not train our young children. I would submit that in the newborn/infant stage, a baby is so new to the world that her cries are not demanding her will over the will of her parents. Rather, those cries are God's gift to parents to let us know of baby's needs. A baby just born, by the mercy of God and His perfect design, has the ability to cry to let parents know when that baby has a need. Although baby may cry sometimes to be held, is this so wrong, to pick up and reassure our newborns of our continued presence and caretaking? As the infant grows, so does the time in which baby may be left to "fuss" while mom makes dinner. Avoiding our newborns as a way of training is not conducive to providing a secure and loving foundation for the parent/child relationship. Our Father has provided us with a strong foundations of love and provision upon which He builds our spiritual growth with training. Can we not provide a similar foundation for training for these blessings from Him?

It is of interest to me that the Bible makes a distinction between brand new converts or followers of Jesus and those who are "grown up" so to speak in maturity and knowledge in the Lord. In the book of Acts, chapter 15, Peter admonishes the council at Jerusalem saying that to expect the new Gentile Believers to follow all of the law of the Torah and make them become circumcised is overly burdensome to them and misleading of their hearts about the grace of the Lord Jesus Christ. It is decided that they will only lay the necessary things upon them as requirements: *abstain from meats offered to idols, and from blood, and from things strangled, and from fornication…*" (Acts 15:29). Did this mean that forever Gentiles could practice sin (the law as a standard of right or righteousness and wrong or sin) by ignoring the law? Paul replies to that question in Romans 6, verse 15, "*God forbid.*" I personally believe this holds true for our brand new babies as well. We must not lay upon them overly burdensome structure or rules. The time will come (all too soon within a few months) when they will begin to exert their will or demands upon us, their parents. At such a time when the rebellious sin nature becomes apparent in their little hearts and when they want what they want when they want it and how they want it (from several months old - it is different with each child), this is the time to begin the training unto submission process. Newborn infants are only able to communicate what they need when they need it.

The major disadvantage I see with this method is the divisiveness caused by its leaders who promote this method of feeding as the *only* biblical method of child training. While I may feel strongly that scheduling is physiologically wrong for newborns and infants until they are at least a couple of months old, I cannot and will not condemn scheduling parents as being sinful in this matter. I do encourage moms and dads to study breastfeeding physiology and God's Word to see how He responds to our needs as a guide for responding to our baby's needs. Anytime someone writes a book or leads a seminar or speaks about God's design and admonishes readers or listeners not to question his advice or practice and not to discuss these ideas with others who disagree, beware. I would encourage anyone interested in following someone's stated idea of the only God's Way to do something to check with that person's church standing to make certain they are willing to submit themselves and their ministry to appropriate church authority.

Demand Feeding

Demand feeding is the method of feeding the baby whenever he wants as long as he wants and wherever he wants. This normally includes nighttime nursing also. Usually parents following the "demand" philosophy continue supplying the same amount of giving throughout the newborn/infant period into later childhood. Many times, those who promote this method of breastfeeding feel that the two-year old child should get his wants met as quickly as a parent would naturally respond to the newborn baby. This method is physiologically sound for mother and infant, not necessarily so for mother and toddler. The advantages of demand feeding are: mom's breasts perfectly adjust to the needs of her infant by supplying what baby's body demands; baby is adequately nourished and satisfied; mom's menstrual cycles are naturally delayed to allow time to get to know her new blessing as well as allows healing and strengthening time before another pregnancy; mom and baby get to know one another well; and because baby usually sleeps with mom and dad, mom and dad get to sleep at night instead of getting up to nurse or dad having to bring baby to mom to nurse. The disadvantages are: parents sometimes give way to the demands of the one-year old as they would and should a one-week old, baby's breastfeeding needs are not always consistent with mom's or dad's desire for other activities, and spoiled children may be yielded due to a lack of discipline on the parents' part to deny their child anything.

The major advantage of demand feeding is that it supports a healthy interaction between mom and baby. Baby suckles at mom's breast as needed, mom's breasts produce more milk for baby, baby grows and thrives in mother's arms. Baby learns through this supply of need that mom and dad give love as needed in the form of physical nourishment. How does dad physically supply this love since it is at mom's breasts baby nurses? He is giving selflessly of his wife for her to meet the needs of this new life God has entrusted him with. He also has a very satisfied infant to cuddle with and bond with after mom has delivered the meal.

The major disadvantage of this method is the propensity of parents with little self-control to neglect training an older child to wait for a momma-meal when he is physically able to wait. I speak as one who has been there. My own lack of self-discipline caused me to have a two-year old I neglected to say "No" to when needed. This resulted in struggling to keep my shirt pulled down in public situations because she thought she ought to get "ninny" when she wanted "ninny." It was at this point that I knew I had stepped over the line into that parental zone of "Don't ever let them cry." This was a fine attitude for her as a newborn who needed to eat. It was not for a willful two-year old. Perhaps if I had let her know that "Wait a minute for Mommy," was okay in her first year, she might not have been so set in her willfulness (by the way, she is a respectful, obedient, very pleasant six-year-old now).

Responsive Breastfeeding

Responsive breastfeeding is a term that has been used by those wishing to make a distinction between being ruled by the growing child's desires and rigidly refusing a newborn's needs. Responsive breastfeeding seems to be identical to demand feeding in the newborn/infant stage, yet it is different in that the method is based on responding to a baby's *needs* and discerning when to say "No" to the growing child's wants. A toddler can be expected to wait until mom finishes directing brother's homeschool phonics lesson. A newborn cannot physiologically wait. A mom responsive to her baby's cues knows when baby just wants to nibble and when baby is hungry. If mom is busy, nibbling can wait, nourishing cannot. The advantages of this methods are the same as those of demand feeding plus mom can know that she is not following another man or woman's interpretation of what is right, rather she can be secure in the knowledge that she is responding to her baby's needs as the Lord consistently responds to our needs, even our needs for self-discipline. The disadvantages are: selflessness to baby is hard for parents to come by in our "Me, me, me" society and parents have to have the self-control and discernment to ascertain the older child's needs from wants and know how to lovingly respond with "You'll just have to wait a few minutes, little one" as he climbs into mom's lap for yet another sip. Parental discipline is more important to child-training than child-discipline.

The major advantage of responsive breastfeeding is establishing a lasting relationship of trust and yes, order, in baby's life. Baby finds his world to be ordered in that when he needs to eat, food is provided, when he is wet, a dry diaper is provided, and when he is frightened, mom's arms and breasts are a comfort to him. How easy it is to trust in one who is there when we need them! How blessed to not have to worry if or when we will eat or be clothed! How love-filled is the one who provides comforting arms when we are hurt, sad or bewildered! Sounds like our Creator, doesn't it?

> *"The Lord is gracious, and full of compassion; slow to anger, and of great mercy. The Lord is good to all: and his tender mercies are over all his works. All thy works shall praise thee, O Lord; and thy saints shall bless thee. They shall speak of the glory of thy kingdom, and talk of thy power; to make known to the sons of men his mighty acts, and the glorious majesty of his kingdom. Thy kingdom is an everlasting kingdom, and thy dominion endureth throughout all generations. The Lord upholdeth all*

that fall, and raiseth up all those that be bowed down. The eyes of all wait upon thee; and thou givest them their meat in due season. Thou openest thine hand, and satisfiest the desire of every living thing. The Lord is righteous in all his ways, and holy in all his works. The Lord is nigh unto all them that call upon him, to all that call upon him in truth. He will fulfill the desire of them that fear him: he also will hear their cry, and will save them." Psalm 145: 8 - 19

Is it not our goal to emulate His love for us in the way we love and care our children? Responsive breastfeeding rightfully imposes on parents responsibility for their children. The parents have to decide according to their discernment what each individual child needs and provide for those needs. These parents do not rely on any expert other than the Lord for knowing their child and responding to that child. This is true parental responsibility. Responsive breastfeeding is not unlike the model of biblical hospitality. A guest may arrive unscheduled during the family dinner hour. We have available food for them to eat, and we can see that they haven't eaten dinner already. Do we graciously offer them a meal or do we deny them because they forgot to schedule this visit?

"For I was ahungered, and ye gave me meat: I was thirsty, and ye gave me drink: I was a stranger, and ye took me in: Naked, and ye clothed me: I was sick, and ye visited me: I was in prison, and ye came unto me. Then shall the righteous answer him, saying, Lord, when saw we thee ahungered, and fed thee? or thirsty, and gave thee drink? When saw we thee a stranger, and took thee in? or naked, and clothed thee? Or when saw we thee sick, or in prison, and came unto thee? And the King shall answer and say unto them, Verily I say unto you, Inasmuch as ye have done it unto one of the least of these my brethren, ye have done it unto me." Matthew 25: 35 - 40

Would we deny our children that which we are expected by the Lord to provide for even strangers? Hospitality begins at the breast.

BREASTFEEDING ANATOMY AND PHYSIOLOGY

by Becky Law, R.N., Certified Lactation Consultant

During pregnancy the breasts take on many changes. They become larger as the alveoli mature and prepare for milk production. The nipple and the area around it known as the areola darken in color. Around the nipple on the areola, the Montgomery glands can be noted. These glands produce oil that inhibits bacteria growth and provides lubrication. Near the end of the pregnancy, the breasts begin making colostrum which is the first milk the baby will receive. The colostrum is golden yellow in color. Colostrum contains antibodies for the baby and is rich in protein and fat; the perfect food for a newborn baby.

Prolactin is the hormone that is released for milk production. The suckling action of the baby's mouth on the mother's areola stimulates the nerve pathways from the nipple to the brain to release prolactin into the bloodstream. In response to the release of prolactin, the alveolar cells make milk. Each time the baby nurses, the prolactin level rises creating the demand and supply principle off breastfeeding. It is not hormones, however, that regulate the supply of breastmilk; rather, it is the quantity and quality of infant suckling. A common adage that expresses this concept is "The more the mother breastfeeds, the more milk there will be."[356]

In response to the baby nursing, the hormone oxytocin is released. Oxytocin causes the "let down" or milk ejection reflex. The cells around the alveoli contract causing the secreted milk to be ejected into the milk ducts and move down to the lactiferous sinuses. The sinuses are little holding tanks for the milk. As the baby compresses them with suckling, the milk is obtained through several nipple openings. The oxytocin level remains elevated during the nursing session.

Another important function of oxytocin is to contract the uterus which helps to reduce bleeding and aid in uterine involution (the return of the uterus to pre-pregnancy size). Some mothers may feel uncomfortable, or even painful, cramps during the time the baby nurses and for a short time afterwards. The cramps are generally uncomfortable only the first few days after delivery.

Nipple Preparation

Preparing the nipples during pregnancy used to be frequently recommended to moms in the belief that nipple preparation would eliminate nipple soreness. It is no longer recommended that prenatal preparation of the nipple be done prior to breastfeeding. Rubbing the nipples with a towel tends to remove the natural oils that keep the nipple supple. Soap may cause the nipple to become dry and increase tenderness. The size of the breast has very little to do with the ability to lactate (produce milk). Many women even have one breast that is slightly larger than the other. This is common and not a cause for concern in breastfeeding.

The First Feeding

The breastfeeding relationship needs to begin as soon after birth as possible. The intent of the first feeding is not solely to obtain nutrition but to foster a relationship that will last for years to come. There are advantages to both mother and child when breastfeeding is initiated immediately after delivery. The baby's most wakeful, alert time is within the first hour to hour and one-half after birth. This is when the baby is smelling, feeling and focusing on her parents. By introducing breastfeeding at this time, you begin meeting the infant's need of warmth, nutrition and suckling. After the quiet, alert state, the baby falls into a twelve hour (average) sleep phase that allows mom and dad the rest they need. The advantages to mom with that first feeding are: the earlier she nurses, the sooner her milk will come in; the release of oxytocin caused by breastfeeding contracts her uterus which minimizes bleeding; baby gets a dose of colostrum before a long-sleep cycle.

Breastfeeding Techniques

Although breastfeeding is a very natural process that God has designed for women to nourish and mother their children, there are a few techniques that may be helpful in getting started. The positioning of both mother and baby are important in helping to prevent sore nipples.

Begin by getting mother comfortable using many pillows. As mentioned, the first feeding will likely occur soon after birth, so whether mom is in her own bed, a hospital bed or the hallway of the bathroom (where Shonda's little Ellie was birthed), get comfortable. When sitting up in bed, use a pillow on the lap, one under the elbow and one behind the back if needed.

Frequently, when in a chair to nurse, a footstool is a necessity. This footstool may be an "official" nursing footstool, a child's step stool or a couple of large telephone books. By using a stool, the lap is brought up to mom which relieves strain on her back. Mom will then need a pillow on her lap and under her elbow.

Even more pillows are needed for nighttime nursing. While mom is lying on her side, a pillow behind her knees to level her hips, a couple under her head and one behind her that helps cradle the baby are needed.

When positioning the baby for a feeding in the cradle hold, place baby's head in the crook of mom's elbow and her arm along baby's back with her hand on baby's bottom. Baby's chest will be facing mom, causing baby's ear, shoulder and hip to be in alignment. By allowing the baby to face mom, baby will not have to turn his/her head to swallow thus preventing tugging on the nipple which can lead to soreness.

When using the clutch hold, the baby's head will be in mom's hand with his body alongside mom's arm. Baby's bottom will be up against the back of the chair and his legs will be crossed and directed up the back of the chair. While nursing lying down, the baby will again be cradled in mom's arm with their bodies facing each other. After mom and baby are comfortable, dad can snuggle in beside them.

After deciding upon body positioning, it is time to offer the baby the breast. Begin by supporting the breast with the opposite hand in a "C" shape. The fingers will be underneath the breast with the thumb on top, being careful not to touch the areola (the dark part around the nipple). Enhance the protractibility of the nipple by rolling it between the finger and thumb. Tickle the baby's lips with the nipple until his mouth opens wide. Do not allow the baby to nibble on it. This can lead to sore nipples. When baby opens wide, pull him close. His lips should be flanged out and his tongue cupping the nipple. If it hurts, take him off and try again. Be sure the baby is not latching on to just the tip of the nipple. He needs to get most of the areola in his mouth in order to compress the lactiferous sinuses where the milk pools and to obtain a sufficient amount of milk. To remove the baby from the breast, mom should insert her finger into his mouth alongside the nipple and break the suction before pulling him off; otherwise, she'll get an "Ouchie!"

Frequency and Duration

Although the topic of responsive and scheduled feeding methods is covered in another area of this book, I feel it is important to have a few guidelines to reassure parents in the feeding method they have chosen. In general, newborn babies are going to nurse 8 - 12 times in a 24-hour period. This figures to be about every 2 - 3 hours; however, it is normal/moral for some babies to nurse as often as every 1 1/2 hours at times.

A baby needs to nurse at least ten minutes on each breast to assure he or she is getting the right mixture of milk. The foremilk comes first and is thin, watery and satisfies the baby's thirst. The hindmilk comes later, is richer in fat and protein and helps the baby grow.

For the best feeding "schedule," watch baby for cues such as: baby mouthing his hands, rooting and sucking on his tongue, hands, fingers or thumbs. There are times in a day when a baby will nurse as frequently as every 30 minutes; this is known as cluster nursing. Babies nurse not only for nourishment but for comfort as well. What better place for comfort than in mother's arms feeling her warmth and love.

The composition of mother's milk changes throughout the day as does the quantity. This allows baby to nurse for comfort and remain comfortable by not getting the tummy overly full of milk. Cluster nursing is often seen in the evening time proving once again that God is in control as He provides a much needed rest time for mom.

Is Baby Getting Enough?

To reassure mom that baby is receiving adequate nutrition, the following are some signs of which mom should be aware. When the baby is latched on and suckling correctly, mom will feel a rhythmic sucking and hear swallowing. In the early days, it will take about 15 sucks to obtain a swallow. When the milk supply increases after about the third day, the ratio is one suck to one swallow. When the baby requests feedings every 2 - 3 hours, nurses for 20 to 30 minutes at each feeding and is satisfied after the feedings, this is a good clue the baby is receiving enough.

Watching the diapers is another sign the baby is taking in enough milk. In the first few days, the baby will have dark, sticky bowel movements called meconium. Once the meconium has passed and the milk supply increases, the bowel movements will change to a more liquid consistency and be mustard yellow in color. It is not unusual for baby's BMs to have small curds in them, which some people define as "seedy-looking." It is not uncommon for babies to have a bowel movement every time they nurse. Parents should be aware if the baby is having less than three bowel movements in a 24-hour period. At times, it is difficult to note how many times the baby has wet when using disposable diapers. Mom or dad may want to place a tissue in the diaper to ascertain if baby is having a sufficient amount of wet diapers per day. Cloth diapers solve this problem by being obviously wet! A good range would be 6 - 8 wet diapers each 24-hour time period. The baby will usually wet with each feeding.

Newborns will lose a small percentage of their weight after birth; however, if they are nursing well, they will regain back to birth weight by two weeks of age. This can be checked by baby's doctor, mom's midwife or a lactation consultant. Parents will notice baby is "filling out" his clothes and that the newborn diapers are fitting tighter, if fitting at all. Some mothers also notice that their breasts feel full before a feeding and softer after the feeding. Others state that they knew their baby was getting milk when they saw it dribbling out of baby's mouth. If mom is seeing these signs, she can relax and enjoy her baby.

"Troubleshooting" Common Breastfeeding Concerns:

Engorgement

Engorgement occurs between the second and fifth day when the milk is changing from colostrum to the mature milk. The breasts increase in size and may become firm, painful and warm to the touch. The skin may take on a shiny transparent look. The nipple can become flat due to the swelling. The cause of the engorgement is increased blood supply, swelling of lymph tissue as well as the increase of the milk supply. Although heat feels good, it should be avoided between feedings. Be cautious of hot showers and bath. Heat increases the blood flow and swelling actually making the breast more uncomfortable after the heat is discontinued. Heat is sometimes suggested immediately before a feeding in combination with massage to enhance the flow of milk and soften the nipple. Between and after feedings, cool compresses or ice packs can be used. Packages of frozen vegetables work very well as instant ice packs. I prefer the frozen peas, they conform the best. If mom thinks applying frozen pea packages to her breasts sounds strange, the use of cabbage leaves may be more than she can handle! If mom is game, she can apply cold cabbage leaves from the refrigerator with holes cut out to keep the nipple dry. She should leave them on for approximately 30 minutes and repeat this procedure four times daily. The research shows there may be some beneficial effects from this treatment with *no* harmful effects.[357]

Frequent nursing is the best prevention against engorgement. Nursing the baby often (every 2 hours in a 24-hour period) helps to regulate the milk supply. Be sure to offer both breasts at each feeding switching from side to side if needed. This "every 2 hours around the clock" does not have to be continued after engorgement passes, but it is an excellent way to firmly establish an adequate milk supply for the newborn.

Clogged Milk Duct

A clogged milk duct is characterized by a tender area on the breast. The area may feel firm like a lump and be reddened. The best treatment is to nurse frequently along with the use of heat and massage. It may be helpful to use different positions and place the baby so his chin is near the clogged duct. This will allow the affected duct to be emptied better. The nursing mother must increase her rest to help ward off an infection. She may boost her immune system with *Echinacea* herb and be sure to drink at least 80 ounces of water per day. Most often the cause for a clogged duct is stress and fatigue. Remember, God has designed breastfeeding as a way for mothers to get extra rest.

Mastitis or Breast Infection

The symptoms of mastitis are that of a clogged milk duct accompanied by fever. A fever, achiness and chills are noted along with a reddened sore spot on the breast that may even appear to be streaked. A mother with mastitis needs to take her nursing baby, a pitcher of water and go to bed. To maintain rest and allow mom to use heat on the infected area, she can take a crock pot and fill it with several warm wash cloths. She can then change out wash cloths as needed to keep a warm one on the affected area. A zip lock baggy can be used to help keep her clothing dry. Some moms may choose to call their doctor for an antibiotic; however, I have always been able to get mastitis under control by using heat, rest, frequent nursing, increased fluids, *Echinacea*, and *Garlic*. The garlic also helps with the frequent nursing because babies like the taste of mama's milk after mom ingests garlic.

If needed, mom must be willing to ask for and accept help with her other children and chores. A good idea for mom is to always have an extra casserole in the freezer for days when she needs extra rest. When dad arrives home from work, he can throw a salad together and a good nutritious meal is underway.

Sore Nipples

Usually the cause of sore nipples is related to poor positioning of the baby at the breast or poor latch-on. The first thing to do is check to be sure these two causes are not the culprit. If they are, correct them. Mom may need to call for help from her local La Leche League chapter or an area lactation consultant if needed. The following are some comfort measures that may lessen the discomfort and allow healing to occur. Shorter, more frequent feedings may help lessen the soreness. To aid in healing, allow the nipples to air dry for a few minutes after the feeding , then apply lansinoh. Breast shells may be used for comfort. They help by keeping the bra and clothing away from the nipple. Avoiding tight bras and bra pads with plastic liners will speed healing. Warm tea bags can be used to make mom more comfortable. Remember, soreness is a sign that something is not going quite right and to call for help if it persists.

Sleepy Baby

Occasionally, mom will get what is known as a "sleepy baby." At times, they are referred to as "good babies," "lazy nursers," or "easy babies." These babies do not wake up every 2 - 3 hours for feedings; they fall asleep a couple of minutes after nursing; and they are quite content to just sleep. These babies need to be awakened at least every three hours and encouraged to nurse. This can be done by undressing baby and nursing him in only his diaper. A cold washcloth to the forehead or tickling their feet may help to arouse them. Avoiding pacifiers and supplemental bottles is a must in these babies. A breast pump may be needed to help mom achieve or maintain supply. If the baby will not nurse at the breast, the expressed breast milk can be given in a spoon, cup, or eyedropper to maintain nutrition in the baby. It is imperative that babies get enough nutrition. Again, if help is needed, do not hesitate to call the local LLL chapter or lactation consultant.

Low Milk Supply

For several reasons, a mother may experience a decrease in her milk supply. If this occurs, moms may try the following actions to increase their supply: increase the frequency of feedings and nurse a minimum of 10 minutes on each side; increase mom's rest and decrease her activity; insure a 2000-2500 calorie nutritious diet; and avoid artificial feeding supplements. If feeding supplements are needed in order to maintain proper nutrition in the baby, they can be given with a supplemental nutritional system which allows the baby to take the feeding supplement while at the breast. If mom is having trouble encouraging the baby to increase her milk supply, she may need to get a double electric breast pump from a lactation consultant.

Jaundice

Normal newborn jaundice, also known as physiologic jaundice, is a common condition. Mom will see the yellowish-color of the skin due to the high level of bilirubin in the bloodstream. Because the baby's liver is immature, he cannot eliminate the bilirubin from his sytem quickly enough thus resulting in jaundice. Reabsorption of bilirubin from the meconium may take place. The best thing to do for jaundice is feed the baby frequently every 2 hours. The colostrum has a laxative-type effect which moves the meconium through baby's system and helps prevent jaundice. There is no reason that breastfeeding needs to be interrupted because of physiologic jaundice.

Growth Spurts

As we all know, babies grow very quickly, doubling their birth weight in about four to six months. In order for them to do so, they eat very often. There are times that babies work to boost mama's milk supply; this is know as a "growth spurt." Characteristically, they occur at about 10 days, 6 weeks, 3 months and 6 months of age. Unfortunately, many babies are switched to artificial baby milk at these times because mothers fail to recognize the symptoms of a growth spurt. Growth spurts are another time for mom to break out one of those frozen meals she has tucked away because much of her time will be spent nursing during this short period. The baby is generally labeled fussy and wants to spend a lot of time at the breast. This is none other than his signal that he is trying to increase the supply of milk. The reason many moms feel they do not have enough milk is due to the fact that at 10 days, the initial engorgement is subsiding and the breasts are feeling softer. This, in combination with the frequent nursing, leads mom astray. Again, at six weeks, the baby nurses frequently and the breast takes on more changes, becoming somewhat softer and leaking tends to diminish greatly. When a growth spurt arises, mom can grab a good book, a large glass of water, her nursing baby and snuggle up for some quality time. The growth spurt will last for about 24 - 48 hours. It is important not to artificially supplement at this time for the baby will not increase mom's supply if she does so.

Nighttime Nursing

Just because the sun sets and the lights are turned off does not mean we stop being parents. I will admit that there are times when it can be very trying to be parents twenty-four hours a day; however, God has entrusted us with a gift and will provide us with the ability to be successful parents. Since we know baby will be nursing frequently even during the night, the best place for them to sleep is near their parents. There are many different views on this topic, and as parents, mom and dad will need to prayerfully choose what God would have them do. Society puts a lot of pressure on parents to purchase all the little gadgets supposedly needed to have a baby in the home, particularly the crib. I,

Becky, tend to agree with Dr. William Sears when he states that a king-size bed is the most important piece of baby furniture for parents to buy.

One option parents have is not owning a crib and keeping the baby in mom and dad's bed at all times until a new baby arrives or the child is ready for a "big" bed. Dr. William Sears has an entire book on this type of parenting called *Nighttime Parenting*. Another option is keeping the baby close to mom at night by placing his crib or cradle near her bed. This allows moms the ease of not having to get up at night. She can still nurse the baby while lying down (maybe even sleeping!), and the baby still has his own bed. Other parents choose to take their babies into their bed while they are young and nursing very frequently (say the first 9 months or so). As baby gets older, they will put the baby down in his own bed and when baby wakes up, they get him and nurse him in their bed and return him to his bed when nursing is over (if mom and baby are not asleep by then). There are many options for parents, and they must choose what is best for their family.

A Closing Note:

This information is for educational purposes only and should not be construed as medical advice. Women having breastfeeding concerns are best served by contacting a local lactation consultant in order to gain insight and help for her own personal situation. While some of the preceding information may seem a bit technical, as mom pulls that sweet, warm baby to her breast and baby begins to suckle, technique worries fade in light of the wonder and beauty of God's perfect design.

Decrease Milk Flow

After baby weans, mom will want to decrease milk production. This process can be more speedily accomplished through natural measures.

Lifestyle/Dietary Recommendations:

1. Cold compresses can relieve the discomfort during the process.

Nutritional Supplement Recommendations:

1. Sage and parsley are the most common herbs used to "dry up" mother's milk. Frequent doses are necessary to achieve a decrease in milk production. 1 to 2 capsules of each every two to three hours.

Increase Milk Flow

Some mothers may want or need to increase their milk production to ensure baby's satisfaction and nourishment. Many mothers worry needlessly about their milk production, assuming that baby must get in as much breastmilk as a bottlefed baby gets of formula per feeding. Breastfeeding is quite different from bottlefeeding in ways other than the obvious. A breastfed infant will physically need to nurse every two to three hours for the first few months of life. As food is introduced (with the appearance of teeth), nursings may be "stretched out" to every four hours and so on as baby grows to toddlerhood and begins eating with the family. Herbs have long been used successfully in increasing milk and providing a healthful nutrient addition for momma's milk.

Some common signs that baby is not receiving enough food are: crying often between nursings without other reasons, lack of weight gain, infrequent nursings (which causes mom's breasts not to produce an adequate supply when baby does nurse), lethargy and dehydration.

Lifestyle/Dietary Recommendations:

1. Nurse at least every two to three hours. Every two hours is important for the first week at least to establish a good milk supply.
2. Do not allow baby to sleep longer than a 5-6 hour stretch at night until she is, at the very minimum, two months old. This is the time when baby becomes physiologically capable of sleeping through the night without needing milk nourishment. Some babies may sleep 5-6 hours from birth naturally. Mom need not wake them unless they are not gaining well or her milk supply is not firmly established and flowing.
3. Breastfeed at each breast for 20 minutes each to allow the baby prolonged suckling time on the aerola which "tells" mom's body to produce more milk. This also allows baby to get the "hind" milk which is the fat-rich, more filling milk.

Nutritional Supplement Recommendations:

1. Chaste tree berry (Vitex agnus-castus) and milk thistle are herbs that have been clearly shown to increase milk production. 3 capsules of each per day should result in greater milk flow.
2. Other herbs commonly used to increase milk production are: fennel, marshmallow, Goat's rue, blessed thistle.
3. *Mega-Mam* (Mother's Choice™) contains milk thistle, chasteberry, fennel, red raspberry, borage and lemon balm to enhance milk production and relax mom for happy breastfeeding!

Mastitis (Breast infection)

A breast infection, or mastitis, is the bane of new motherhood. Mom is transformed from a busy new mother into a prone individual with flu-like symptoms with an additional red, firm area on her breast that aches. The busy of "a busy new mother" may be the clue into prevention of this condition. Mothers who "overdo" their "extra-Mommy" duties may find themselves forced to rest because of a breast infection. There are many factors that can be the cause of repeated breast infections. If mom experiences frequent breast infections, she would do well to consult with a certified lactation consultant for an evaluation of her individual condition.

Many times a breast infection gives a warning sign in the form of a clogged milk duct, mom experiences a firm, slightly red, achy spot on the breast without fever, fatigue or body aches. If mom will be diligent to follow the measures listed below, she may avert full-blown mastitis.

Lifestyle/Dietary Recommendations:
1. Rest is imperative. Mom should go to bed to rest just as she would in the flu except she will have her baby beside her nursing frequently, favoring the affected breast. Baby will not be harmed by nursing during a breast infection. If baby does not nurse during a breast infection, mom will be harmed in that her breast infection will worsen requiring greater intervention. The milk may taste more "salty" to baby during the infection.
2. Fresh cabbage leaves may be applied to the breast by placing in the bra and leaving there as a poultice. Sounds odd, but works.
3. Mom should be drinking 8 ounces of water per hour during a breast infection to keep her well hydrated and, hopefully, push the "plug" out of the clogged duct.
4. Moist heat is helpful with tender massage starting at the outer portion of the breast massaging down toward the nipple to try to loosen the plug.

Nutritional Supplement Recommendations:
1. Echinacea may be used for immune stimulation as well as garlic; fresh cloves are always best, tablets or capsules; these may be used 1 tablet or capsule of each every two hours.
2. An herbal combination containing: echinacea root, goldenseal root, red clover blossom, violet, poke root (or red root), and licorice root may be taken three times daily for 5-7 days for its antibacterial, immune-modulating, antiinflammatory and antiseptic action.
3. Vitamin C, 1,000mg, every couple of hours with vitamin A and zinc. Mastitis risk may be increased in those who are vitamin A deficient.[358]

PART SEVEN

The Return of Menstruation and Family Planning

"When you eat the labor of your hands, You shall be happy, and it shall be well with you. Your wife shall be like a fruitful vine In the very heart of your house, Your children like olive plants All around your table." Psalm 128:2,3

Family Planning

"Lo, children are an heritage of the Lord: and the fruit of the womb is His reward. As arrows are in the hand of a mighty man; so are the children of youth. Happy is the man that hath his quiver full of them: they shall not be ashamed, but they shall speak with enemies in the gate." Psalm 127:3-5

BIRTH CONTROL—
THE NAME SAYS IT ALL

The very mention of the words "birth control" usually ignites a response in the listeners or readers. I certainly have no desire to set off a powder keg in this latter portion of my book; however, there are physiologic consequences to various forms of birth control that merit a brief synopsis at the very least. I humbly submit that I am no expert in this area. There are others considerably more knowledgeable than I in this subject area. Please read the books listed in the Resource section on Family Planning. These books will provide information which can then be prayed over as the Holy Spirit directs each family to their personal conviction.

The personal conviction concerning family planning of the Keith Parker family may not be that of the Jones family. While we may desire for the Jones the freedom we have found in our planning method, we know that our Lord is Great and Mighty enough to change the Joneses if He wills, when *He* decides it needs changing. We know our job is not to change hearts or personal convictions. We only pray that God might use us, our experiences, our growing wisdom as His Spirit desires. 'Cause we do not know it all; in fact, we find daily we need to know so much more.

Birth Control Methods:

"Birth control" is a method by which a man and woman seek to prevent the birth of a child by: preventing the passage of sperm from man to woman (condom, cervical cap, diaphragm, coitus interruptus), killing the sperm inside the body of woman (spermicidal gel, foam, suppository, or sponge, diaphragm), aborting by preventing the implantation of a developing baby still in early development inside the woman (IUD, birth control pill, morning-after pill), preventing the passage of sperm through surgical intervention (vasectomy and tubal ligation) or utilizing instruments or chemicals to terminate the life of the developing baby (abortion). Apart from moral judgment (which would conclude, at the very least, abortion to be grievously wrong) as to the aforementioned birth control methods, said methods do not align themselves with the thrust of this book which is to seek the normal physiologic processes of healing and living.

All methods of birth control cause mom and dad to interfere with the natural, God-given process of conception which is His blessing on the physical union of husband and wife. Not only do the two become one spiritually and physically with the act of marital intercourse, God divinely chooses when to bless the two with an extra one, or two, or three, or…well, the picture is clear. Any time we choose to alter our Creator's divine purpose for our bodies, there are health consequences. Each method of birth control will be briefly described with the possible health risks thereof.

Coitus Interruptus

This method of birth control is notoriously unreliable. It is the process in which the husband withdraws his penis from his wife's vagina prior to ejaculation. For those trying to avoid pregnancy, this method is unreliable. Even if a husband and wife are willing to practice this form of birth control, a small amount of semen is leaked from the penis during sexual arousal prior to ejaculation. While the number of sperm contained in this seminal fluid is much less than the 25 to 200 million that are in a normal ejaculate, it only takes one to penetrate an ovum and create a new life. If repeated acts of intercourse occur within several hours time, live sperm may be in the male urethra and passed into the vagina during sexual relations. Actual penetration into the vagina is not even necessary for pregnancy to occur. Seminal fluid that comes into contact with the wife's labia can travel through the fertile mucous up the vagina, through the cervix, into the uterus and fallopian tubes to fertilize a descending egg. This method does not reap negative health consequences, but it can be frustrating for husband and wife, and reap emotional and spiritual consequences.

Condom

A condom is used as a covering of the husband's erect penis to prevent seminal fluid from entering the vagina. Most condoms are made of latex (rubber) to which some women and men are allergic. Several brands are made of sheepskin which can be used by those allergic to latex; however, the sheepskin brands are not as durable and do not provide protection from sexually-transmitted disease (latex condoms are not completely reliable protection from STDs either). The latex material of the condoms can irritate the delicate lining of the vaginal walls even in those with no latex allergy. The powder residue on the surface of the condoms may increase the wife's risk of reproductive cancers. Condoms also reduce pleasure in both husband and wife, cannot be used with oil-based lubricants, and only have a two-year shelf life (less in heated places). User-effectiveness is 70% to 90% for condom-use. If used improperly, leakage of seminal fluid from the condom may occur resulting in a surprise blessing (pregnancy). As of July 1995, a new material is being used for condoms, polyurethane. I am not familiar with the effectiveness of this material, but it may be more durable than sheepskin and less allergenic than latex.

Diaphragm

Diaphragms are used as a barrier form of birth control although they actually do not function effectively as a barrier. For diaphragms to be effective (71% to 85%), they must be combined with spermicidal cream or jelly. Diaphragm users must leave the diaphragm in place at least six hours after intercourse. The health risks with diaphragm use are: increased risk of bladder infection due to the diaphragm's pressure on the bladder causing irritation; dusting the diaphragm as manufacturers suggest with powder may increase reproductive cancer risk; spermicidal creams and jellies may increase the risk of a "defective" sperm penetrating the released ovum and increase miscarriage or birth defect risk; diaphragms are made of latex to which some women are allergic; as well as not being a highly effective form of birth control when health conditions necessitate a wait for a baby.

Cervical Cap

The cervical cap is a rigid, latex (rubber) dome that fits over the cervix by suction. It is not a common form of birth control in the U.S and must be fitted by a professional fitter (midwife, nurse-midwife, physician). The rate of user-effectiveness is an average of 85%. The cervical cap, when fitted properly, does serve as a barrier. Most caregivers recommend the use of spermicidal cream or jelly in combination with the cervical cap for maximum effectiveness. Although the cervical cap does not carry an increased risk of bladder infections as does the diaphragm, the other health risks associated with the diaphragm are also present with use of the cervical cap. Users of cervical caps must have two pap smears within six months of beginning this method of birth control due the observation of cellular changes in pap smears in women utilizing the cervical cap. As with any device left in the vagina for several hours, there is an increased risk of toxic shock syndrome.

Spermicides

Spermicides are available in several forms: foam, gel or suppositories. The foam seems to be the most effective since it bubbles into the crevices of the vaginal wall; however, a spermicide alone only has an effectiveness rate of 64% to 90%. Spermicide can be irritating to the delicate tissues of the vagina and penis, causing a burning sensation in some individuals. There is a theoretical risk of miscarriage or birth defect due to spermicide-injured spermatozoa fertilizing the released ovum.

Sponge

The sponge is a soft, doughnut-shaped piece of polyurethane foam that is filled with spermicide. It functions as a foam barrier over the cervix as well as a spermicide. The reliability of this method is similar to that of the diaphragm and cervical cap. There is an increased risk of toxic shock syndrome with its use since it must be left in place for at least six hours after intercourse. See the risks of spermicide for more health risk information.

Intrauterine Device (IUD)

The IUD is a device that is inserted through the cervix into the uterus. The IUD is not a barrier method. It works by preventing implantation into the endometrium of the uterus of a developing baby (abortifacient). As is logical with a procedure that destroys a tiny human life, the health risks for mom are abundant: pelvic infection (can be chronic, Pelvic Inflammatory Disease, and sterilize mom); irregular bleeding; cramping; uterine perforation; and for those IUDs which release birth-control hormones, all the risks attendant with oral contraceptive use should be added. Some women have died as a result of IUD use.

Oral Contraceptives (the Pill)

The function of oral contraceptives is two-fold: to suppress ovulation (however, ovulation will periodically occur) and by changing hormone levels to create an "unfriendly" environment (thin endometrial lining where baby needs to implant) for the developing baby thus aborting the developing child. The lower the dosage of hormones present in the pill used, the higher the incidence of "breakthrough" ovulation. Most BC pills currently sold are low-dosage pills. The "mini-pill" or progesterone-only type is almost totally abortifacient. There are numerous health concerns when taking the pill: nausea, vomiting, breast engorgement, headache, vertigo, fluid retention, depression, changes in sexual desire, irregular menstrual bleeding, delayed resumption of menstruation after discontinuing oral contraceptives, thromboembolism, heart attacks, cerebrovascular accidents, hypertension, increased cholesterol and triglyceride levels, blood clots from coagulation, diabetogenic effect similar to pregnancy, cholecystitis and cholelithiasis, liver tumors, benign proliferative adenomatous growth on the cervix, increased risk of congenital anomalies in children born to mothers who had recently discontinued oral contraceptives, increased risk of miscarriage among women who conceive shortly after discontinuing oral contraceptives.[359] These health risks should cause any of us to question whether this form of birth control is appropriate for those seeking to follow the Creator's design for our bodies, but combined with its abortifacient effects, Christians desiring to follow God's Word regarding "Thou shalt not kill" should avoid this form of birth control completely. The effectiveness rate of oral contraceptives is .34 to 1% pure method failure rate (theoretic effectiveness) and a 4 - 10% user-effectiveness failure rate (in actual use).

Tubal Ligation

Tubal ligation refers to a surgical process to cut or block the fallopian tubes thereby attempting to prevent pregnancy by blocking meeting of spermatazoa and egg. All risks attendant with any surgery are present in a tubal ligation. After tubal ligation, a large percentage of women require further gynecological surgery because the blood supply to the ovaries may be cut off or decreased. There has also been reported that 22% to 29% of sterilized women report increased (heavier) menstrual bleeding and menstrual pain. The effectiveness rate is .04% for tubal ligation; however, when pregnancy does occur after the surgery, ectopic (tubal) pregnancy occurs in as many as 50% of pregnancies following tubal ligation. Tubal ligation should be thought of as permanent birth control even though some may be later reversed.

Hysterectomy

Hysterectomies should be a rare surgery performed for the removal of cancer, not for the removal of fertility. A hysterectomy is surgery which removes a woman's uterus making it impossible to ever carry a child again; therefore, the birth rate after the procedure is zero. The uterus is not a disposable organ. The complications associated with hysterectomy include all complications associated with major surgery as well as post-hysterectomy depression and hormonal fluctuations similar to menopausal changes.

Vasectomy

A vasectomy refers to surgery performed on the male genitalia that involves interrupting or cutting out a section of the vas deferens. The surgery is a permanent procedure although many who find they regret their decision have had a reversal performed that has at best a 50/50 success rate. Additional forms of birth control must be practiced for a period of time after the vasectomy due to stored sperm in the reproductive tract beyond the interrupted vas deferens. This period of time may be a couple of weeks up to several months. Two sperm counts registering zero should be done before eliminating other birth control methods. In the past few years, more reports of health risks associated with vasectomies have appeared in health journals. The risks are: increased risk of coronary-artery disease, immune dysfunction creating autoimmune problems, as well as an increased risk of prostate problems. The birth rate following vasectomy is approximately 1%.[360]

Herbal Contraceptives

I am including this section for those women who would like to avoid herbs with contraceptive activity. Herbs that exhibit contraceptive activity:

Aloe - 7.5% and 10% concentrations of lyophilized aloe barbadensis exhibited spermicidal activity, suggesting use as a vaginal contraceptive.[361]

Hibiscus rosa-senensis - May act as abortifacient through implantation failure. Avoid completely for baby safety.

Fo-Ti, Polygonum multiflorum, had a reference in a particularly objectionable book called *Herbal Birth Control* that historically the herb had been used to achieve permanent sterility. Moms may want to avoid use of this herb during childbearing years.

Natural progesterone, processed from wild yam - I am including this due to the mini-
pill, which is almost entirely progesterone, causing implantation failure thus acting as an abortifacient. If a natural progesterone is used all month long rather than
only in the second half of the cycle as intended, implantation failure and miscarriage may result.

Natural Family Planning

Natural family planning generally refers to the observation of body signals or "signs"
of fertility to achieve or avoid pregnancy. Most of the time when we mention natural
family planning, people automatically think of the "rhythm method" which is not the
same thing as natural family planning (NFP). The form of natural family planning we
will discuss here is the sympto-thermal method. The sympto-thermal method involves
checking cervical mucous and taking the basal body temperature of mom each day to
ascertain fertile days. This method has a user-effectiveness rate of 99.2% when applied
by trained and motivated spouses. There are no known physiologic dangers from
employing this method of limiting or spacing pregnancies.

The signs of fertility are easily recognizable, so husband and wife can together make
a decision to abstain or engage in relations on a fertile day, knowing that should they
choose to engage, a pregnancy is possible. Although these signs are easily recognizable,
we have to learn what we are "recognizing" before we can know effectively use natural
family planning. For this reason, *I heartily encourage parents wishing to utilize NFP to
attend classes together to learn how to observe the signs of fertility.* These classes are available through the Couple-to-Couple League, Cincinnati, OH. The Couple-to-Couple
League is a non-profit organization (from a Roman Catholic background) that offers
classes and a home study course in natural family planning. *Please do not attempt to practice NFP from the guidelines offered in this book.* There is so much more to know.

The basics of how the sympto-thermal method work follow: Each day after mom
uses the toilet, she can check her cervical mucous by noticing when the toilet paper is
slick after wiping or by manually reaching a finger inside the vagina and sweeping out
some mucous for observation. Fertile mucous is very slick and clear, being the consistency of raw egg white. On the peak fertile days, when ovulation is likely to be occurring,
the cervical mucous will stretch at least an inch, possibly two inches or more between
finger and thumb. Fertile mucous must be present for sperm to be able to "swim" up
through the uterus into the fallopian tubes in search of the released egg. The general rule,
if one wishes to avoid pregnancy, is to cease relations on the day of beginning fertile
mucous and abstain from relations until the fourth or fifth day after observing dry (zero-
amount) mucous.

Combined with cervical mucous observation, mom and dad also check mom's basal

Combined with cervical mucous observation, mom and dad also check mom's basal body temperature each morning to observe when the thermal shift occurs that signals ovulation has taken place. The term basal body temperature refers to body temperature taken each morning at a constant time before mom has arisen from bed with a special thermometer appropriately called a basal body temperature thermometer. Thermal shift refers to the post-ovulation rise in temperatures sustained in an overall rising or elevated pattern for at least three days, reaching and staying at a level usually .4 (4/10) of 1(F above the pre-shift base level.[362]

Observing the signs of fertility through the sympto-thermal method provides a natural form of limiting or spacing pregnancies that does not interfere with the natural processes of mom's body. She and dad can choose whether to engage in relations or not, based on the signs of fertility and their desire, knowing that a pregnancy is always possible as a result of sexual relations. The downside of this method is that mom's peak time of desire usually coincides with ovulation.

Children as Blessings

Some parents choose simply to acknowledge God as the Giver of Life, yield all control of their sexual relations to the Lord, and He chooses when to bless them with children. I do firmly believe that it is not we who fill our wombs with children or cause them to be empty. We do participate in the means (sexual relations) through which God creates life. As I have talked with persons unfamiliar with this trust in God's Sovereignty in the area of pregnancy and birth, they almost inevitably ask what I think God meant for us to do with our brain if not to use it to decide when having a child is appropriate. The issue is not about our brain. A brain cannot create life or deny life; only the Sovereign God can. For me, I suppose it came down to a question of trust. Can I trust God when He tells me in His word that children are a blessing, that my way may seem right in my eyes but is not necessarily the best for me, that He alone is worthy to decide matters of life and death, and that He provides for the children He sends? I do not know what tomorrow will bring; God does. I do not know whether I will be able to "manage" another child; God does. Not only does He know if I can "handle" another child, He will supply me with all that I need to love, train up, and educate this child He has given as my reward for faithfulness.

I find great comfort in seeing the natural physiology of a woman's body which God created. The design of woman enables us to become pregnant, carry and nourish the child in our wombs, birth that child and then nourish that child with our breasts. The time of breastfeeding, if done as God intended the breastfeeding the relationship to be, naturally grants a woman a period of amenorrhea for an average of 14.5 months.[363] Some women with high levels of estrogen do not have a very long period of amenorrhea; others may go three or four years without ovulation occurring. I firmly believe in responsive breastfeeding, responding to the child's needs for physical and spiritual nourishment through a caring breastfeeding relationship. I believe man-made rigid schedules to be apart from God's perfect design and will (See Part 6). When we assert our will whether it is in the form of rigid schedules or forced weaning or the practice of birth control, this assertion of *our* will still defines iniquity, and iniquity leads to sin.

Even as I say this, I want to say that I know that God's plan for our families will not be thwarted even if we "take control." If our quiver is not yet full and we choose to place a barrier to another child, God can, and does, override our barriers to bring His fruit into our families. We do miss out on the blessing of viewpoint about children when we look at what He has called a blessing as a burden.

Yielding our will to God's will is the hardest task for us in all areas of life, yet walking in faith and trusting in His Sovereignty yields for us the greatest reward: His pleasure and blessing of spiritual growth. I love Psalm 128:

> *"Blessed is every one that feareth the Lord; that walketh in his ways.*
> *For thou shalt eat the labor of thine hands: happy shalt thou be, and it shall*
> *be well with thee.*
> *Thy wife shall be as a fruitful vine by the sides of thine house: thy children*
> *like olive plants round about thy table.*
> *Behold, that thus shall the man be blessed that feareth the Lord.*
> *The Lord shall bless thee out of Zion: and thou shalt see the good of*
> *Jerusalem all the days of thy life.*
> *Yea, thou shalt see they children's children, and peace upon Israel."*

What an incredible blessing!

Keith and I often use this Psalm as the basis for responding to the question of "How many more children are you going to have?" We just tell them that we have a large table with chairs around it to fill up! The family planning issue is one most of us never consider in the light of God's Word. The information presented here is intended to be an encouragement to study the word of God about family planning, not simply follow what the world is doing or saying. Family planning is a part of our lives we want to prayerfully consider with our husbands, to allow the Holy Spirit to lead the way He would have us follow. There are some excellent books exploring what the Bible says about family planning. Please see Part 8, Resource section, for titles and authors.

The downside of this method occurs when parents welcome all the children God will bless them with only to be remiss in their training of those blessings. For an excellent look at family structure, please read Douglas Wilson's book, *Reforming Marriage* and Nancy Wilson's (his wife's) book, *The Fruit of Her Hands* available from CanonPress.

Amenorrhea

Amenorrhea is the term used for lack of (not having) menstrual periods. There are two types of amenorrhea: primary—never started periods; and secondary—periods were normal and have stopped. I will discuss secondary amenorrhea in this section. If periods are merely irregular (having one every 2 months or so), treatment may not be necessary. If a cycle does not occur for three or more months, the following recommendations may be implemented. These recommendations are based on herbs that supply the necessary building blocks to enable our glands to produce the hormones that regulate menses. The nutritional focus will be to support the body's function with high-quality proteins and fats.

The most obvious cause of amenorrhea is pregnancy, and a pregnancy test should be performed to rule out pregnancy before mom does any of the following supplementation. Another cause of amenorrhea that needs no nutritional intervention is the very normal period of postpartum amenorrhea which occurs in breastfeeding moms. This postpartum amenorrhea may be only six weeks in mothers who do not breastfeed; however, mothers who breastfeed exclusively (no other foods, water or pacifiers and breastfeed at least every two to three hours until baby is eating other foods besides "momma-milk") experience an average of 15 months of having no periods (as well as no ovulation). Please see the Family Planning, as well as the Breastfeeding, section for a more complete explanation on postpartum amenorrhea and natural child spacing.

Lifestyle/Dietary Recommendations:

1. We can become so focused on limiting fats and meats that we deprive our body of these *necessary* foods. The Whole Foods diet will supply the correct amount of protein and fat without overloading the body.
2. Limit exercise. Long-distance runners and ballet dancers, as well as some swimmers, experience amenorrhea due to the amount of exercise they do. If amenorrhea began after beginning a weight-loss regimen, mom may want to limit exercise to 30 minutes three to five times weekly.
3. If basal body temperature is consistently low, rule out hypothyroidism as a factor (See Hypothyroidism).
4. Emotional stress can be a cause of amenorrhea or irregular cycles. Prayer, relaxation techniques and discussing matters of concern with husband and church elders may prove helpful.

Nutritional Supplement Recommendations:

1. Chaste tree berry, in preliminary investigations, has shown the ability to adjust the production of female hormones by the presence of several compounds, including a progesterone-like compound.[364] [365] Chaste tree berry is now believed to have

dopaminergic properties, meaning it inhibits the secretion of the peptide hormone prolactin (produced in large amounts while breastfeeding, thought to be responsible for the above-mentioned postpartum amenorrhea associated with breastfeeding) by the pituitary gland.[366] Some women, who are not breastfeeding, have high levels of prolactin which cause the normal menstrual cycle to cease. A dosage of at least 20mg standardized tablets or capsules daily.

2. Mugwort has been used in many different countries, including the United States, to assist and promote menstruation. Test-tube experiments confirm that it does contract uterine tissue, but human studies are lacking.[367] 2 capsules daily.

3. In my own counseling on herb use, I have found a product, Fem-a-Gen by Rainbow Light to regulate the menses even in cases where women were previously using strong medications to bring on their menstrual cycles. Dosage on the bottle may be followed.

4. Dong quai has a tonic effect on the uterus making it useful for many menstrual disorders including amenorrhea. 2 - 3 capsules daily.

5. One study showed that 2g per day of acetyl-L-carnitine for six months had a positive impact on menstruation.[368]

Please Note: I sincerely hope that those reading this book would not consider ending the life of their baby. I do feel compelled to state this warning in the event that someone misinterprets the above to mean they could "bring on a period" (bring death to their baby) through the use of herbs after becoming pregnant. These herbs are not abortifacients or true emmenagogues (herbs that promote menstruation). Even the words "true emmenagogues" are not very accurate as even the "true" emmenagogue herbs do not consistently produce abortion. In the quantities that some books or herbalists recommend these herbs as abortifacients, they would be more likely to cause serious harm to mother (perhaps death) and malformation in baby rather than death. If an herb reference says "will bring on a period" or "emmenagogue," avoid completely during pregnancy.

Dysmenorrhea

Dysmenorrhea is the medical term used to describe painful periods—menstrual cycles—with cramps in the lower abdominal area. While most women experience some discomfort during menstruation, those who must restrict normal activities due to cramping are diagnosed with dysmenorrhea. Approximately 50% of women of child-bearing age experience dysmenorrhea. Out of these 50%, one in five are incapacitated 1 to 3 days of each month due to pain.[369] Herbs have been found to be of great benefit to women who seek relief from monthly menstrual pain.

Lifestyle/Dietary Recommendations:
1. Foods containing arachidonic acid should be limited or avoided during the week of menstruation. Arachidonic acid is converted in the body to the PGE prostaglandin which causes the uterine muscles to contract Animal foods are the primary (almost only) source of arachidonic acid. (Humans produce arachidonic acid, but we won't be eating our neighbor.)
2. Limit dairy products. They contain arachidonic acid and calcium which cause muscles to contract.
3. Increase foods containing magnesium: whole grains, beans, nuts. Magnesium causes muscles to relax.
4. A warm lavender, chamomile or passion flower bath may be helpful for some women to aid relaxation.
5. A hot water bottle, warm towels, warm clothing is always preferable to cold items which cause all tissues to contract.

Nutritional Supplement Recommendations:
1. Evening primrose oil capsules are an excellent choice for women with dysmenorrhea due to its high gamma-linolenic acid (GLA) which converts to the "good" prostaglandins which cause the uterine muscles to relax. One to two, 500mg capsules three times daily.
2. Red raspberry leaf tea or capsules have long been used for reduce cramping during menstrual cycles. 2 to 6 capsules daily.
3. Valerian root and cramp bark are two valuable herbs scientifically documented to relax smooth muscle. 1 to 2 capsules of each may be taken every 2 to 3 hours while experiencing cramps.
4. **CrampEase** by Mother's Choice™ company works very well for cramps and after-birth pains. The herbs contained in this combination are Cramp Bark or Black Haw, Valerian, Skullcap, Hops, Catnip, Chamomile. 1/2 to 1 teaspoon every 2 to 3 hours during painful cycle.

5. Female Formula by Mother's Choice™ are both helpful for relieving painful menstruation.
6. FemCare by Enzymatic Therapy was specifically formulated for use during menstruation to relieve pain.

Fibrocystic Breast Disease

Fibrocystic Breast Disease, also known as cystic mastitis, is a sometimes painful, although benign, cystic swelling of the breasts. The term disease is really unfair and scary. It is a set of symptoms that commonly occur in healthy women (lumpy, swollen breasts with sometime nipple discharge) and is NOT a precursor to breast cancer.[370]

Fluctuating estrogen levels may aggravate the condition as well as caffeine in coffee, teas and colas, theophylline in tea and theobromine in chocolate. Infrequent bowel movements may also have a direct bearing on cystic mastitis. Women who have fewer than three bowel movements per week are more likely to have this condition. This may be due to reabsorption of estrogens that the liver has sent to be eliminated through the bowels.

Lifestyle/Dietary Recommendations:

1. Consume plenty of fruits and veggies. Eat more plant-based proteins rather than meat to encourage regular bowel movements. Animal fat may contribute to growth.
2. Eliminate coffee, tea, chocolate and caffeinated sodas.
3. Eat sea fish or sea vegetables rich in iodine.
4. Do regular breast self-exams and alert health care provider to any new lumps.
5. Rule out wheat allergy by eliminating all wheat products for two weeks, then reintroduce wheat to see if allergy symptoms develop.

Supplement Recommendations:

1. Vitamin E, 400 - 600 IU daily.
2. Beta-carotene, 10,000 - 25,000 IU daily.
3. Evening Primrose Oil has been used successfully in Europe to reduce the size of cysts.[371] 1 - 2 capsules three times daily.
4. Gotu kola has been clinically documented as an effective treatment for fibrocystic breast disease.[372] 500 to 1,000mg daily.
5. Vitamin B6 - 50 - 200mg in a B complex of other B vitamins in 25mg amounts.
6. Magnesium - 200mg daily.
7. Zinc - 10 - 40mg daily.
8. Cold-pressed flax seed oil - 1 to 2 tablespoons daily.
9. Vitamin C - 60mg daily.
10. Iodine from sea kelp either as food or 4 to 6 capsules daily.

Menorrhagia (Excessive Menstrual Flow)

Menorrhagia refers to a heavy blood loss during menstrual periods. This excessive flow may occur because of prolonged bleeding meaning a menstrual flow lasting longer than six or seven days. This can be due to a variety of factors: endometriosis, uterine fibroids, low thyroid function, nutrient deficiencies, post-birth control pill hormone changes, or reproductive tract tumors or cysts. Heavy bleeding can lead to anemia if left unchecked. Nutritional changes should be coupled with medical testing to rule out a more serious health condition.

Lifestyle/Dietary Recommendations:

1. A large salad of dark, green leafy vegetables should be eaten daily to supply vitamin K, iron, folic acid, vitamin A, and chlorophyll which are all needed in greater amounts when bleeding has occurred.
2. Including sea vegetables in the diet such as kelp, dulse, spirulina, etc. provides nutrients for the endocrine (glandular) system.
3. Commit to the whole foods diet for at least six months to allow time for the body to recuperate and adjust to better quality foods.

Nutritional Supplement Recommendations:

1. There are several formulas that nourish the female endocrine system. A formula containing the following herbs has proven beneficial for many women: Chasteberry (Vitex agnus castus), wild yam, dong quai, licorice, ginger, blue cohosh (may elevate blood pressure) or black cohosh, as well as liver supportive herbs such as dandelion, milk thistle, burdock and/or yellow dock.
2. Several herbs have traditionally been used to halt uterine bleeding. The following herbs have demonstrated the ability to curb bleeding: shepherd's purse, yarrow, cayenne pepper (may stimulate bleeding later if not used in combination with a styptic herb such as shepherd's purse), bayberry. These herbs are contained in the *HemHalt*™ by Mother's Choice™ (See Resource section, Part 8).
3. Chlorophyll has long been used for bleeding because of its similar molecular structure to human blood. Whether this is why chlorophyll works well in slowing down bleeding or re-building blood supply after bleeding episodes is unknown. Midwives have long used it in cases of hemorrhage. 2 to 3 capsules daily or 1/2 to 1 cup of liquid daily.
4. A high-quality vitamin supplement is a must for women with excessive bleeding. The brands I like best are: *NF Prenatal Formula* by NF Formulas, *Opti-Natal* by Eclectic Institute, and *Professional Prenatal Formula* by LifeTime Pharmacy. There may be other quality formulas I am unaware of; please see resource section for the contents of these formulas for comparison with other brands. The supplement chosen must have an adequate amount of vitamin A as vitamin A deficiency has been shown to be a causative factor in menorrhagia.[373]

Premenstrual Syndrome (PMS)

Premenstrual syndrome (PMS) is a complex of symptoms including: headache, breast swelling and tenderness, abdominal bloating, peripheral edema, fatigue, irritability, tension and depression. Other common symptoms are increased thirst and appetite, constipation and acne. PMS symptoms generally begin after ovulation and linger until menstrual bleeding begins. In severe cases, symptoms may last virtually all month. While the medical community generally maintain this is a syndrome with "no cause," leading researchers into PMS name nutritional deficiencies and imbalances as the cause.

Dr. Guy Abraham is the United States' leading PMS researcher. He divided PMS sufferers into four categories:

- PMT (PreMenstrual Tension)-A (for Anxiety) - characterized by nervous tension, mood swings, irritability and anxiety;
- PMT-H (for hyperhydration) - which includes weight gain, swelling of the extremities, breast tenderness, and abdominal bloating;
- PMT-C (for carbohydrate craving) - characterized by headaches, craving for sweets, increased appetite, heart pounding, fatigue, and dizziness or faintness;
- PMT-D (for depression) - which involves depression, forgetfulness, crying, confusion and insomnia.[374]

Dr. Abraham found that the dietary intake of nutrients in women with premenstrual symptoms is often less than in healthy women with no premenstrual symptoms. Since dietary factors are so important, Dr. Abraham's suggestions for treating PMS are:

Lifestyle/Dietary Recommendations:
1. Limit consumption of refined sugar, salt, red meat and alcohol.
2. Eat fish, poultry, whole grains and legumes as major sources of protein and rely less on red meat and dairy products.
3. Reduce or abolish tobacco consumption.
4. Consume only minimal quantities of coffee, tea, chocolate and cola-based drinks.
5. Reduce intake of fats, avoiding particularly animal fats, fried foods and hydrogenated margarine.
6. Increase intake of fiber in the form of complex carbohydrates such as green, leafy vegetables, legumes and fruits.
7. Reduce weight, if you are obese, by avoiding refined carbohydrates, reducing animal fat intake and increasing fiber intake.
8. For those with sugar or other food cravings, high-quality protein snacks (e.g. nuts, seeds, peas, beans, lentils) as well as animal protein in the form of fish, eggs or poultry.

9. Exercise outdoors regularly.
10. Reduce stress.
11. Avoid making major decisions during PMS time of month.

Nutritional Supplement Recommendations:

1. A high-quality multivitamin such as Optivite by Eclectic Institute is recommended. Optivite has proven scientific value in treating PMS. Make certain the vitamin contains between 40-100mg of vitamin B6.
2. Evening primrose oil - 4 to 8, 500mg capsules per day beginning two weeks before menstrual bleeding begins.
3. Vitamin E - 300-500 IUs daily especially for breast swelling and tenderness.
4. Magnesium - 200-300mg of magnesium aspartate or citrate every day of the month combined with the above multivitamin.
5. Pycnogenols, particularly endotelon, improved or eliminated PMS symptoms in 60.8% of women after 2 cycles and 78.8% after 4 cycles. Symptoms improved were: breast tenderness and swelling, abdominal swelling, pelvic pain, weight variations and venous problems of the legs.[375]
6. Gingko biloba helps to relieve the breast symptoms of PMS.[376]
7. Dr. Abraham recommends following a supplement regimen for three months before deciding if PMS is getting better.
8. Fem-a-Gen by Rainbow Light has also been successfully used to regulate and balance the female hormones.

Weight Loss

Most new mothers are very concerned about the weight left after delivering baby. We are inundated with a cultural bias toward "skinny." Even with the abundance of research indicating the risk to mom and baby of limiting weight gain during pregnancy to an "appropriate" 20 - 25 lbs for all women regardless of nutritional status, I have found authors and physicians who still advocate "appropriate" weight gain. I certainly am not suggesting mom become gluttonous and gain useless weight from low-nutrient, high-calorie foods. I am strongly recommending mom eat at least 2500 calories daily from a whole foods diet, and I encourage moms to wait until baby is at least one year old to begin any weight-loss regimen.

New mothers need a little added weight to keep up with the physical demands of breastfeeding. Baby's nourishment should come first. After the baby is one year old and baby is being introduced to food, mom may begin a sensible weight-loss program.

Lifestyle/Dietary Recommendations:
1. Decrease calories and add exercise. Caloric intake should not go below 1,200 calories daily. One can "afford" 1,500 to 2,000 calories if the amount of exercise is increased.
2. There is no "miracle diet." The key to overcoming fat cells' set point appears to be increasing the fat cells exposure to insulin.
3. Eat more high-nutrient foods. If the body feels starved, metabolism will slow down and less fat will be burned.
4. Snacking should be avoided unless it is with foods that expend the same amount of calories to eat as they contain.
5. Exercise should be 15 to 20 minutes of aerobic activity three to four times weekly.

Nutritional Supplement Recommendations:
1. Fiber supplements seem to be beneficial by providing bulk in the stomach to decrease food requirements. Supplementation may come from psyllium, guar gum, glucomannan, or pectin - up to 5 grams daily.
2. Michael T. Murray, N.D., in his excellent book *Natural Alternatives to Over-the-Counter and Prescription Drugs*, recommends thermogenic herb formulas for weight-loss. The thermogenic formulas work by activating the sympathetic nervous system which increases metabolism and thermogenesis. Moms who are still breast-feeding need to be cautious because of the stimulant activity of these herbs. If baby responds to the herbs passed through mom's breastmilk, mom should discontinue the thermogenic formula immediately. Herbal combinations with synergistic (combining two or more substances to create a stronger action) effects: ephedra (ma huang) is amplified by green tea (Camellia sinesis) or cola nut (Cola nitida)

(ma huang) is amplified by green tea (Camellia sinesis) or cola nut (Cola nitida) and coffee or black tea. Ephedrine from the Ephedra plant (ma huang) promotes weight loss in experimental and clinical studies by increasing the metabolic rate of fat tissue and decreasing appetite. Ephedrine's action is greatly enhanced by caffeine. 22 mg of ephedrine to 80mg caffeine is Murray's recommended dosage. This should be taken early in the day and all other stimulants should be eliminated. **Thermogenic formulas should not be used in people with high blood pressure, heart disease or those on antidepressants without consulting their physician.** There have been cases of young women using ephedrine in very large doses with fatal effects. For those interested in using thermogenic formulas, I strongly recommend the purchase of Dr. Murray's book, *Natural Alternatives to Over-the-Counter and Prescription Drugs* published in 1994 by William Morrow and Company in New York, New York.

3. Meal-replacement formulas should only be used after baby has weaned (This does not mean wean baby so mom can go on a diet!). When using meal-replacement formulas, the following guidelines will help keep the diet complete:
   - The product should contain high-quality protein from grains, legumes, whey or hydrolyzed lactalbumin. Avoid casein-based formulas because casein is difficult to digest.
   - The formula should contain at least a 5-gram combination of soluble and insoluble dietary fiber per serving.
   - Balanced high-quality nutrition with enhanced levels of nutrients critical to weight-loss, such as chromium picolinate.
   - Formula should have a low total fat content and should supply some essential fatty acids (EFAs).
   - The product should contain no sweeteners, artificial flavors or other artificial food additives.[377]

Part Eight

Resources for Healthful Living

"The heart of him that hath understanding seeketh knowledge…" Proverbs 15:14a

"The simple believeth every word: but the prudent man looketh well to his going." Proverbs 14:15

RESOURCES

Childbirth Education Resources:

Midwifery Institute of America
R.R. #2, Box 409
Rome, PA 18837
(717) 395-3192

Resident training or correspondence course in midwifery with a Christian instructor. Excellent and affordable.

NAPSAC
Rt. 1, Box 646
Marble Hill, MO 63764

Education on safe childbirth alternatives through a quarterly newsletter, bookstore, telephone counseling and referrals.

Apple Tree Family Ministries
P. O. Box 2083
Artesia, CA 90702-2083

Certifying organization for Christian childbirth educators founded by Helen Wessel and currently led by Kathy Nesper. Publishes *The Joy of Natural Childbirth: Fifth Edition of Natural Childbirth & the Christian Family, Under the Apple Tree* as well as other educational materials.

Christian Homesteading Movement
Anna Marie and Richard Fahey
Rd. #2 N
Oxford, NY 13830

Information on homesteading, midwifery/homebirth skills and herbal care primarily taught in week-long intensives. Some of their courses are taught by correspondence.

International Childbirth Education Assoc.
(ICEA)
Box 20048
Minneapolis, MN 55420

A federation of childbirth education groups worldwide which sponsors regional conferences and a biennial convention. Wide selection of books and other educational materials (including PennyPress materials). Certifies childbirth educators.

American Academy of Husband-Childbirth
Box 5224
Sherman Oaks, CA 91413

Certifies childbirth instructors Coached in the Bradley Method of natural childbirth.

Apprentice Academics
P.O. Box 788
Claremore, OK 74018-0788

Excellent midwifery training program by Carla Harley. Name of program may have recently changed.

Christian Midwives International
P.O. Box 21621
Eugene, OR 97402

Formed by Jan Tritten of *Midwifery Today* to provide quarterly newsletters and CMI prayer meetings at *Midwifery Today* Conferences.

Birth Supplies:

Spirit-Led Childbirth
PO Box 1225
Oakhurst, CA 93644
(209) 683-2678
toll-free 1-888-683-2678 (orders)

Excellent resource for birth supplies under the new ownership of Leslie Parish, a Believer committed to service of the Lord Jesus Christ. Expanded selection (at good prices) of birth supplies, books and nutritional products to meet the needs of practicing midwives as well as moms and dads.

Cascade Healthcare Products, Inc.
141 Commercial St. NE
Salem, OR 97301
(800) 462-4784

Birth supply house. Also owns Birth & Life Bookstore and Moonflower Birthing Supply-"Mystical" perspective of birth and healing.

BIRTH Video
Box 475
Aptos, CA 95001
(408) 761-3388

Excellent video by Veronica Wagner, R.N.,C.N.M. Veronica is a Christian midwife who has delivered thousands of babies in over 20 years of practice. This video is wonderful and available for only $32.50

Nutritional Supplement Companies:

The companies listed sell primarily to health food stores or professional providers. Some sell directly to consumers. These are noted with an asterisk (*).

American Health
15 Dexter Plaza
Pearl River, NY 10965
(800) 445-7137

Maker of Super Papaya digestive enzymes as well as other products.

bio/chem Research
865 Parallel Dr.
Lakeport, CA 95453
(800) 225-4345

Producers of Citricidal, a grapefruit seed extract antimicrobial.

Biotec Foods
2639 S. King St. #206
Honolulu, HI 96826
(800) 331-5888

High-potency, enteric-coated antioxidant enzyme formulas to include superoxide dismutase and glutathione peroxidase.

Blessed Herbs
109 Barre Plains Rd.
Oakham, MA 01068
(800) 489-HERB

Company providing herb tinctures, bulk herbs, oils, salves, tea bags, soaps, shampoos and books.

Cardiovascular Research/
Ecological Formulas
106 "B" Shary Circle
Concord, CA 94518
(800) 888-4585
(510) 827-2636 (in CA)

Advanced nutritional medicine line specializing in immune support, yeast problems and allergies.

Eclectic Institute, Inc.
11231 S.E. Market St.
Portland, OR 97216
(800) 332-HERB

Maker of Opti-Natal prenatal vitamins as well as other multiple vitamin and mineral formulas specifically designed for certain health conditions. Only source I know of that carries the freeze-dried herbal products such as nettles that has received so much research attention in the past few years.

*The Pure Body Institute
423 East Ojai Ave. #107
Ojai, CA 92303
(800) 952-PURE

Makers of the best internal cleansing program I've tried. It is gentle yet very effective. "Nature's Pure Body Program" is my personal choice for pre-pregnancy detoxification.

Enzymatic Therapy
825 Challenger Dr.
Green Bay, WI 54311
(800) 648-8211

Top-quality line of nutritional products. Michael Murray, N.D. is on their Scientific Advisory Board which tells me this company is committed to excellence. ET has been the first to provide U.S. consumers with nutritional supplements common on the European market because of their research-proven benefits.

*Frontier Cooperative Herbs
Box 299
Norway, IA 52318

Full-line of bulk herbs. Now expanding their encapsulated product line.

Kal Healthway Vitamins
P.O. Box 4023
Woodland Hills, CA 91365
(818) 340-3035

Nutritional product company that has been around for a long time. Many times available through food co-ops.

McZand Herbal, Inc.
P.O. Box 5312
Santa Monica, CA 90405
(310) 822-0500

A limited line of herb supplements primarily designed for immune and respiratory support.

Metagenics, Inc./Ethical Nutrients
971 Calle Negocio
San Clemente, CA 92672
(800) 692-9400

Quality and excellence are found in this company's products that are sold under the brand of Metagenics for practitioners, Ethical Nutrients for health food stores. I especially like their line of Intestinal Care products. They have the only milk thistle extract tablets standardized to contain 80% silymarin that I have been able to find.

Miracle Exclusives, Inc.
P.O. Box 349
Locust Valley, NY 11560
(800) 645-6360

Floradix liquid vitamin and herb supplements are made by this company including Floradix Liquid Iron mentioned in the section on anemia.

*Mother's Choice™
P.O. Box 829
North San Juan, CA 95960
1-888-HERB-MOM, toll-free

Excellent liquid line of herbal TincTracts™ sold directly to mother's at wholesale cost. Sister line of the Liquid Light™ herbs. Carries my midwife formulas.

Natren
3105 Willow Lane
Westlake Village, CA 91361
(800) 992-3323
(800) 992-9292 (CA)

Maker of probiotics such as "Life Start" containing *Bifidobacterium infantis* and "Bio Nate," an improved strain of *acidophilus*.

Nature's Apothecary
997 Dixon Road
Boulder, CO 80302
(303) 581-0288

Source of herbal products.

Nature's Sunshine Products, Inc.
P. O. Box 1000
Spanish Fork, UT 84660

A line of products sold through distributors in a multi-level organization.

Nature's Herbs
P.O. Box 335
Orem, UT 84059
(800) HERBALS

Owned by Twinlab, a company producing excellent herbal products certified both for potency and organic.

Nature's Way
10 Mountain Spring Pkwy.
Springville, UT 84663
(800) 9-NATURE

Superior quality nutritional and herbal products easily found in the health food store and in many food co-ops.

NF Formulas, Inc.
805 S.E. Sherman
Portland, OR 97214
(800) 547-4891

A full line of naturopathic products including my favorite prenatal supplement, Prenatal Forte. Their Echinacea products are some of the best. Sold only through practitioners and midwives.

Phyto-Pharmica

(see Enzymatic Therapy)

Progressive Labs/ *Kordial Products
1701 W. Walnut Hill Lane
Irving, TX
(800) 527-9512

Extensive line of dietary supplements certain to please both health practitioners and consumers due to their commitment to excellence in product and customer service.

Rainbow Light Nutritional Systems
207 McPherson St.
Santa Cruz, CA 95060
(800) 635-1233

Maker of a quality line of supplements to include one of my favorite menstrual cycle regulators, Fem-a-Gen.

Schiff Products
180 Moonachie Ave.
Moonachie, NJ 07074
(800) 526-6251

Full line of products available in many health food stores.

Standard Process Laboratories
12209 Locksley Lane, Ste. 15
Auburn, CA 95603
(800) 662-9134
(916) 888-1974 (in CA)

Extensive line of naturopathic formulas sold only to chiropractors and naturopaths. Some midwives may be able to distribute them.

Traditional Medicinals
4515 Ross Road
Sebastopol, CA 95472

A quality line of herbal teas sold for specific health conditions such as "Pregnancy Tea" and "Mother's Milk."

Tri-Light, brand name Liquid Light™
14618 Tyler Foote Road
Nevada City, CA 95959
(800) HERB-KID

My personal favorite for liquid herbs. This company uses a unique multi-staged process that captures the optimum benefits from the herbs while preserving enzymes and preventing oxidation. Children love the flavor (glycerine is naturally sweet) and adults like the potency. No alcohol, no sugar, in handy squeeze bottles—standard glycerites, these are not. Yes, they do process my Midwife Formulas, and no, I do not receive any financial gain from their sales. Lyle and Mary are kind, generous Believers concerned with family health.

Twin Labs
2120 Smithtown Ave.
Ronkonkoma, NY 11779
(800) 645-5626

A complete line of nutritional supplements commonly found in health food stores and food co-ops.

UAS Laboratories
9201 Penn Ave. S., #10
Minneapolis, MN 55431
(800) 422-DDS-1

Maker of the DDS Acidophilus, a high-potency strain.

Magazines and Journals:

Herbalgram
American Botanical Council
Austin, TX 78720
(512) 331-8868

Published quarterly by the American Botanical Council and the Herb P.O. Box 201660 Research Foundation. Subscriptions: $25/yr. This is THE best source for up-to-date research news, legal and regulatory information regarding nutritional supplements and the ABC mail-order bookstore offerings include basic herbals as well as more scientific works for the professional herbalists (or consumers desiring to truly educate themselves for family herbal care). No home considering botanical medicine should be without this journal.

Herb Research Foundation
10007 Pearl St., Ste. 200
Boulder, CO 80302

*Membership to HRF is $35/yr and includes a subscription to *Herbalgram*. Both ABC and HRF are non-profit educational organizations and need our support to continue their very valuable work. HRF members also receive the *Herb Research News* quarterly edited by Rob McCaleb, HRF President.
**For a small increased member donation, the Herb Research Foundation will

also include a subscription to *Herbs For Health*, my very favorite herb magazine!

Protocol Journal of Botanical Medicine
Herbal Research Publications
12B Lancaster County Road
Harvard, MA 01451

A peer-reviewed publication offering current and thoroughly referenced material for use in both clinical and educational settings. Each issue offers therapeutic protocols with descriptions of contra-indications, underlying chemistry and pharmacology and complete citations from research from around the world. Subscriptions: $96/yr. Quarterly.

Quarterly Newsletter of
The American Herb Association
P.O. Box 1673
Nevada City, CA 95959

This 20-page newsletter is always packed with an array of information from case studies and research news to book reviews—my personal favorite section. AHA is an association of medical herbalists; however because of AHA's commitment to promoting the use, understanding and acceptance of herbs, anyone interested in herbs will benefit from regular reading of the *Newsletter*. Subscriptions: $20/yr. Quarterly.

Digest of Alternative Medicine
P.O. Box 2049
Sequim, WA 98382
(360) 385-0699 (FAX)

An offshoot of the *Townsend Letter for Doctors* that is designed for use by patients. Write for subscription information.

Townsend Letter for Doctors
Townsend Letter Group
911 Tyler Street
Port Townsend, WA 98368
(360) 385-6021

This 150+ page journal is written for and by health care providers. Published 10 times per year at $49 subscription price, it is an incredible value to those interested in the technical, scientific side of nutritional healing. Many naturopathic researchers publish their findings in this journal.

Medical Herbalism
P.O. Box 33080
Portland, OR 97233

This 12-page newsletter is published six times per year for $18 subscription fee. Focus is primarily case studies and practical application of herbal medicine.

Books:

Botanical Medicine

The ABC Herbal by Steven Horne. Wendell Whitman Co., 302 E. Winona Avenue, Warsaw, IN 46580. 1992. 82 pp. $7.95.

A quick afternoon read that will give parents the very basics of herbal care with an obvious leaning to Thomsonian practice. The aspect I like best about this book is the guidelines for using the Tri-Light Liquid Light TincTracts (the formulas mentioned in the book are those that Tri-Light processes).

The Alternative Health & Medicine Encyclopedia by James E. Marti.

The Encyclopedia is basically a guide to alternative therapies. The botanical and nutritional medicine information is good; however, there are therapies I personally have a caution about using.

Botanical Influences on Illness: A Sourcebook of Clinical Research by Melvin R. Werbach, M.D. and Michael T. Murray, N.D., Third Line Press, Tarzana, CA. 1994. 344 pp. $39.95

This book is not a guide as to what to use or how to use it; rather, it is more an annotated bibliography that most herbalists will find most helpful when called upon to cite scientific safety and efficacy documentation for clients.

The Complete Botanical Prescriber by John A. Sherman, N.D.

A wonderful book for those who counsel others in use of herbs or for those consumers who wish to be highly informed. The price is a little steep at $59.95, but well worth it for professionals.

Encyclopedia of Natural Medicine by Michael Murray, N.D. and Joseph Pizzorno, N.D.

Dr. Murray and Dr. Pizzorno, authors of *The Textbook of Naturopathic Medicine* which is the definitive text for naturopathic physicians, have written this book as a comprehensive guide for consumers detailing how to use herbs, vitamins, minerals as well as diet and other nutritional supplements. The book employs an easy-to-use style which lists health conditions followed by natural treatments for said conditions.

Foundations of Health: The Liver & Digestive Herbal by Christopher Hobbs. Botanica Press, P.O. Box 742, Capitola CA. 1992. 321 pp. $12.95

Most of us might skip this book thinking we do not have a problem with our livers. How much we would miss if we did. The longer I practice herbal health care with an emphasis on pregnancy and childbirth, I find the liver to be an organ not to be ignored if one seeks a healthy pregnancy. Mr. Hobbs does an excellent job of explaining liver and digestive function, and his recommendations for keeping our liver happy and healthy are superb.

Gynecology and Naturopathic Medicine, A Treatment Manual by Tori Hudson, N.D.

An excellent "treatment manual" is what I would call this spiral-bound book. All practitioners who combine botanical medicine with women's health care will want this one in their library. Consumers who want to participate more in their preventive health plan than simply doing what someone else recommends without knowing why will also benefit from the reading of this book.

The Healing Herbs by Michael Castleman.

This is one of my most-valued books in my personal library. It was a wonderful introduction to the "scientific" side of herbal medicine. Castleman lists the historical usage of herbs, herbal healing information based on scientific research, safety concerns for specific herbs where appropriate as well as herb-growing guidelines. The only thing I do not agree with in this book is the advice to not give herbal medicines to children under 2 years of age or older people over 65 or pregnant women. My own family has chosen to inform ourselves of the risks versus benefit of both herbal medicine and modern pharmaceuticals and choose herbal medicine (wise and prudent use) the majority of the time.

The Healing Power of Herbs by Michael T. Murray, N.D.

The subtitle of this book is "The Enlightened Person's Guide To The Wonders Of Medicinal Plants." Dr. Murray does not mean mystically enlightened; rather, this title appropriately refers to the scientific enlightenment that occurs when we begin to dip into the great body of research regarding botanical medicines. After reading this book, which is so well documented, one will know botanical medicine yields results that not only compete with modern pharmaceuticals, but actually outperform them in many instances.

Herbs for Health and Healing by Kathi Keville, Director of the American Herb Association.

Easy to read. Plenty of make-your-own formulas. Kathi is an authority in the professional herbalist field, and it shows in her book.

Herbal Prescriptions for Better Health by Donald J. Brown, N.D.

Currently one of my favorite herbals. Excellent scientific documentation along with well-researched toxicity information. A very readable writing style makes this book one of the most essential for families who are practicing herbal medicine at home.

Herbal Tonic Therapies by Daniel B. Mowrey, Ph.D.

Another great book due to the abundance of scientific citations for each herb discussed. The format follows herbal support for the body systems which does include a section on gynecological health which I have found particularly helpful.

Herbs of Choice by Varro Tyler, Ph.D., ScD.

Although Dr. Tyler and I would not agree on every point of what defines herbalism, I feel this book will serve as a bridge between the informed natural health community and the all-too-often misinformed medical community. This is not a "starter" book into herbal healing unless one has a command of pharmaceutical terms and a good knowledge of biochemistry. Dr. Tyler does present meticulous documentation that makes further study a breeze.

Herbs That Heal by Michael A. Weiner, Ph.D. and Janet Weiner.

This book is extremely user-friendly. A number of herbs are presented complete with their history, recent scientific findings, preparation instructions and some caution information. Since the material is not foot- or end-noted, further study proves difficult for those of us who want to see the source.

Natural Alternatives to Over-the-Counter and Prescription Drugs by Michael T. Murray, N.D.

This book is my favorite book to recommend to those who are new to botanical medicine. Dr. Murray provides excellent information about drugs commonly used for the health complaints he addresses in the book, and then he follows this with excellent lifestyle/dietary and nutritional supplement recommendations. Must have this book when practicing herbal medicine.

Natural Prescriptions by Robert M. Giller, M.D. and Kathy Matthews.

I found this book to be more about vitamins, minerals and other nutritional supplements than about botanical medicine; however, I have included it in this section because I liked the background information given on each health condition. Health problems are listed alphabetically with treatment options in a shaded box at the end of each section.

The Natural Pharmacy by Skye Lininger, D.C., Editor-in-Chief, Jonathan Wright, M.D., Steve Austin, N.D., Donald Brown, N.D., Alan Gaby, M.D.

An excellent sourcebook for specific illness recommendations, detailed information, including toxicity risk, of nutritional supplements.

Nutrition:

Fertility, Cycles and Nutrition by Marilyn M. Shannon. The Couple-to-Couple League Int'l. Cincinnati, OH. 1992. 167 pp. $10.95.

Marilyn Shannon offers in this book the basics of nutrition coupled with specific nutritional recommendations to positively affect fertility. I especially like the tone of this book — favorable to large families, breastfeeding and natural family planning.

Food - Your Miracle Medicine by Jean Carper. HarperCollins Publishers, Inc., 10 E. 53rd St., New York, NY. 1993. 528 pp. $25.00.

This is my favorite and most-often reached for book on nutritional healing. The format listing disorders by body system and then alphabetically within that system is so easy to use. Even critics of "alternative medicine" cannot argue with research proving Grandma's chicken soup really is good for respiratory bugs.

Encyclopedia of Nutritional Supplements by Michael T. Murray, N.D.

Murray completely covers all nutritional supplements with information on how to obtain through diet and supplementation, correct dosages and toxicity information.

The Healing Power of Foods by Michael T. Murray, N.D. Prima Publishing, P.O. Box 1260BK, Rocklin, CA. 1993. 438 pp. $16.95.

Yes, I do have every one of this man's books, and the reason is I have found every single one of them to be a source of solid education on nutrition and herbs. This particular book educates one on the nutrient content of different foods as well as provides an ample section on health conditions that may be treated with food recommendations given.

What Every Pregnant Woman Should Know by Gail Sforza Brewer with Tom Brewer, M.D. Penguin Books, 375 Hudson St., New York, NY. 1985. 260 pp. $9.95.

This information contained in this book arms women with the nutritional guidelines that helps to prevent the pregnancy complication, metabolic toxemia of late pregnancy. While I do believe protein is important to prevent MTLP, I believe that it is beneficial to obtain said protein from a variety of sources that excludes liver.

Pregnancy and Childbirth

A Good Birth, A Safe Birth by Diana Korte & Roberta Scaer.

This is a must read for a thorough understanding of the risks and benefits regarding the technology of birth especially for those planning a hospital birth. Those planning a home birth will also benefit from this information. Do not assume having a midwife will mean no intervention; be informed.

The Birth Book. William Sears, M.D. and Martha Sears, R.N.

This is a comforting and reassuring book about the natural-ness of childbirth. The Sears clearly and simply share with us the benefits of "low-tech, high-touch" birth. Options are discussed openly and honestly. Illustrations are some of the best I've seen of birth positions. My favorite quote from the book, "While you can't totally orchestrate the perfect birth—birth is full of surprises—you can create the conditions that increase your chances of having the birth you want."

Childbirth Without Fear by Grantly Dick-Read.

Helen Wessel Nickel has revised this edition of Mr. Dick-Read's classic on natural childbirth. An excellent book for the parent-to-be.

Emergency Childbirth. Gregory White.

A small, basic manual for those who are concerned about not making it to the hospital or their midwife not making it to the home for delivery. Step-by-step instructions are clear and easy to understand.

Heart and Hands. Elizabeth Davis.

A guide written for midwives, but useful for mothers planning home-birth, on caring for pregnant women.

The Joy of Natural Childbirth, A Revised Edition of Natural Childbirth and the Christian Family. Helen Wessel-Nickel.

Helen walks one through the beginning of pregnancy to the completion of a joy-filled birth in this book. An essential book to understand God's design for birth. Keep in mind that while His design is perfect, our fallen world may yield a not-quite-perfect birth. I suppose what I am trying to say is that although pain in childbirth may not be a curse from God, most women do experience some (or a great deal) pain during their childbirth experience. The perception of pain in daily life has an impact on the perception of pain during birth.

Under the Apple Tree. Helen Wessel Nickel.

Once again, Helen imparts to us her expansive knowledge of Christian parenting and birth. Her personal style of writing makes the book a very easy read.

Birth After Cesarean. Bruce Flamm, M.D.

Extensive documentation of the safety of vaginal birth following a cesarean section. De-bunks the myth of "Once a cesarean, always a cesarean."

Understanding Diagnostic Tests in the Childbearing Year. Anne Frye.

This 1995 revised edition is Frye's best yet. While I do not practice midwifery, therefore am not the book's target group, I do prefer to have my own information available at home to go over my lab results and aid in self-diagnosis where possible. I found this book to be the one most referred to during my childbearing years (my midwife kept calling me for the answers—she didn't own the book until I sold her one of her own).

Breastfeeding

Bestfeeding. Renfrew, Fisher and Arms.

A basic guide to breastfeeding. Accurate information and helpful pictures.

Breastfeeding and Natural Child Spacing. Sheila Kippley.

Discusses and details the "ecological" method of natural child spacing. The information is accurate and scientific on the natural amenorrhea imparted through breastfeeding which I believe is God's perfect design for a woman's healing and rest for baby's first year.

Keys to Breastfeeding. William and Martha Sears.

Practical advice for new and expectant moms on nutrition, dietary needs and advantages of breastfeeding.

The Womanly Art of Breastfeeding. La Leche League International.

Don't throw out the baby with the bath water. While I may disagree with much of the childrearing information promoted through La Leche League, this organization should be recognized for being highly instrumental in a resurgence in breastfeeding in this country. Their breastfeeding support is invaluable for many women. I was told to call La Leche League when I had my first child prematurely. I did not. I now wish I had as he was bottle-fed, developed allergies and chronic ear infections until I finally got him off formula and cow's milk.

Marriage and Family

Titles by Patrick L. Hurd: *Separation of Church and Family; Sexual Purity; Covenant Succession: Transferring Godly Convictions to our Children; The High Calling of Covenantal Fatherhood; Training Godly Rulers: Apprenticing in Statecraft; Solidarity vs. Separatism: In Search of Effectual Alliances; Our Heritage of Citizenship; The Effectual Kingdom Family.*

Reforming Marriage by Douglas Wilson.

This is a wonderful book on marriage. I've never seen a clearer presentation of the Christ-Bride/Husband-Wife relationship.

The Fruit of Her Hands by Nancy Wilson.

This is an excellent book for women on "our part" in the marriage relationship.

Other family titles by Douglas Wilson: *Her Hand in Marriage, Standing on the Promises.*

Family Planning

All the Way Home by Mary Pride

The Art of Natural Family Planning. John and Sheila Kippley.

The Bible and Birth Control. Charles D. Provan.

A Full Quiver: Family Planning and the Lordship of Christ. Rick and Jan Hess.

Letting God Plan Your Family. Samuel A. Owen, Jr.

Children: Blessing or Burden (Exploding Myth of the Small Family). Max Heine.

Grand Illusions: The Legacy of Planned Parenthood. George Grant.

The Way Home by Mary Pride

Child Training

I recommend the books below knowing that they offer practical suggestions to loving our children by training our children; however, I want to add that whatever training we do, we need to realize that the sin nature of our children cannot be trained out. Our children can learn to obey, but they will disobey (sin) because of their flesh's cry for willfulness. Do not be discouraged! God is at work in all of us. Let us be diligent in our daily training and be not angry when they fail.

Seminars by Jonathan Lindvall.

My church family has benefited from the shared wisdom of this man's experience with child training and suggestions for protecting our children.

Shepherding a Child's Heart by Ted Tripp.

This book gets to the heart of the disobedience matter. A good book to provide some insight for our children into the "why" of their behavior.

Hints on Child Training. Henry Clay Trumbull.

A classic written over a hundred years earlier, this book still hits right on target. The truth of: discipline-only promoting wrath, love-only promoting self-adoration is clear as Trumbull promotes a loving discipline method of child training.

To Train Up a Child. Michael and Debi Pearl.

The Pearls have written a concise book on building family ties and gentle use of the rod for training. I do not particularly promote the early toilet training exampled in this book (I think it's parent-training; if parents want to be trained this way, fine). This book offers very practical "remedies" to rebellious behavior.

PART NINE

Nutritional and Botanical Medicine

"And God said, Behold, I have given you every herb bearing seed, which is upon the face of all the earth, and every tree, in the which is the fruit of the tree yielding seed: to you it shall be for meat." Genesis 1:29

NUTRITIONAL AND BOTANICAL MEDICINE

Why Should You Read This Section

The information contained in this section of the book will help moms and caregivers make the best and safest choices in supplements today. Nutritional and botanical medicine are not immune to problems within the industry. There are irresponsible supplement companies and herbalists just as there are irresponsible physicians. Fortunately for us all, these irresponsible members of both groups are few in number.

I think it important that we inform ourselves as much as possible since there is disagreement in the herb community as to the safety and/or efficacy of different herbs. The same admonition that has been carried throughout this book applies here: Do not simply trust what is said in any one book other than THE book, the Word of God, our Holy Bible; do your own research, ask questions, make certain that the author is giving a correct representation of the topic of discussion.

Certainly, I have attempted here to at least give you a sampling of how one uncovers the truth about herbs that have been called into question in terms of safety or efficacy. When I read about herbs that are being banned or called "unsafe," yet those same herbs have a long history of historical safety, I dig further to try to find out if the problem is only a contamination problem or if it is only unsafe for a certain group of people with known health disorders, etc.

Always, when I reach an impasse in my research, I call upon information provided by the *Herb Research Foundation*, a non-profit organization dedicated to providing accurate information about herbal medicine. Their address and phone number may be found in Part 8, Resources, Magazines and Journals.

Safety Questions

The safety of certain herbs has been questioned particularly in the past few years as more consumers choose to employ herbal medicine as part of their health care program. It never ceases to amaze me when television news shows or newspapers and magazines vilify herbal medicine because of a limited number of herbs that may have contributed to pre-existing health problems. These same media sources ignore the overwhelming confirmed and documented evidence of health problems created by over-the-counter and prescription drugs.

The concern about herb safety appears to arise from several different reasons: the inherent toxicity of certain herbs, the presence of potentially toxic chemical constituents in certain herbs, and the potential for adulteration in the herb industry. These are valid concerns that should warrant our investigation into the herbs we plan to consume; however, we need not toss the baby out with the bathwater. All of these concerns can be addressed and our risks limited through wise and prudent use.

Inherent Toxicity

There are definitely certain herbs that have toxic effects; most of us would call them poisons. These plants, while certainly herbs, would not be present in the category of medicinal herbs. These herbs primarily function as the basis for pharmaceutical preparations. One example of an inherently toxic plant is belladonna or deadly nightshade. Belladonna toxicity depends largely on the presence of the alkaloids Hyoscyamine and Atropine. Some scopolamine is present in the leaves. This is not an herb to be used as part of home health care because it is classified as a poison. Belladonna instead performs as the basis for pharmaceutical preparations because of its narcotic, diuretic, sedative, antispasmodic and mydriatic effects. Other examples of poisonous or inherently toxic herbs that should not be used without professional preparation and guidance would be: poke root, mandrake, ipecac, opium, rauwolfia, foxglove, ergot. This list is by no means exhaustive; rather, it is a sampling of toxic herbs some of us may be familiar with because of their pharmaceutical preparations.

Potentially Toxic Constituents

Many herbs and foods have chemical constituents (chemical parts of their make-up) that are toxic if that chemical alone is administered. This concern has created the most debate. Even some professional herbalists differ in their opinions as to whether an herb with potentially toxic constituents should be consumed in any quantity. While it would certainly not be prudent to ingest these isolated chemicals, does it necessarily follow that these chemicals when found in the whole herb (or portion of the plant that is generally used) constitute a direct threat to the general public? The answer to this question appears to be simple, yet because each of us is unique in design by our Creator, each individual must weigh the risk versus benefit for oneself and seek the counsel of others with wisdom in order to come to a decision regarding usage.

Several herbs have come under fire from the FDA because of their pyrollizidine alkaloid (PA)-content, namely, comfrey, borage, coltsfoot and life root. Pyrollizidine alkaloids have been linked as a contributing factor in several individuals who developed a disorder called hepatic veno-occlusive disease (HVOD), also known as Budd-Chiari syndrome. HVOD occurs when blood flow from the liver becomes obstructed which then impairs liver function. HVOD can lead to liver damage of varying degrees and, still later, can lead to cancerous liver tumors. This is a serious disorder that might, at first glance, convince anyone that any use of herbs containing pyrollizidine alkaloids would mean certain disease. The problem with this assumption is that these herbs have been used for several thousand years by a great number of people without the end result of all of them contracting HVOD. Why did only these people contract the disease and not all or even most of the world's other comfrey users?

I am not trying to minimize the ill effects of pyrollizidine alkaloids. They can be destructive to the body. The first point to consider when evaluating PA-containing herbs for safety is that we must recognize that some of those who contracted HVOD appeared to already have liver or digestive system problems. Another point to consider is that PA-containing herbs were not definitely identified as the cause; they were linked to the disease because a few of the people who contracted HVOD had consumed comfrey in the form of comfrey/pepsin tablets. Lastly, the people who were using comfrey were ingesting large quantities above the standard recommended dosage. One boy had Crohn's disease, a chronic intestinal disorder. This young boy drank comfrey tea daily for two years before he developed HVOD. Another woman developed HVOD after four months of taking six comfrey/pepsin capsules daily in addition to drinking a quart of comfrey tea each day.[378] All of these factors make the case against any use of PA-containing herbs less clear. In point of fact, there has never been reported a case of HVOD in people taking recommended amounts of herbs containing pyrollizidine alkaloids for brief periods.

Since these herbs do have beneficial properties as well as the PA content, a cautious approach would make sense until some definitive research combined with the long history of use clears up this PA/HVOD relationship.

The following people should exercise caution or avoid the use of herbs containing pyrollizidine alkaloids (comfrey, borage, coltsfoot, life root):

- Persons with a history of liver disease, alcoholism, or general digestive problems;
- Children under two because their immature digestive systems might possibly be unable to process any absorbed alkaloid;
- Pregnant women because pregnancy places a greater burden on the liver's detoxifying process;
- Nursing mothers because whatever mom eats or drinks, baby absorbs while nursing.

Comfrey has also been accused of being carcinogenic. What a bad reputation this once highly-regarded herb is now gaining! A different picture is painted once again with a little investigation into the experiments upon which this ill repute is based. The experiment that deemed comfrey carcinogenic was one in which lab rats or mice were fed very large doses of comfrey roots for 600 days. After 130 days, they began to show liver toxicity. By the end of the study, liver cancer appeared in even the rats fed the lowest dosage of comfrey. Comfrey roots contain 10 times the pyrollizidine alkaloids that the leaves contain, and these rats were (as usual for toxicity studies) being fed doses many times greater than the human equivalent daily dosage. The result extrapolated from this study cannot be equated to human consumption or application of comfrey since we do not exist solely on a diet of mega-doses of comfrey roots for almost two years (at least we certainly should not be existing in this manner).

Tons of comfrey are grown each year to be used as fodder for horses, cattle and pigs with no ill effects observed. Our human history of comfrey use has no reports of harm to the average person. In a 1987 study published in Science, Dr. Bruce Ames, Ph.D., chariman of the Biochemistry Department at the University of California at Berkeley, estimated the lifetime cancer risk from exposure to typical man-made and naturally-occurring carcinogens. His estimations concluded that one cup of comfrey tea posed:

- about the same risk as one peanut butter sandwich, which contains traces of the natural carcinogen aflatoxin;
- about half the risk of eating one raw mushroom, which contains traces of the natural carcinogen, hydrazine;
- half the risk of one diet soda containing saccharin;
- and about one one-hundredth the risk of a standard beer or glass of wine, which contains the natural carcinogen ethyl alcohol.

He did conclude that comfrey-pepsin tablets carry 4 to 200 times the risk of comfrey tea.[379] The tablets can be avoided because there are so many other herbs that may be used to supplement the digestive process with lesser risk.

Another herb that came under attack and was banned by the FDA several years ago was chapparal. The FDA banned it until it could be proven that it did not cause kidney and liver failure in four cancer patients undergoing extensive chemotherapy treatments. Chapparal contains the chemical NDGA (nordihydroguaiaretic acid) which is approved by the U.S. Department of Agriculture as a preservative in lard and animal shortenings. NDGA has an antiseptic and antioxidant action that kills bacteria and microorganisms that turn fat and oils rancid. This antiseptic action reduces cavities by 75%, according to a study done on chaparral mouthwash published in the *Journal of Dental Research*.[380] Medical literature has several case reports of tumor shrinkage in people who used chapparal.

The FDA removed NDGA from the list of substances generally regarded as safe (GRAS) in 1968 because experimental animals fed large amounts for long periods developed kidney and lymph-system problems. No human kidney or lymphatic disease has ever been documented in chaparral users until this recent questioning of its safety.[381] The most baffling aspect is that over the long history of chaparral use, this problem has not appeared before even when being used by other cancer patients. All four of the individuals who experienced kidney and liver failure while taking chaparral were also taking extremely toxic drugs known to cause failure of the body's systems. These pharmaceuticals were not blamed, nor were they banned or even investigated; their toxicity was already established in their clinical drug trials. Chaparral seems to have been in the wrong body at the wrong time.

Yet another herb has a lingering cloud of controversy over its name, lobelia. I read in one book on pregnancy and childbirth that lobelia was a very dangerous herb to be avoided by all. The book claimed that lobelia can cause convulsion, coma and even death due to the toxic alkaloid, lobeline. As I looked up the research done on the herb, lobelia, I found these danger claims were made on drug provings for the isolated constituent of the herb, lobeline, not on the whole herb, lobelia. As already mentioned, the toxic alkaloid, lobeline, can cause convulsion, coma and even death. Well, this toxic alkaloid, lobeline, is the active ingredient in some over-the-counter (OTC) drugs used as nicotine deterrents.

I phoned a Poison Control Center to inquire about common effects of the herb lobelia. I was told common effects are: vomiting, transient slowing of the heart rate, increase in blood pressure, and an increase in the respiratory or breathing rate.[382] These effects are most often associated with large doses of the herb, not standard recommended dosages. In the history of lobelia use, the emetic (induces vomiting) effect is clearly noted and actually honored. This emetic effect makes overdose (with recommended amounts) extremely unlikely. The OTC preparations containing lobeline do not have this built-in protective device (emetic property); therefore, lobeline-containing OTCs *do* represent an overdose risk. They have not been banned, but they have the FDA stamp of approval.

St. John's Wort, an herb with increasingly recognized beneficial effects, was included in a March 1977 USFDA "unsafe herb list" due to toxic reactions in cattle. These reactions were not in humans, just in cattle. St. John's Wort may have phytotoxic activity (increases sunburn risk) in humans when used in large quantities. There has never been any report that this is the case; however, we might choose to follow the lead of our Eastern neighbors. European consumers who have long used this herb confine their use to moderate doses and restrict their exposure to sunlight while medicinally using the herb.[383]

Sassafras is another herb with unsavory reputation due to its content of the chemical compound safrole. Safrole was isolated from the whole plant sassafras and fed to mice in the 1960s. A high percentage of the mice had liver damage and liver cancer by the end of the study. This is why the FDA banned the whole herb's internal use. It has been found since that time that safrole itself does not cause cancer in animals; it first must be converted to another compound that is known to be carcinogenic. We do not have adequate research to show that safrole does or does not pose a significant cancer risk in humans. We do know that sassafras has long been popular and is still in use despite its ban with no ill effects being reported.[384]

After all this investigation, it seems that beyond the issue of potentially toxic constituents, the issue really is one of prudent use in recommended amounts for limited periods of time when dealing with those herbs whose safety has been called into question.

Adulteration and Contamination in the Herb Industry

Adulteration of herbal products (accidentally or deliberately substituting one herb for another or processing in such a way as to allow contaminants into the product) is a problem that has plagued the herb industry as long as there has been herb use. The situation is certainly getting better in that there are quite a few reputable companies processing herbs that have a definite commitment to ascertaining that the herb they are processing and labeling as herb X is indeed herb X. The problem with adulteration is that it can give an herb a bad name because the effects of the herb taken were not the effects expected or wanted. In the worst case scenario, the adulterating or contaminating agent can actually cause disease, as in the case of the l-trytophan controversy.

One quite excellent herb, ginseng, is still characterized in some herbals as causing an abuse syndrome. This accusation began with a 1979 study published in the *Journal of the American Medical Association* that linked ginseng to a "ginseng abuse syndrome" which supposedly included symptoms such as nervousness, sleeplessness, and raised blood pressure. The researcher also stated that his subjects (psychiatric patients) used caffeine regularly during the study. Caffeine is well known for the symptoms described in the "ginseng abuse syndrome."[385] In addition to the caffeine consumption, the subject's methods of consuming the herb were rather bizarre when compared to traditional ginseng use: they inhaled and injected it. This strongly suggests that the patients could also have been abusing illicit drugs during the two-year study, which could certainly skew the results.

"Morning diarrhea" was another of the symptoms of GAS. This could possibly be due to adulteration of the herb. The researcher admitted that he made no attempt to verify that his "ginseng" was, indeed, the herb ginseng. It certainly was fact that adulteration was rampant in the health food industry in the 1970s.[386] During the '70s, Wild Red American Ginseng or "desert ginseng" became popular. "Desert" ginseng is an impossibility because ginseng is a shade-loving, moisture-demanding plant. The phony ginseng was actually red dock, a laxative plant that contains anthraquinones (chemicals that stimulate intestinal peristalsis).[387]

As mentioned before, the worst of the adulteration/contamination cases was the l-tryptophan contamination that occurred between October 1988 to June of 1989 resulting in cases of EMS (eosinophilia-myalgia syndrome) in a number of individuals taking l-tryptophan products. The cases of EMS were not a result of taking l-tryptophan per se; rather, they were a result of taking contaminated l-tryptophan from Japanese supplier, Showa Denko.[388] The FDA removed products containing more than 100mg of l-tryptophan from the market due to the cases of EMS in November of 1989 before it became widely known that Showa Denko's contaminated l-tryptophan was the problem.

Despite the findings of contamination, the FDA has continued to refuse to lift the ban on uncontaminated l-tryptophan. This situation is a tragic one both for those who developed EMS and their families as well as for those for whom uncontaminated l-tryptophan had been effectively treating their insomnia and depression.[389] The irony and greater tragedy in the tryptophan ban is research reported in 1990 showed uncontaminated l-tryptophan to be one of the most effective treatments for EMS.[390]

As we have looked at the safety issues surrounding herbal products, our directives for safe, responsible use become clear:

- Avoid known toxic (poison) herbs or use only under a professional health care provider's guidance, completely avoid during pregnancy and lactation;

- Use herbs in medicinal amounts only in recommended dosages for limited periods of time; consult with a professional herbalist regarding use during pregnancy and lactation;

- Purchase herbal products only from reputable sources (see Part 8, Resources);

- Gather and process herbal medicines at home only after receiving instruction and education regarding identification of herbs in the wild.

APPENDIX:
THE PROFESSIONAL HERBALIST

What exactly *is* a Professional Herbalist? I wish the answer were as easy as saying "One who has certification in such and such areas;" however, this is not the case. Currently in the United States, there is no "official" certifying body for herbalists. Translated, this means that we are basically self-taught and self-governed.

While I do not see a problem with being self-taught (I am primarily self-taught), I think there are a few guidelines to follow when seeking a professional herbalist for herbal medicine recommendations. Since anyone could "hang out their herbalist's shingle" without actually being well-versed in the properties and actions of herbs, the consumer must shoulder the responsibility for making certain his/her herbalist is truly knowledgeable in the field of botanical medicine. I have set forth a few suggestions for the herbal consumer as he/she seeks professional herbal care:

1. Where did the herbalist receive his/her training?
   - Herbal Correspondence Course - What texts were used? Training in anatomy and physiology? Biochemistry? Herbal pharmacognosy? Basic pharmacology? Actual medicine-making with the herbs?
   - Apprenticeship - Who with? Were the above areas studied in addition to field work with the plants?
   - Self-Taught - Same questions as with herbal correspondence course as well as clinical experience? Can the herbalist work with the actual plant? Years of study?

2. Does the herbalist only work with one brand of herbal supplements?
   - While preferring certain supplements is actually the norm in botanical medicine, is the herbalist willing to concede that one company does not hold the "corner" on the "best" of medicines? One company cannot fill every need. Some will have better products in one area than another and vice versa. A willingness to explore a variety of company's products is essential to achieving the best for the client. Does the herbalist receive financial compensation for only recommending one certain brand? While this is not necessarily bad, this should be taken into consideration as being a financial incentive to get the consumer to purchase their product. Many herbalists make supplements available to their clients and receive the profit from wholesale to retail price for the supplement; however, the time for concern is when the herbalist tries to convince the consumer that no other product is "quality."

3. Does the herbalist read only books from a folklore/historical use standpoint or is he/she also knowledgeable in the scientific findings regarding herbal medicine?
   - While we certainly would not want to ignore the historical data, we must as herbalists strive to integrate scientific evidence with the clinical data we compile.

4. Is the herbalist willing to refer out to other specialists, including physicians, when necessary?
   - There are times in acute situations when allopathic medicine or pharmaceuticals could and should be employed; the herbalist must be willing to concede that he/she do not have "all the answers."

5. Are the fees for services reasonable and customary?
   - $ .50 - $1.00 per minute for phone consultations is common with evaluations ranging from $25.00 - $50.00 according to time involved.

6. Is the herbalist aware of the implications and cautions regarding herbal medicine during pregnancy and lactation?

7. Does the herbalist take a complete health history?
   - The whole picture of health must be taken into consideration to arrive at the appropriate measures to be taken.

8. Does the herbalist employ diagnostic techniques such as muscle response testing that may be objectionable to some believers (I, myself do not feel comfortable spiritually with this practice)?
   - The body is flesh, and the flesh does not know what is best for it since the flesh is not an omniscient being. The flesh is fallen and deteriorating until death. Herbs do not halt this process. They may slow or make deterioration less noticeable.

9. Does the herbalist acknowledge God as the Ultimate Healer or does he/she rely on the "power" or "spirit" of the herbs?

Finding a good herbalist is most often accomplished through the recommendation of a friend or other health professional. Consumers still must ask their own questions regarding the issues with which they are most concerned. I find, for myself, that I am primarily a researcher of data and clinical results more than anything else.

For more information about professional herbalists and other natural health care professionals, you may phone toll-free 1-888-HERB 101 to reach the Institute for Family Herbal Care. A free information packet is available as well as a free referral list to health professionals.

About The Author

Shonda Parker is the wife of Keith Parker and mother of five wonderful children (at least at the date of this printing!). Shonda, once a medical assistant, began her journey into natural medicine after the birth of her first child, Zachary, by cesarean section. She has since birthed, naturally, her next four children, Emily, Eryn, Eliana and Zebediah. Shonda learned about herbs through a variety of means: direct-learning under an herbalist, seminar and conference attendance and self-study. Shonda and Keith reside with their children in Weatherford, Texas, where they are members of Heritage Covenant Church.

INDEX

ENDNOTES

1. Pritchard, Jack A. and Paul C. MacDonald. *William's Obstetrics.* 15th Ed. New York, New York: Prentice-Hall, Inc. 1976. p. 257.

2. Beischer, Norman A. and Eric V. Mackay, *Obstetrics and the Newborn*, 2nd Ed. Artamon, NSW: CBS Publishing Australia Pty Limited, 1986. p. 197.

3. Giller, M.D., Robert M. and Kathy Matthews. *Natural Presciptions.* New York, New York: Crown Publishers, Inc., 1994. p. xxi.

4. Murray, N.D., Michael T. *Natural Alternatives to Over-the-Counter and Prescription Drugs.* New York, New York: William Morrow & Co., 1994. pp. 115 & 237.

5. Weiner, Ph.D., Michael A. & Janet A. Weiner. *Herbs That Heal.* Mill Valley, CA: Quantum Books, 1994. p. 181.

6. Davies, Dr. Stephen and Dr. Alan Stewart. *Nutritional Medicine.* New York, New York: Avon Books, 1987. p. 132.

7. Rinzler, Carol Ann. *The Safe Pregnancy Book.* New York, New York: New American Library, 1984. p. 106.

8. Davies, *Nutritional Medicine*, p. 132.

9. Ibid, p. 324.

10. Crawford, Amanda McQuade. *Herbal Remedies for Women.* Rocklin, CA: Prima Publishing, 1997. p. 136.

11. Weiner, *Herbs That Heal.* pp. 113-114.

12. Ibid, p. 151.

13. Ibid, p. 276.

14. Ibid, p. 339.

15. Castleman, Michael. *The Healing Herbs.* Emmaus, PA: Rodale Press, 1991. p. 77.

16. F. Umeda, et al., "Effect of Vitamin E on Function of Pituitary-gonadal Axis in Male Rats and Human Subjects," *Endocrinol Jpn*, 29(3), June 1982, p. 287-292.

17. Crawford, *Herbal Remedies* for Women, p. 138.

18. Scalzo, Richard. "Therapeutic Protocol for Premenstrual Syndrome," *The Protocol Journal of Botanical Medicine*, Spring 1996: 184-185.

19. Calloway, D. H. "Nutrition in reproductive function of man," *Nutrition Abstracts and Reviews, Reviews in Clinical Nutrition*, 53:5 (1983), 361-82.

20. Piesse, J. "Zinc and human male infertility," *International Clinical Nutrition Reviews*, 3:2 (1983), 4-6.

21. Jungling, M.D. and Bunge, R.G. "The treatment of spermatogenic arrest with arginine," *Fert. Ster.* 27 (1976), 282.

22. Davies, *Nutritional Medicine*, p. 318.

23. E. Kessopoulou, et al., "A Double-blind Randomized Placebo Cross-over Controlled Trial Using the Antioxidant Vitamin E to Treat Reactive Oxygen Species Associated Male Infertility," *Fertil Steril*, 64(4), October 1995, p. 825-831.

24. S. Palmero, et al., "The Effect of L-acetylcarnitine on Some Reproductive Functions in the Oligoasthenospermic Rat," *Horm Retab Res* (1990 Dec) 22(12):622-6.

25. A. Lenzi, et al., "Glutathione Therpay for Male Infertility," *Arch Androl*, 29(1), July-August 1992, p. 65-68.

26. C.Y. Hong, et al., "Astragalus Membranaceus Stimulates Human Sperm Motility in Vitro," *Am Jnl of Chin Med*, 20(3-4), 1992, p. 289-294.

27. Willson, J. Robert & Carrington, Elsie Reid. *Obstetrics & Gynecology.* St. Louis: MO: The C.V. Mosby Co., 1987. p. 210.

28. Mowrey, Daniel B., Ph.D. *Herbal Tonic Therapies.* New Canaan, CT: Keats Publishing, Inc., 1993. pp. 312-14.

29. Weiner, Michael A., Ph.D., & Janet A. *Herbs That Heal.* Mill Valley, CA: Quantum Books, 1994. p. 135.

30. Castleman, Michael. *The Healing Herbs.* Emmaus, PA: Rodale Publishing, 1991. p. 79 - 81.

31. Castleman, p. 295.

32. Weiner, p. 51.

33. Weiner, p. 339.

34. Kurzepa, S. & Samojlik, E. Studies on the effects of extracts from plants of the family rosaceae on gonadotropin and thyrotropin in the rat. *EndoKrinol Pol.* 14: 143- , 1963.

35. Phone conversation with DeAnn Domnick. Ms Domnick was unable to recall the naturopathic school from which the students came; therefore, I have been unable to trace the origin of the students "saying."

36. R.S. Shah, et al., "Vitamin E Status of the Newborn in Relation to Gestational Age, Birth Weight and Maternal Vitamin E Status," *British Jrnl of Nutrition*, 58(2), September 1987, p. 191-198.

37. Null, Gary, Ph.D. *The Clinician's Handbook of Natural Healing* NY, NY: Kensington Publishing Corp. 1997. P.693.

38. Bassett I.B., Pannowitz D. L. and Barnetson RSC, "A comparative study of tea tree oil versus benzoyl peroxide in the treatment of acne," *Med J Australia* 153: 455 - 458, '90.

39. Lininger, Skye, Wright, Jonathan, Austin, Steve, Brown, Donald, Gaby, Alan. *The Natural Pharmacy*. Rocklin, CA: Prima Publishing, 1998. p. 6.

40. L.H. Leung, "Pantothenic Acid Deficiency as the Pathogenesis of Acne Vulgaris," *Med Hypoth*, 44(6) June 1995, p. 490-492.

41. M.G. Longhi, et. Al., "Activity of Crataegus Oxyacantha Derivatives in Functional Dermocosmesis," *Fitoterapia*, L,(2), 1984, P. 87-99.

42. Shirakawa, T. and Morimoto, K.: "Lifestyle effect on total IgE," *Allergy*, 46:561-569, 1991.

43. Freedman, B.J. A diet free from additives in the management of allergic disease. *Clin Allergy*, 7:417-421, 1977.

44. Lindahl, O. Lindwall, L., Spangberg, A., et al. Vegan diet regimen with reduced medication in the treatment of bronchial asthma. *J Asthma*, 22:45-55, 1985.

45. Johnston, C.S., Retrum, K.R., and Srilakshmi, J.C. Antihistamine effects and complications of supplemental vitamin C. *J Am Diet Assoc*, 92:988-989, 1992.

46. Foreman, J.C. Mast cells and the actions of flavonoids. *J Allergy Clin Immunol*, 127:546-50, 1984.

47. Taussig, S. The mechanism of the physiological action of bromelain. *Med Hypoth*, 6:99-104, 1980.

48. Simon, S.W. Vitamin B-12 therapy in allergy and chronic dermatoses. *J Allergy*, 2:183-185, 1951.

49. Garrison, R. and E. Somer. *The Nutrition Desk Reference*, Chapter 5 - Vitamin Research: Selected Topics. New Canaan, CT: Keats Publishing, 1985. pp93-94.

50. Collip, P. J., Goldzier, S.III, Weiss, N., et al. Pyridoxine treatment of childhood asthma. *Ann Allergy*, 35:93-97, 1975.

51. Kasahara, Y., Hikino, H., Tsurufuji, S., et al. Anti-inflammatory actions of ephedrines in acute inflammations. *Planta Medica*, 54:325-331, 1985.

52. Weil, M.D. Andrew. *Natural Health*, Natural Medicine. Boston, Mass: Houghton Mifflin Co., 1990. p.254.

53. Weiner, PhD, Michael and Janet A. Weiner. *Herbs that Heal*. Mill Valley, CA: Quantum Books, 1994. p166. Actual studies listed p. 358.

54. Fu, J.S. Measurement of MEFV in 66 cases of asthma in the convalescent stage and after treatment with Chinese herbs. *Chinese Journal of Modern Developments in Traditional Medicine*, 9(11): 658-659, 644, 1989.

55. Li, Y.P. & Wang, Y.M. Evaluation of tussilagone: a cardiovascular repiratory stimulant isolated from Chinese herbal medicine. *General Pharmacology*, 19(2): 261-263, 1988.

56. Frye, Anne. *Understanding Diagnostic Tests in the Childbearing Year*. New Haven, CT: Labrys Press, 1993.

57. Frye, p. 132-133.

58. el-Chobaki, F.A., Saleh, Z.A., & Saleh, N. The effect of some beverage extracts on intestinal iron absorption. *Journal of Nutritional Sciences*, 29(4): 264-269, 1990.

59. Null, Gary, Ph.D. *A Clinician's Handbook for Natural Healing*, p. 831.

60. Weiner, Michael, A. Ph.D. & Janet A. *Herbs That Heal*. Mill Valley, CA: Quantum Books, 1994.

61. Null, Gary Ph.D. *The Clinician's Handbook of Natural Healing*. p. 450.

62. Murray, Michael, T. N.D. *The Healing Power of Foods*. Rocklin, CA: Prima Publishing, 1993. p. 273-74.

63. Ellis, J.M., Folkers, K. Shizukuishi, S., et at., Response of Vit B6 Deficiency & the Carpal Tunnel Syndrome to Pyridoxine. *Proceedings of National Academy of Science*, USA. 79:749-98, 1982.

64. Ellis, J., Folkers, K., Watebe, I., et.al. Clinical Results of a Cross-over Treatment with Pyridoxine and Placebo of the Carpal Tunnel Syndrome. *American Journal of Clinical Nutrition*, 32: 2040-46, 1979.

65. Ellis, J.M., Azuma, J. Watanebe, T. et.al. Survey and New Data on Treatment with Pyridoxine of Patients Having a

Clinical Syndrome Including the Carpal Tunnel and Other Defects. *Research Committee on Clinical Pathology & Pharmacology*, 17: 165-67, 1977.

66. Hamfelt, A. Carpal Tunnel Sundrome & Vit B6 Deficiency. *Clinical Chemistry.* 28:721, 1982.

67. Phalen, G.S. The Birth of a Syndrome, or Carpal Tunnel Syndrome Revisited. *Journal of Hand Surgery.* 6:109-10, 1981.

68. Frye, Anne. *Understanding Lab Work in the Childbearing Year.* New Haven, CT: Labrys Press, 1990. p. 305.

69. Murray, N.D. Michael T. Pharmaceuticals Used in the Treatment of Inflammatory Disease and Their Botanical Alternatives, Part II: Botanical Alternatives to NSAIDS *1995 Gaia Symposium Proceedings of "Clinical Applications of Botanical Medicine"* p. 14-17, 1995.

70. Fraser, G.E., Sabate, J. Beeson, W.L., and Strahan, T.M. A possible protective effect of nut consumption on risk of coronary heart disease. *Arch Int Med* 152: 1416-24, 1992.

71. Satyavati, G.V. Gum guggal (Commiphora mukul) - The success story of an ancient insight leading to a modern discover. *Ind J Med Res* 87: 327-35, 1988.

72. Nityanard, S., Srivastava, J.S., & Asthana, O.P. Clinical trials with gugulipid, a new hypolipidaemic agent. *J Assoc Phys India* 37: 321-28. 1989.

73. Lau, B.H., Adetumbi, M.A. & Sanchez, A. Allium sativum (garlic) & atherosclerosis: a review. *Nutr Res* 3:119-28, 1983.

74. Carper, Jean. *The Food Pharmacy.* NY,NY: Bantam Books, 1989.

75. Murray, Michael T., N.D. *The Healing Power of Foods.* Rocklin, CA: Prima Publishing, 1993. p. 115-17.

76. Arsenio, L. Bodria, P., Magnati, G., et al. Effectiveness of long-term treatment with pantethine in patients with dyslipidemias. *Clin Ther* 8: 537-45, 1986.

77. Gaddi, A., Descovich, G., Noseda, G. et. al. Controlled evaluation of pantethine, a natural hypolipidemic compound, in patinets with different forms of hyperlipoproteinemia. *Atheroscl* 50:73-83, 1984.

78. Murray, Michael T., N.D. *Natural Alternatives to Over-the-Counter and Prescription Drugs.* NY,NY: Wilaim Morrow & Co., Inc., 1994. p. 140.

79. Beischer, Norman A. and Mackay, Eric V. *Obstetrics and the Newborn.* 2nd Ed. Artarmon, NSW: CBS Publishing Australia Pty Ltd, 1986. p. 237.

80. Varney, Helen. *Nurse-Midwifery.* 2nd Ed. Boston, Mass.: Blackwell Scientific Publications, 1987. p. 322-25.

81. Frye, Anne. *Understanding Lab Work in the Childbearing Year.* New Haven, CT: Labrys Press, 1990. p. 311.

82. B.M. Barrett, et al., "Potential Role of Ascorbic Acid and Beta-carotene in the Prevention of Preterm Rupture of Membranes," *Int Jrnl of Vit and Nutrit Res,* 64(3), 1994, p. 192-197.

83. Giller, Robert M. & Matthews, Kathy. *Natural Prescriptions.* NY,NY: Carol Southern Books, 1994. p. 84.

84. Eby, G.A., Davis, D.R., & Halcomb, W.W. Reduction in duration of common colds by zinc gluconate lozenges in a double-blind study. *Antimicrob Agents Chemother* 25: 20-24, 1984.

85. Murray, Michael T., N.D. *Natural Alternatives to Over-the-Counter and Prescription Drugs.* NY,NY: William Morrow & Co, Inc., 1994.

86. Murray, Michael T., N.D. *The Healing Power of Herbs.* Rocklin, CA: Prima Publishing, 1994.

87. Weiner, Michael A., & Janet A. *Herbs That Heal.* Mill Valley, CA: Quantum Books, 1994. p. 213 & p. 73-74.

88. Murray, Michael T., N.D. *The Healing Power of Foods.* Rocklin, CA: Prima Publishing, 1993. p. 60-63.

89. Frye, Anne. *Understanding Lab Work in the Childbearing Year.* New Haven, CT: Labrys Press, 1990. p. 226.

90. Murray, Michael T., M..D. *Natural Alternatives to Over-the-Counter & Prescription Drugs.* NY,NY: William Morrow & Co., 1994, p. 174.

91. Ibid, p. 174.

92. Anderson, J.W. & Ward, K. High carbohydrate, High Fiber Diets for Insulin-treated Men with Diabetes Mellitus. *American Journal of Clinical Nutrition* 32: 2312-21, 1979.

93. Anderson, J. Diabetes: *A Practical Approach to Daily Living.* NY,NY: Arco Press, 1981.

94. Vahouny, G. & Kritchersky, D. *Dietary Fiber in Health and Disease.* NY, NY: Plenam Press, 1982.

95. Hughes, T., Gwynne, J. Switzer, B., et.al. Effects of Caloric Restriction and Weight Loss on Glycemic Control, Insulin Release and Resistance and Atherosclerotic Risk in Obese Patients with Type II Diabetes Mellitus. *American Journal of Medicine* 77: 7-17, 1984.

96. Murray, N.D., Michael T. *Natural Alternatives to Over-the-Counter and Prescription Drugs.* NY,NY: William Morrow & Co., 1994.

97. Carper, Jean.*Food - Your Miracle Medicine.* NY,NY: HarperCollins Publishers, Inc., 1993. p. 120.

98. Carper, p. 124-125.

99. Ibid, p. 125.

100. Ibid, p. 124.

101. Ibid, p. 123.

102. Pedersen, Mark. *Nutritional Herbology.* Bountiful, UT: Pedersen Publishing, 1991. p. 154.

103. Castleman, Michael. *The Healing Herbs.* Emmaus, PA: Rodale Press, 1991. p. 60.

104. Casteman, Michael. *The Healing Herbs.* Emmaus, PA: Rodale Press, 1991, p. 187.

105. Ibid, p. 191.

106. Giller, Robert M, M.D. & Matthews, Kathy. *Natural Prescriptions.* NY,NY: Carol Southern Books, 1994. p. 128.

107. Castleman, Michael. *The Healing Herbs.* Emmaus, PA: Rodale Press, 1991. p. 152.

108. T. Ovesen, et at., "Local application of N-acetylcysteine in Secretory Otitis Media in Rabbits," *Clinical Otolaryngol,* 17(4), August 1992, p., 327-331.

109. Murray, Michael T., N.D. *The Healing Power of Foods.* Rocklin, CA: Prima Publishing, 1993. p. 290.

110. F.A. Bahmer & J. Schafer, "Treatment of Atopic Dermatitis with Borage Seed Oil (Glandol) - A Time Series Analytic Study," *Kinderarztl Prax,* 60(7), October 1992, p. 199-202.

111. Evans, F.Q. The Rational Use of Glycyrrhetinic Acid in Dermatology. *British Journal of Clinical Practice* 12:269-74, 1958.

112. Mann, C., and Staba, E.J. The Chemistry, Pharmacology and Commercial Formulation of Chamomile. *Herbs, Spices, and Medicinal Plants: Recent Advances in Botany, Horticulture and Pharmacology* 1: 235-80, 1986.

113. Weiner, Michael A., Ph.D. & Janet A. *Herbs That Heal.* Mill Valley, CA: Quantum Books, 1994. p. 131.

114. Castleman, Michael. *The Healing Herbs.* Emmaus, 1991. p. 134.

115. Giller, Robert.M., M.D. & Matthews, Kathy. *Natural Prescriptions.* NY,NY: Carol Southern Books, 1994. p. 133.

116. Murray, Michael T., N.D. *Natural Alternatives to Over-the-Counter & Prescription Drugs.* NY,NY: William Morrow & Co., 1994.

117. Frye, Anne. *Understanding Lab Work in the Childbearing Year.* New Haven, CT: Labrys Press, 1990. p322.

118. Hanshaw, James B., Dudgeon, John A. & Marshall, William C. *"Viral Diseases of the Fetus & Newborn.* Philadelphia, PA: W.B. Saunders Co., 1985. p. 209.

119. Carper, Jean. *Food - Your Miracle Medicine.* NY,NY: HarperCollins Publishers, 1993. p. 362-65.

120. Haas, Elson M., MD. *Staying Healthy with Nutrition.* Berkeley, CA: Celestial Arts Publishing, 1992. p. 272.

121. Weiner, Michael A., Ph.D. & Janet A. *Herbs That Heal.* Mill Valley, CA: Quantum Publishers, 1994. p. 213.

122. Haas, *Staying Healthy with Nutrition,* p. 288.

123. Mowrey, Daniel B., Ph.D. *Herbal Tonic Therapies.* New Canaan, CT: Keats Publishing, Inc., 1993. p. 78.

124. Campos, R., Garrido, A., Guerra, R. & Valenzuela, A. Silybin dihemisuccinate protects against glutathione depletion & lipid peroxidation induced by acetaminophen on rat liver. *Planta Medica* 55: 417-19, 1989.

125. Weiner, Michael A., Ph.D. & Janet A. *Herbs That Heal.* Mill Valley, CA: Quantum Books, 1994. p. 333.

126. Castleman, Michael. *The Healing Herbs.* Emmaus, PA: Rodale Press, 1991. p. 252, 371.

127. Murray, Michael T., N.D. *The Healing Power of Foods.* Rocklin, CA: Prima Publishing, 1993. p. 201.

128. Heinerman, John. *Science of Herbal Medicine.* Orem, UT: Bio-World Publishers, 1984. p. 125.

129. Castleman, Michael. *The Healing Herbs.* Emmaus, PA: Rodale Press, 1991. p. 86.

130. Mowrey, Daniel B., PhD. *Herbal Tonic Therapies.* New Canaan, CT: Keats Publishing, Inc., 1993. p. 56.

131. Castlleman, *The Healing Herbs,* p. 152.

132. V. Esanu, et al., "The Effect of an Aqueous Propolis Extract, of Rutin and of a Rutin-quercetin Mixture on Experimental Influenza Virus Infection in Mice," *Virologie,* 32(3), July-September 1981, p. 213-215.

133. Conversation regarding gallbladder attacks with Chris Marquart, M.D., June 30, 1992.

134. Carper, Jean. *Food - Your Miracle Medicine.* NY,NY: HarperCollins Publishers, Inc., 1993. p. 187.

135. Ibid.

136. Carper, *Food - Your Miracle Medicine,* p. 188.

137. Ibid.

138. Carper, *Food - Your Miracle Medicine,* p. 189.

139. Hobbs, Christopher. *Foundations of Health.* Capitola, CA: Botanica Press, 1992. p. 226.

140. Murray, Michael T., N.D. *The Healing Power of Herbs.* Rocklin, CA: Prima Publishing, 1992. p. 74-75.

141. M.S. Hussain & N. Chandrasekhara, "Effect on Curcumin on Cholesterol Gall-stone Induction in mice," *Indian Journal Medical Research,* 96, October 1992, p. 288-291.

142. Niu & B.F. Smith, "Addition of N-acetylcysteine to Aqueous Model Bile Systems Accelerates Dissolution of Cholesterol Gallstones," *Gastroenterology,* 98(2), February 1990, p. 454-463.

143. Carper, Jean. *Food - Your Miracle Medicine.* NY,NY: HarperCollins Publishers, In.c, 1993. p. 139-141.

144. Carper, p. 142.

145. Carper, p. 141.

146. Hobbs, Christopher. *Foundations of Health.* Capitola, CA: Botanica Press, 1992. p. 197.

147. Frye, Anne. *Understanding Lab Work in the Childbearing Year.* 4th Ed. New Haven, CT: Labrys Press, 1990. p. 314.

148. Varney, Helen. *Nurse-Midwifery.* 2nd Ed. Boston, Mass.: Scientific Publications, 1987. p. 172.

149. Weiss, Rudolf F. *Herbal Medicine.* Beaconsville, England: Beaconsville Publishers, Ltd., 1991. p. 337.

150. Ibid.

151. Ody, Penelope. *The Complete Medicinal Herbal.* NY,NY: Dorling Kindersley, 1993. p. 160-161.

152. Beischer, Norman A. & Mackay, Eric V. *Obstetrics & the Newborn.* 2nd Ed. Artarmon, NSW: CBS Publishing Australia Pty Ltd., 1986. p. 242.

153. Pritchard, Jack A. & MacDonald, Paul C. *William's Obstetrics.* 15th Ed. NY,NY: Prentice-Hall, Inc., 1976. p. 816.

154. Ibid.

155. Beischer, *Obstetrics & the Newborn,* p. 242.

156. Ibid.

157. Beischer, p. 243.

158. Beischer, p. 591.

159. Frye, Anne. *Understanding Lab Work in the Childbearing Year.* New Haven, CT: Labrys Press, 1990. p. 367.

160. H. Hertel, et al., [Low Dosage Retinol and L-cystine Combination Improve Alopecia of the Diffuse Type Following Long-term Oral Administration], *Hautarzt,* 40(8), August 1989, p. 490-495.

161. Murray, Michael T., N.D. *Natural Alternatives to Over-the-Counter & Prescription Drugs.* NY,NY: William Morrow & Co., 1994.

162. Ibid.

163. Ibid.

164. Ibid.

165. Weiner, Michael A. Ph.D. & Janet A. *Herbs That Heal.* Mill Valley, CA: Quantum Books, 1994. p. 154-55.

166. Carper, Jean. *Food - Your Miracle Medicine.* NY,NY: HarperCollins Publishers, Inc., 1993. p. 311

167. Carper, p. 314.

168. Carper, p. 321.

169. Castleman, Michael. *The Healing Herbs.* Emmaus, PA: Rodale Pres, 1991. p. 188.

170. Carper, *Food - Your Miracle Medicine,* p. 322.

171. Carper, Jean. *Food - Your Miracle Medicine.* NY,NY: HarperCollins Publishers, Inc., 1993. p. 149-153.

172. Weiner, Michael A., Ph.D. & Janet A. *Herbs That Heal.* Mill Valley, CA: Quantum Books, 1994. p. 227.

173. Mowrey, Daniel B., Ph.D. *Herbal Tonic Therapies.* New Canaan, CT: Keats Publishing, Inc., 1993. p. 188.

174. Murray, Michael T., N.D. *The Healing Power of Foods.* Rocklin, CA: Prima Publishing, 1993. p. 156.

175. Frye, Anne. *Understanding Lab Work in the Childbearing Year.* New Haven, CT: Labrys Pres, 1991. p. 215.

176. Weiner, Michael A., Ph.D. & Janet A. *Herbs That Heal.* Mill Valley, CA: Quantum Books, 1994. p. 196, 241, 247, 340-41.

177. Frye, p. 215.

178. Weiner, p. 102.

179. Weiner, p. 84.

180. Hanshaw, James B., Dudgeon, John A., & Marshall, William C. *Viral Diseases of the Fetus & the Newborn.* Philadelphia, PA: W.B. Saunders Co., 1985. p. 184.

181. Ibid.

182. Frye, Anne. *Understanding Lab Work in the Childbearing Year.* New Haven, CT: Labrys Press, 1991. p. 332.

183. Hanshaw, p. 185.

184. Hanshaw, p. 186.

185. Hanshaw, p. 188 - 191.

186. Frye, p. 335.

187. Hanshaw, p. 190 - 191.

188. Hanshaw, p. 195-96.

189. Hanshaw, p. 196.

190. Frye, Anne. *Understanding Diagnostic Tests in the Childbearing Year.* New Haven, CT: Labrys Press, 1993. p. 387.

191. Willson, J.Robert & Carrington, Elsie Reid. *Obstetrics and Gynecology.* 8th Ed. St. Louis, MO: The C.V. Mosby Co., 1987. p. 330.

192. Weiner, Michael A., Ph.D. & Janet A. *Herbs That Heal.* Mill Valley, CA: Quantum Books, 1994. p. 139, 234.

193. Mowrey, Daniel B., Ph.D. *Herbal Tonic Therapies.* New Canaan, CT: Keats Publishing, Inc., 1993.

194. Ibid.

195. Mowrey, p. 40-45.

196. Castleman, Michael. *The Healing Herbs.* Emmaus, PA: Rodale Press, 1991. p. 152-53.

197. Weiner, Michael. A. Ph.D., & Janet A. *Herbs That Heal.* Mill Valley, CA: Quantum Books, 1994. p. 142-42.

198. Mowrey, p. 55-59.

199. Weiner, p. 73-75.

200. V.I. Komar, [The Use of Pantothenic Acid Preparations in Treating Patients with Viral Hepatitis A], *Ter Arkh,* 63(11), 1991, p. 58-60.

201. S. Iwarson & J. Lindberg, "Coenzyme-B12 Therapy in Acute Viral Hepatitis," *Scandinavian Jounal of Infectious Disease,* 9(2), 1977, p. 157-158.

202. I.V. Komar, [Use of Vitamin B12 in the Combined Therapy of Viral Hepatitis], *Vopr Pitan,* (1), February 1982, p. 26-29.

203. W. Li, et atl, [Preliminary Study on Early Fibrosis of Chronic Hepatitis B Treated with Ginkgo Biloba Composita], *Chung Kuo Chung His I Chieh Ho Tsa Chih,* 15(10), October 1995, p. 593-595.

204. Shonda Parker as noted while working as a medical assistant for Dr. James R. Bergeron in Shreveport, LA - 1984.

205. Frye, Anne. *Understanding Lab Work in the Childbearing Year.* New Haven, CT: Labrys Press, 1990. p. 338.

206. Willson, J. Robert and Carrington, Elsie Reid. *Obstetrics and Gynecology.* St. Louis, MO: The C.V. Mosby Co., 1987. p. 609-10.

207. Varney, Helen. *Nurse-Midwifery.* St. Louis, MO: Blackwell Scientific Publications, Inc., 1987. p. 169.

208. Frye, Anne. *Understanding Lab Work in the Childbearing Year.* New Haven, CT: Labrys Press, 1990. pp. 339-40.

209. Carper, Jean. *Food - Your Miracle Medicine.* NY,NY: HarperCollins, Inc., 1993. p. 362.

210. Murray, Michael T., N.D.*The Healing Power of Foods.* Rocklin, CA: Prima Publishing, 1993. p. 307.

211. Murray, *The Healing Power of Foods,* p. 307.

212. Giller, Robert M., M.D. & Matthews, Kathy. *Natural Prescriptions.* NY,NY: Carol Southern Books, 1994. p. 184.

213. Weiner, Michael A. & Janet A. *Herbs That Heal.* Mill Valley, CA: Quantum Books, 1994. p. 79.

214. Weiner, p. 84.

215. Weiner, p. 97.

216. Weiner, p. 141-42.

217. Weiner, p. 276-77.

218. Weiner, p. 296.

219. Mowrey, Daniel B., Ph.D. *Herbal Tonic Therapies.* New Canaan, CT: Keats Publishing, Inc., 1993. p. 67, 323.

220. Weiner, p. 126, 319.

221. D.B. Mowrey, *The Scientific Validation of Herbal Medicine,* New Canaan, CT, Keats Publishing, 1986, p. 73.

222. M. Amoros, et al., "Comparison of the Anti-herpes Simplex Virus Activities of Propolis and 3-methyl-but-2-enyl Caffeate," *Journal of Nat Prod,* 57(5), May 1994, p. 644-647.

223. IuF Maichuk, et al., [The Use of Ocular Drug Films of Propolis in the Sequelae of Ophthalmic Herpes], *Voen Med Zh,* (12), December 1995, p. 36-39.

224. Frye, Anne. *Understanding Lab Work in the Childbearing Year.* New Haven, CT: Labrys Press, 1990. p. 258.

225. Willson, J. Robert & Carrrington, Elsie Reid. 8th Ed. *Obstetrics and Gynecology.* St. Louis, MO: The C.V. Mosby Co., 1987. p. 308.

226. Mowrey, Daniel B., Ph.D. *Herbal Tonic Therapies.* New Canaan, CT: Keats Publishing, Inc., 1993. pp. 55-58.

227. Castleman, Michael. *The Healing Herbs.* Emmaus, PA: Rodale Press, 1991. pp. 58, 353.

228. Weiss, Rudolf F., M.D. *Herbal Medicine.* Beaconsfield, England: Beaconsfield Publishers, Inc., 1991. p. 279.

229. Murray, Michael T., N.D. *The Healing Power of Foods.* Rocklin, CA: Prima Publishing, 1993. p. 313.

230. Giller, Robert M., M.D. & Matthews, Kathy. *Natural Prescriptions.* NY,NY: Carol Southern Books, 1994. p. 203.

231. Frye, Anne. *Understanding Lab Work in the Childbearing Year.* New Haven, CT: Labrys Press, 1990. p. 250.

232. Giller, Robert M., M.D. & Matthews, Kathy. *Natural Prescriptions.* NY,NY: Carol Southern Books, 1994. p. 205.

233. Frye, p. 256.

234. Willson, J. Robert, & Carrrington, Elsie Reid. *Obstetrics & Gynecology.* 8th Ed. St. Louis, MO: The C.V. Mosby Do., 1987. p. 308.

235. Frye, Anne. *Understanding Lab Work in the Childbearing Year.* New Haven, CT: Labrys Press, 1990. p. 262.

236. Frye, p. 261.

237. Murray, Michael T., N.D. *The Healing Power of Foods.* Rocklin, CA: Prima Publishing. p. 70.

238. Frye, p. 261.

239. Mowrey, Daniel B., Ph.D. *Herbal Tonic Therapies.* New Canaan, CT: Keats Publishing, Inc., 1993. pp. 194-99.

240. Jones, V.; McLaughlin, P.; Shorthouse, M.; et al. Food Intolerance: A Major Factor in the Pathogenesis of Irritable Bowel Syndrome. *Lancet* 2: 1115-18, 1982.

241. Petitpierre, M.; Sumowski, P.; and Dirard, J. Irritable Bowel Sundrome and Hypersensitivity to Food. *Annals of Allergy* 54: 538-40, 1985.

242. Carper, Jean. *Food - Your Miracle Medicine.* Ny,NY: HarperCollins Publishers Inc., 1993. p. 163.

243. Ibid.

244. Carper, p. 167.

245. Murray, Michael, T., N.D. *The Healing Power of Foods.* Rocklin, CA: Prima Publishing, 1993. p. 320.

246. Ibid.

247. Murray, *Natural Alternatives to Over-the-Counter & Prescription Drugs,* p. 201.

248. Brochure Nutritional Research News Issue 2 provided by the Foundation for the Advancement of Nutritional Education, PO Box 4621, San Clemente, CA 92672.

249. Murray, Michael T., N.D. *Natural Alternative to Over-the-Counter and Prescription Drugs.* NY,NY: William Morrow & Co., 1994.

250. Giller, Robert M., M.D. & Matthews, Kathy. *Natural Prescriptions.* NY,NY: Carol Southern Books, 1994. p. 213.

251. Ibid.

252. Carper, Jean. *Food - Your Miracle Medicine.* NY,NY: HarperCollins Publishers, Inc., 1993. p. 134.

253. Murray, Michael T., N.D. *The Healing Power of Foods.* Rocklin, CA: Prima Publishing, 1993. pp. 147, 149.

254. Murray, *The Healing Power of Foods,* p. 114.

255. Murray, Michael T., N.D. *Natural Alternatives to Over-the-Counter & Prescription Drugs.* NY,NY: William Morrow & Co., 1994. p. 226.

256. Giller, Robert, M., M.D. & Matthew, Kathy. *Natural Prescriptions.* NY,NY: Carol Southern Books, 1994. pp. 218-19.

257. Trowell, H.; Burkitt, D.; and Heaton, K. *Dietary Fibre, Fibre-Depleted Foods and Disease.* NY,NY: Academic Press, 1985.

258. Murray, Michael T., N.D. *The Healing Power of Food.* Rocklin, CA: Prima Publishing, 1993. p. 321.

259. Trowell, H. & Burkitt, D. *Western Diseases: Their Emergence and Prevention.* Cambridge, Mass.: Harvard University Press, 1981.

260. Carper, Jean. *Food - Your Miracle Medicine.* NY,NY: HarperCollins Publishers, Inc., 1993. p. 192.

261. Murray, pp. 322-23.

262. Rose, G., and Westbury, E. The Influence of Calcium Content of Water, Intake of Vegetables and Fruit and of Other Food Factors Upon the Incidence of Renal Calculi. *Urological Research* 3: 61-66, 1975.

263. Shaw, P., Williams, G. and Green, N. Idiopathic Hypercalciuria: Its Control with Unprocessed Bran. *British Journal of Urology* 52: 426-29, 1980.

264. Seeling, M.S. Vitamin D - Risk vs Benefit. *Journal of American College of Nutrition* 4: 109-10, 1983.

265. Murray, p. 323.

266. Prien, E. and Gershoff, S. Magnesium Oxide-Pyridoxine Therapy for Recurrent Calcium Oxalate Calculi. *Journal of Urology* 112: 509-12, 1974.

267. Gershoff, S. andPrien, E. Effect of Daily MgO and Vitamin B6 Administration to Patients with Recurring Calcium Oxalate Stones. *American Journal of Clinical Nutrition* 20: 393-99, 1967.

268. Giller, Robert M., M.D. & Matthews, Kathy. *Natural Prescriptions.* NY,NY: Carol Southern Books, 1994. p. 228.

269. Weiner, Michael A., Ph.D. & Janet A. *Herbs that Heal.* Mill Valley, CA: Quantum Books, 1994. p. 132.

270. Weiner, p. 136.

271. Weiner, p. 156.

272. Weiner, p. 197.

273. Mowrey, Daniel B., Ph.D. *Herbal Tonic Therapies.* New Canaan, CT: Keats Publishing Inc., 1993. p. 270.

274. Weiss, Rudolf F., M.D. *Herbal Medicine.* Beaconsfield, England: Beaconsfield Publishers Ltd., 1991. p. 185.

275. Frye, Anne. *Understanding Lab Work in the Childbearing Year.* New Haven, CT: Labrys Press, 1991. p. 192.

276. Weiner, Michael A., Ph.D., & Janet A. *Herbs That Heal.* Mill Valley, CA: Quantum Books, 1994.

277. Murray, Michael T., N.D., p. 56.

278. Mowrey, Daniel B., Ph.D. *Herbal Tonic Therapies.* New Canaan, CT: Keats Publishing, Inc., 1993. p. 8.

279. Weiner, Michael A., Ph.D. , p. 169.

280. Murray, Michael T., N.D. *The Healing Power of Herbs.* Rocklin, CA: Prima Publishing, 1992. p. 4 - 6.

281. Castleman, Michael. *The Healing Herbs.* Emmaus, PA: Rodale Publishing, 1991. p. 191.

282. Frye, Anne. *Understanding Diagnostic Tests in the Childbearing Year.* New Haven, CT: Labrys Press, 1990. p. 472.

283. Frye, p. 474-476.

284. Mowrey, Daniel B., Ph.D. *Herbal Tonic Therapies.* New Canaan, CT: Keats Publishing, Inc., 1993. p. 219-227.

285. Weiner, Michael A., Ph.D. & Janet A. *Herbs That Heal.* Mill Valley, CA: Quantum Books, 1994. p. 234.

286. Willar, Terry, Ph.D. *Textbook of Advanced Herbology.* Calgary, Alberta, Canada: Wild Rose College of Natural Healing, Ltd., 1992. p. 135-37.

287. Hobbs, Christopher. *Foundations of Health.* Captola, CA: Botanica Press, 1992. p. 274-75.

288. Mowrey, Daniel B., Ph.D. *Herbal Tonic Therapies.* New Canaan, CT: Keats Publishing, Inc. 1993. p. 245-49.

289. Ibid.

290. Giller, Robert M., M.D. & Matthews, Kathy. *Natural Prescriptions.* NY,NY: Carol Southern Books, 1994. p. 65-67.

2. Pizzorno, Joseph & Murray, Michael. *An Encyclopedia of Natural Medicine.* Rocklin, CA: Prima Publishing, 1991. p.467.

291. P. J. Leggott, et al., "Effects of Ascorbic Acid Depletion and Supplementation on Periodontal Health and Subgingival Microflora in Humans," *Jrnl of Dental Res*, 70(12), December 1991, p. 1531-1536.

292. R. I. Vogel et al., " The Effect of Folic Acid on Gingival Health," *Jrnl of Periodont*, 47(11), November 1976, p. 667-668.

293. Murray, Michael T. *Natural Alternatives to Over-the-Counter & Prescription Drugs.* NY,NY: William Morrow & Co., 1994. p. 228.

294. Murray, Michael T., N.D. *The Healing Power of Foods.* Rocklin, CA: Prima Publishing, 1993. p. 191.

295. Carper, Jean. *Food - Your Miracle Medicine.* NY,NY: HarperCollins, 1993. p. 444.

296. C. Miyares, et al., [Clinical Trial with a Preparation Based on Propolis "propolisina" in Human Giardiasis], *Acta Gastroenterol Latinoam*, 18(3), 1988, p. 195-201.

297. Weiner, Michael A., Ph.D., & Janet A. *Herbs That Heal.* Mill Valley, CA: Quantum Books, 1994. p. 259.

298. Mowrey, Daniel B., Ph.D. *Herbal Tonic Therapies.* New Canaan, CT: Keats Publishing, Inc., 1993. p. 78-79.

299. Castleman, Michael. *The Healing Herbs.* Emmaus, PA: Rodale Press, 1991. p. 156.

300. Frye, Anne. *Understanding Lab Work in the Childbearing Year.* New Haven, CT: Labrys Press, 1990. p. 187.

301. Murray, Michael T., N.D. *Natural Alternatives to Over-the-Counter & Prescription Drugs.* NY,NY: William Morrow & Co., 1994. p. 101.

302. Murray, p. 102.

303. Ibid.

304. Murray, p. 113.

305. Ibid.

306. Berkow, Robert, M.D. *The Merck Manual.* Rahway, NJ: Merck Research Laboratories, 1992. p. 2428.

307. Weiss, Rudolf Fritz. *Herbal Medicine.* Beaconsfield, England: Beaconsfield Publishers, LTD, 1991. p. 337.

308. Sherman, John A., N.D. *The Complete Botanical Prescriber.* 1993. p. 411.

309. Weiss, p. 337.

310. J. DeBersaques, "Vitamin A Acid in the Topic Treatment of Warts," *Acta Derm Venereol Suppl*, 55(74), 1975, p. 169-170.

311. C Trenkwalder, et al., "L-dopa Therapy of Uremic and Idiopathic Restless Legs Syndrome: A Double-Blind, Crossover Trial," *Sleep*, 18(8), October 1995, p. 681-688.

312. Schmidt, Michael A., Smith, Lendon H. & Sehnert, Keith W. *Beyond Antibiotics.* Berkeley, CA: North Atlantic Books, 1993. p. 30

313. Hoffman, R.L. *Seven Weeks to a Settled Stomach.* NY,NY: Pocket Books, 1990. p. 6.

314. Frye, Anne. *Understanding Lab Work in the Childbearing Year.* New Haven, CT: Labrys Press, 1990. p. 362.

315. Giller, Robert M., M.D. & Matthews, Kathy. *Natural Prescriptions.* NY,NY: Carol Southern Books, 1994. p. 305-307.

316. Carper, Jean. *Food - Your Miracle Medicine.* NY,NY: HarperCollins, Inc., 1993. p. 338-39.

317. Murray, Michael T., N.D. *The Healing Power of Herbs.* Rocklin, CA: Prima Publishing, 1992. p. 183-84.

318. Weiner, Michael A., Ph.D. & Janet A. *Herbs That Heal.* Mill Valley, CA: Quantum Books, 1994. p. 141-42.

319. Castleman, Michael. *The Healing Herbs.* Emmaus, PA: Rodale Press, 1991. p. 152-53.

320. Schmidt, Michael A., Smith, Lendon H. & Sehnert, Keith A. *Beyond Antibiotics.* Berkeley, CA: North Atlantic Books, 1992.

321. Schmidt, Smith, & Sehnert, p. 246.

322. Carper, Jean. *Food - Your Miracle Medicine.* NY,NY: HarperCollins, Inc., 1993. p. 342.

323. Carper, p. 343.

324. Castleman, Michael. *The Healing Herbs.* Emmaus, PA: Rodale Press, 1991. p. 171.

325. Weiss, Rudolf F., M.D. *Herbal Medicine.* Beaconsfield, England: Beaconsfield Publishers Ltd., 1991. p. 228.

326. Castleman, p. 343.

327. Mowrey, Daniel B., Ph.D. *Herbal Tonic Therapies.* New Canaan, CT: Keats Publishing, Inc., 1993. p. 55-59.

328. Weiner, Michael A., Ph.D. & Janet A. *Herbs That Heal.* Mill Valley, CA: Quantum Books, 1992. p. 73-75.

329. Weiner, Michael, Ph.D. & Janet A. *Herbs That Heal.* Mill Valley, CA: Quantum Books, 1994. p. 126.

330. G. Hotz, et al., [Antiphlogistic Effect of Bromelain Following Third Molar Removal], *Dtsch Zahnarztl Z,* 44(11), November 1989, p. 830-832.

331. E. Rapisarda & A. Longo, [Effects of Zinc and Vitamin B6 in Experimental Caries in Rats], *Minerva Stomatol,* 30(4), July-August 1981, p. 317-320.

332. Varney, Helen. *Nurse-Midwifery.* 2nd. Ed./ Boston, Mass.: Blackwell Scientific Publications, 1987. p. 168.

333. Beischer, Norman A. & Mackay, Eric V. *Obstetrics & the Newborn.* 2nd Ed. Artamon, NSW: CBS Publishing Australia Pty Ltd., 1986. p. 250.

334. Giller, Robert, M., M.D. & Matthews, Kathy. *Natural Prescriptions.* NY,NY: Carol Southern Books, 1994. p. 101-103.

335. Weiner, Michael A., Ph.D. & Janet A. *Herbs That Heal.* Mill Valley, CA: Quantum Books, 1994. p. 136.

336. Weiner, p. 79, 188, 264-265, 331-332.

337. Frye, Anne. *Understanding Lab Work in the Childbearing Year.* New Haven, CT: Labrys Press, 1991. p. 381.

338. Belaiche P, Treatment of vaginal yeast infections of Candida albicans with the essential oil of Melaleuca alternifolia. *Phytotherapie* 15:15-16, 1985.

339. Brown, Donald J. *Herbal Prescriptions for Better Health.* Rocklin, CA: Prima Publishing, 1996. p. 240.

340. Frye, p. 384.

341. Mowrey, Daniel B. *Herbal Tonic Therapies.* New Canaan, CT: Keats Publishing, Inc. 1993. p. 80.

342. M.S. Litschgi, et al., [Effectiveness of a Lacctobacillus Vaccine on Trichomonas Infection in Women. Preliminary Results], *Fortschr Med,* 98(41), November 6, 1980, p. 1624-1627.

343. J. Starzyk, et al., " Biological Properties and Clinical Application of Propolis. II. Stidus on the Antiprotozoan Activity of Ethanol Extract of Propolis," *Arzneimittelforschung,* 27(6), 1977, p. 1198-1199.

344. Varney, Helen. *Nurse-Midwifery.* 2nd Ed. Boston, Mass: Blackwell Scientific Publications, 1987. p. 387.

345. Varney, p. 387-388.

346. Weiner, Michael A., Ph.D. & Janet A. *Herbs That Heal.* Mill Valley, CA: Quantum Books, 1994. p. 77, 128, 301, 340.

347. Castleman, Michael. *The Healing Herbs.* Emmaus, PA: Rodale Press, 1991. p. 83, 337, 379.

348. Willson, J. Robert & Carrington, Elsie Reid. *Obstetrics & Gynecology.* St. Louis, MO: The C.V. Mosby Co., 1987. p. 553.

349. Dale, A. & Cornwell, S. The role of lavender oil in relieving perineal discomfort. *Journal of Advanced Nursing* 19(1): 89-96, 1994.

350. Willson, J. Robert & Carrington, Elsie Reid. *Obstetrics & Gynecology.* St. Louis, MO: The C.V. Mosby Co., 1987. p. 425.

351. Willson, p. 426.

352. A.G. Rillo, et al., [Uterine Contraction Induced by Carbachol is Inhibited by Melatonin], *Ginecol Obstet* Mex, 61, February 1993, p. 40-44.

353. F. Facchinetti, et al., "L-arginine Infusion Reduces Preterm Uterine Contractions," *Jrnl of Perinat Med,* 24(3), 1996, p. 283-285.

354. Willson, J. Robert & Carrington, Elsie Reid. *Obstetrics & Gynecology.* St. Louis, MO: The C.V. Mosby Co., 1987. p. 591.

355. Weiner, Michael A., Ph.D. & Janet A. *Herbs That Heal.* Mill Valley, CA: Quantum Books, 1994.

356. LaLeche League International, 1991, p. 144.

357. Nikodem, C. et al. "Do Caggage Leaves Prevent Engorgement?" *Birth,* 20:61-64, June 1993.

358. B.P. Chew, et al., "Effect of Vitamin A Deficiency on Mammary Gland Development and Susceptibility to Mastitis through Intramammary Infusion with Staphylococcus Aureus in Mice," *Am Jrnl of Vet Res,* 46(1), January 1985, p. 287-293.

359. Willson, J. Robert and Carrington, Elsie Reid. *Obstetrics and Gynecology.* St. Louis, MO: The C.V. Mosby Co., 1987. pp. 199-203.

360. Cunningham, F. Gary, M.D., MacDonald, Paul C., and Gant, Norman F. *Williams Obstetrics.* Norwalk, CT: Appleton & Lange, 1989. p. 940-41.

361. M.S. Fahim & M. Wang, "Zinc Acetate and Lyophilized Aloe Barbadensis as Vaginal Contraceptive," *Contraception*, 53(4). April 1996, p. 231-236.

362. Kippley, John & Sheila. *The Art of Natural Family Planning*. Cincinnati, OH: The Couple to Couple League Int'l, 1984.

363. Kippley, Sheila K. *Breastfeeding and Natural Child Spacing*. Cincinnati, OH: Couple to Couple League Int'l, 1974. p. 81.

364. Weiner, Michael A., Ph.D. & Janet A. *Herbs That Heal*. Mill Valley, CA: Quantum Books, 1994. p. 138.

365. Mowrey, Daniel B., Ph.D. *Herbal Tonic Therapies*. New Canaan, CT: Keats Publishing, Inc., 1993. p. 334.

366. Tyler, Ph.D., ScD., Varro E. *Herbs of Choice*. Binghamton, NY: Pharmaceutical Products Press, 1994. p. 137.

367. Weiner, p. 240.

368. A.D. Genazzani, et al., "Acetyl-l-carnitine as Possible Drug in the Treatment of Hypothalamic Amenorrhea," *Acta Obstet Gynecol Scand,* 70(6), 1991, p. 487-492.

369. Willson, J. Robert, and Carrington, Elsie Reid. *Obstetrics and Gynecology*. St. Louis, MO: The C.V. Mosby Company, 1987. p. 115.

370. *Women's Health Letter*. August 1994, p. 8.

371. Giller, Robert M., M.D. and Matthews, Kathy. *Natural Prescriptions*. NY,NY: Carol Southern Books, 1994, p. 140.

372. Murray, Michael T., N.D. *The Healing Power of Herbs*. Rocklin, CA: Prima Publishing, 1992, p. 207.

373. D.M. Lithgow and W.M. Politzer, "Vitamin A in the Treatment of Menorrhagia," *South African Med Jrnl,* 51(7), February 12, 1977, p. 191-193.

374. Shannon, Marilyn. *Fertility Cycles and Nutrition*. Cincinnati, OH: Couple to Couple League Int'l, Inc., 1992. p. 47-48.

375. M. Amsellem, et al., "Endotelon in the Treatment of Venolymphatic Problems in Premenstrual Syndrome, Multicenter Study on 165 Patients," *Tempo Medical*, 282, 1987.

376. A. Tamborini & R. Taurelle, [Value of Standardized Ginkgo Biloba Extract (Egb 761) in the Management of Congestive Symptoms of Premenstrual Syndrome], *Rev Fr Gynecol Obstet* 88 (7-9), July-September 1993, p. 447-457.

377. Murray, Michael T., N.D. *Natural Alternatives to Over-the-Counter and Prescription Drugs*. NY,NY: William Morrow & Co., 1994.

378. Castleman, Michael. *The Healing Herbs*. Emmaus, PA: Rodale Press. 1991. p. 135.

379. Ames, Bruce, et al. *Science* 236:271, 1987.

380. Castleman, p. 113.

381. Castleman, p. 112-14.

382. Akron, Ohio Regional Poison Control Center's national database.

383. Weiner, Ph.D., Michael A. & Janet A. *Herbs That Heal*. Mill Valley, CA: Quantum Books, 1994. p. 286-87.

384. Ibid. p. 289-90.

385. Murray,N.D., Michael T. *Natural Alternatives to Over-the-Counter and Prescription Drugs*. New York, NY: William Morrow & Co., Inc., 1994. pp. 114-15, 237-239,224,228.

386. Weiner, p. 95.

387. Castleman, p. 199.

388. Roufs, J.B. Review of L-tryptophan and eosinophilia-myalgia syndrome. *J Am Diet Assn,*92:844-850, 1992.

389. Murray, p. 227, 228.

390. Caston, J.C., Roufs, J.B., Forgarty, C.M., et al. Treatment of refractory eosinophilia-myalgia syndrome associated with the ingestion of L-tyrptophan-containing products. *Adv Ther* 7:206-228, 1990.